The Untold Story of a Fighting Ship

Eugenio Luis Facchin

The Untold Story of a Fighting Ship

One Ship, Two Flags, a Thousand Battles

Eugenio Luis Facchin
School of Marine Sciences of the National
Defence University (Argentina)
Buenos Aires, Argentina

ISBN 978-3-030-92623-6   ISBN 978-3-030-92624-3 (eBook)
https://doi.org/10.1007/978-3-030-92624-3

© The Editor(s) (if applicable) and The Author(s), under exclusive license to Springer Nature Switzerland AG 2022

This work is subject to copyright. All rights are solely and exclusively licensed by the Publisher, whether the whole or part of the material is concerned, specifically the rights of reprinting, reuse of illustrations, recitation, broadcasting, reproduction on microfilms or in any other physical way, and transmission or information storage and retrieval, electronic adaptation, computer software, or by similar or dissimilar methodology now known or hereafter developed.

The use of general descriptive names, registered names, trademarks, service marks, etc. in this publication does not imply, even in the absence of a specific statement, that such names are exempt from the relevant protective laws and regulations and therefore free for general use.

The publisher, the authors and the editors are safe to assume that the advice and information in this book are believed to be true and accurate at the date of publication. Neither the publisher nor the authors or the editors give a warranty, expressed or implied, with respect to the material contained herein or for any errors or omissions that may have been made. The publisher remains neutral with regard to jurisdictional claims in published maps and institutional affiliations.

This Springer imprint is published by the registered company Springer Nature Switzerland AG
The registered company address is: Gewerbestrasse 11, 6330 Cham, Switzerland

To my dear family, my source of inspiration and constant support

Foreword

This work is the faithful and passionate portraying of the history of a warship, the destroyer ARA *Bouchard*, which contributed to mark a milestone in global naval history. It was written by a Navy Officer and Doctor in Political Sciences, who crewed it with professionalism and courage, participating in the Falklands/Malvinas Conflict, and who has researched in depth, for six years, everything concerning its history.

Three critical moments could not make it wreck: 1. In the last days of the Second World War, it participated in the attacks on the islands of Japan's archipelago, where it was hit by a Japanese kamikaze airplane, leaving a balance of 48 dead and 66 injured. 2. In 1982, during the Falklands/Malvinas Conflict, with a courageous crew working as a team, an MK8 torpedo launched by the nuclear submarine HMS *Conqueror* exploded close by, though outside its lethal range, damaging the hull. 3. At the end of its active life, it could not be sunk after being assigned as a target for an aeronautical firing exercise. It did not bend in the face of adversity, leaving lessons behind about an attitude of strength. It took the hits and continued with its positive actions.

In the mentioned South Atlantic Conflict, it patrolled areas where it ran the risk of being attacked by submarines. It also showed patriotic spirit by raising the war flag on the night from May 1 to 2. It was an unforgettable situation, calm and dark, with the whole complement on the bridge and signal bridge, where the decision to go after the usurper's fleet was announced. It headed six times towards hydrophonic noises detected to investigate possible submarine contacts. It endured the explosion from one of the three torpedoes launched from a nuclear submarine, as stated above. In adverse meteorological and mechanical conditions, the survivors of the cruiser ARA *General Belgrano* were rescued using creative manoeuvring, in one of the most successful rescues in history. Authorisation was requested to continue the rescue after it had been finalised, with an almost exhausted autonomy, and no more liferafts were found. This shows that the order to cease given by the Commanding Officer of the destroyer ARA *Piedrabuena* was the right one, which was a balm to all the families of those who were shipwrecked, since today they know that no one was abandoned. Last but not least, the precise attention paid to the sensors and the fast reactions in front of

Río Grande led to the failure of the British Operation "Mikado", saving the lives of pilots and the airplanes with Exocet missiles.

The crew of the *Bouchard* knew how to face wars. These are situations where one has to be ready to fight and give one's life for territorial sovereignty and, if necessary, for liberty and people's dignity. There are situations where the use of force is not only necessary, but also morally justifiable. Before reaching that line of no return, the measures to avoid it must be undertaken: negotiation, politics, diplomacy, persuasion, dialogue, and, lastly, wisdom.

The spirit of *Bouchard*, which still lives on in its crewmembers, also knew and knows about values, that quality that human beings claim for their normal development and perfection. There were many accounts from sailors of different ranks that left indelible impressions. Today, many of them are members of a Civil Association that aims to perpetuate, through the years, the operations executed and extol the values of country and family, and carry out charitable and educational activities.

I would like to finish these reflections with an ardent tribute to the cruiser ARA *General Belgrano* and its dead, the destroyer ARA *Piedrabuena* and their crews that, with the destroyer ARA *Bouchard*, were part of Task Group 79.3, showing the love for Country that, should it continue to prevail in the national spirit, will allow the peaceful and definitive recovery of the "lost southern pearl".

Dr. Washington Bárcena
Captain (Retired) VGM (Falklands/Malvinas War Veteran) Buenos Aires,
República Argentina
Commanding Officer of the destroyer ARA *Bouchard* in 1982

Preface

When this research started, the main purpose was retelling the events that had befallen during the Falklands/Malvinas War, in which the ship had taken part. Shortly after having started, it became noticeable that this vessel had participated in a host of relevant events since the Second World War, both military and general.

This opened a wide spectrum of story lines to research. To avoid straying from the main objective, a brief overview was developed describing the actions the vessel took part in under the flag of the United States of America, and later under the Argentine flag, until the onset of the Falklands/Malvinas War.

The ship's name, in Argentina, honours a hero in the Argentine Independence. He was a French serviceman who had his start as a cavalry officer in General San Martín's renowned Granaderos a Caballo (Mounted Grenadiers). They have a long list of victories to their name, including the Battle of San Lorenzo, where Hipólito Bouchard snatched the flag from the Spanish standard bearer in the middle of the battle. He later returned to his seafarer career, and in 1815, he got his letter of marque, became a privateer and freed slaves captured by a slaver in the south of Africa. He was also able to convince Kamehameha, King of Hawaii, to recognise Argentina as an independent country for the first time in history. He later captured a city in California, over which the Argentine flag flew for a week. He continued privateering throughout Central America and incited uprisings that greatly weakened the Spanish hold on the region, which is why almost every flag of those countries is inspired by the Argentine flag, and the similarities are really striking. When he arrived in Chile, he was a part of the fleet transporting San Martín to Peru, where he made his home and became an Admiral in the burgeoning Peruvian Navy. After he retired, he was assassinated by one of his employees.

To some degree, it seems that its history as *Borie II* under the United States flag where, for instance, it might have been the last ship to be hit by a Kamikaze during the attack on the metropolitan area of Tokyo, Japan, during the Second World War; and the addition of the hallmark left by the name of *Bouchard* it received in Argentina, have marked its fate and made it a privileged and active participant in the naval war during the Falklands/Malvinas conflict.

In the South Atlantic conflict, the vessel was part of a taskforce made up of ships from the Second World War with scarce technical capabilities, on the edge of exhausting their service life and poorly maintained. Standing in opposition to this state of affairs was the superior training of their crews, an enormous feeling of vindication for the sovereignty usurped by the British and the high degree of professionalism of the Argentine Navy.

The account is profusely supported by the official documents researched and the British literature addressing the events described.

The destroyer took part in the capture of the islands.

Of the three torpedoes launched against the cruiser ARA *General Belgrano*, which caused over half the Argentine losses in the war, one exploded under the destroyer severely damaging it, but that did not prevent it from taking part in rescue operations, despite the constant submarine threat.

It later thwarted two boarding attempts executed by the prestigious British Special Forces, SAS and SBS. During one of said attempts, the main gun battery fired on the raiders and became the only main battery of the whole Argentine fleet to have the privilege of firing, with cannons, at the enemy.

Once the war ended, the vessel was sent to dry dock to replace 172.22 ft^2 (16 m^2) of the hull plates, damaged by the torpedo explosion.

Finally, *Bouchard* was excluded from active service and it was used as a target for testing air-sea missiles (launched by aircrafts) and sea-sea missiles (launched by ships).

This account, with supporting documents, contains all the ship's actions, from its launch in New York until its final fate, with special emphasis on the Falklands/Malvinas War.

Buenos Aires, Argentina   Eugenio Luis Facchin

Acknowledgments To my proofreader, Elena Virginia Martin, who helped me shape the texts in Spanish and, as translator, worked as final reviewer of the English version.

To Eduardo Norberto López Professional Photographer and a great Teacher.

To Lexlogos, the company that translated the texts from Spanish into English. (www.lexlogos.com).

To my Navy comrades who fought with honour for the glory of our country.

To the Naval History and Heritage Command (USA).

To The Nav Source Naval History Photographic History of the US Navy.

Prologue

Writing about professional endeavours becomes difficult, especially when one was a party to the events, because the task of balancing one's own personal experiences and the strict usage of research methodology was exhausting at times. Nevertheless, I tried to undertake, with all due rigour, an investigation of events. The results were always greater than what we perceived personally as crewmembers of the ship, both in their dimension and in their historical significance.

I then decided to study the ship's participation in actions since its launching, to add context to the description. This was even harder, and no less enthralling, since, despite the fact that actions in the Second World War have been extensively documented and described, these types of ship were insignificant in the face of the forces deployed by both sides. What are a mere 300 hundred men when compared to the millions that fought? What are 3,000 tonnes of metal in the face of thousands of millions of tonnes that advanced with each battle group? This arduous task showed that this tiny cog in the war machine had been noteworthy in the most standout events in humanity's history between the 1940s and the beginning of the 1970s.

The name that was bestowed in Argentina also deserved to be analysed, since the character of this national hero, Hipólito Bouchard, in some way, marked its performance. He was a decisive, blunt, opinionated, and temperamental man, whose gaze was always fixed on the objective, and who had no petty thoughts about the personal convenience of reaching it or not.

The war for the Falklands/Malvinas still has many aspects that must be analysed, but those who study it will have to rid themselves of prejudice and their own purposes, to arrive at the real incentives, motivations, and valuations that led Argentina to engage in an unproductive war, that faced (at least in the case of the Navy) forces that could not be compared in number, offensive capability, technology, logistical support, maintenance, training, and, especially, war experience. This exposed us to an enemy that far surpassed us by any measurable metric. Besides, we have to add the explicit and notable support of the largest world power, the United States of America, as well as the North Atlantic Treaty Organization, and neighbouring countries that were interested in seeing us weakened and defeated, which diverted a huge amount of resources and weakened our military efforts, by having to respond to threats of a different nature in addition to the military ones.

We were not heroes, in the strict meaning of the word. However, we fully met everything that we were trained and shaped for, giving all of ourselves in service to our country, which is no small thing. Amongst what we were willing to give up, were our very lives, which is, without a doubt, the most precious treasure of a human being, and with that sacrifice, we were also giving our families. Aboard the ship, we shared all material and spiritual wealth we had, without any pettiness. In the spirit of mutual respect and regard, we vigorously worked in teams, trying to meet with professionalism and creativity each of the endless technical issues that appeared every day in systems that, at the time of the war, had been manufactured 40 years before and designed even earlier. During the rescue after the sinking of the cruiser ARA *Belgrano*, as a show of our commitment and comradeship, we offered our own lifejackets (perhaps the only tool that could give us the chance to survive should we be sunk) to the shipwreck survivors that boarded from the liferafts. There was neither inappropriate behaviour nor signs of anxiety or anguish. We were not heroes, but we fulfilled what was expected of us.

Our return and how we were treated later made us feel that we were guilty for the defeat. Time let us understand that we were privileged parties to history.

The Falklands/Malvinas cause and the war veterans have been the object of political use that is often questionable and that on certain occasions embarrasses, irritates and offends us and on other occasions seems excessive. Time will dampen passions and put everything in the place that history assigns to the events that have changed the sense of becoming.

My heartfelt recognition goes to those who gave their lives for the Falklands/Malvinas, in combat or due to the profound effects that the conflict left in them, and to their relatives who continue to wait for a return that will not come, or longing for a presence that will never be replaced.

Contents

1	**Characteristics of the Destroyer ARA *Bouchard***	1
	Machinery	4
	Elements for Deck Operations	6
	Other Elements	7
	Artillery	7
	Anti-submarine Weapons	8
2	***Borie II*, Campaign in the Pacific Ocean (WWII), in the Korean War, in the Vietnam War, in the Mediterranean (July to December, 1956), Miscellaneous, Other Minor Actions**	11
	Campaign in the Pacific Ocean	11
	Iwo Jima	12
	Okinawa	14
	Kamikaze Actions	16
	The Fight Continues in the Pacific	17
	Roosevelt Passes Away	18
	The Forces Go for Tokyo	20
	The End of the War in the Pacific	21
	Borie II in the Korean War	22
	Vietnam War	27
	Beginning of the Conflict	29
	Borie II's Participation	30
	Borie II in the Mediterranean (July to December, 1956)	31
	Miscellaneous, Other Minor Actions	33
	References	34
3	**Hipólito Bouchard: His Origins and Arrival in the Country**	35
	The First Action: San Nicolás de los Arroyos	37
	Bouchard: Grenadier	38
	Return to Sea	39
	War as a Privateer	39
	Argentina in the World (1817–1819)	41

	Ending of the Campaign and Return to Valparaiso	45
	A Tragic End	47
	References	47
4	**Condition of the Destroyer ARA *Bouchard***	49
	Crew and Materials (Bárcena, 1982)	49
	Bouchard's Tactical Procedures	51
	Intelligence	53
	References	54
5	**Background and Outbreak of the Falklands/Malvinas War**	55
	Pertinent Historical Background (Vv. Aa., IRI, 1994) (Rattenbach B., 1983)	55
	The Davidoff Incident	58
6	**The Days Before the War (Vv. Aa. Logbook 1982)**	63
	The Domestic and International Context and the Hostilities (Vv. Aa., IRI, 1994) (Vv. Aa., *Historia de la Fuerza Aérea Argentina* [History of the Argentine Air Force], 1998) (Vv. Aa., informe oficial del Ejército Argentino, *Conflicto Malvinas* [Official Argentine Army report on the Falklands/Malvinas War], 1983) (Rattenbach B., 1983)	64
	February 3, 1982: First Voyage of the Year	69
	February 16: Destination, Ushuaia	69
	March 4 and 5: The First Basic Drills	70
	March 17 to 19: The Drills Continue	71
	March 20 to 25: "Operation Cimarrón VII" With the Uruguayan Navy and Aircraft Carrier Exercises	71
	From March 29 to April 7: To War, Unawares	73
	References	75
7	**We're at War**	77
	The Domestic and International Context and the Hostilities (Vv. Aa., IRI, 1994) (Vv. Aa., *Historia de la Fuerza Aérea Argentina* [History of the Argentine Air Force], 1998) (Vv. Aa., informe oficial del Ejército Argentino, *Conflicto Malvinas* [Official Argentine Army Report on the Falklands/Malvinas War], 1983) (Rattenbach B., 1983)	77
	From April 16 to 27	79

8	**Operation Algeciras (Vv. Aa., Irizar.Org, 2014) (Nicoletti M., 2000)**	85
9	**From Puerto Deseado to the Sinking of *General Belgrano***	89
	The Domestic and International Context and the Hostilities (Vv. Aa., IRI, 1994) (Vv. Aa., *Historia de la Fuerza Aérea Argentina* [History of the Argentine Air Force], 1998) (Vv. Aa., informe oficial del Ejército Argentino, *Conflicto Malvinas* [Official Argentine Army Report on the Falklands/Malvinas War], 1983) (Rattenbach B., 1983)	89
	In the ARA *Bouchard*	90
10	***General Belgrano* Was Sunk!**	99
	The Domestic and International Context and the Hostilities (Vv. Aa., IRI, 1994) (Vv. Aa., *Historia de la Fuerza Aérea Argentina* [History of the Argentine Air Force], 1998) (Vv. Aa., informe oficial del Ejército Argentino, *Conflicto Malvinas* [Official Argentine Army report on the Falklands/Malvinas War], 1983) (Rattenbach B., 1983)	100
	In the ARA *Bouchard*	101
	Distribution of the Rescue of the Belgrano's Survivors	111
11	**Rebuffing the Attacks Attempted by Commandos (From May 14 to May 19, 1982)**	113
	The Domestic and International Context and the Hostilities (Vv. Aa., IRI, 2012) (Vv. Aa., *Historia de la Fuerza Aérea Argentina* [History of the Argentine Air Force], 1998) (Vv. Aa., informe oficial del Ejército Argentino, *Conflicto Malvinas* [Official Argentine Army report on the Falklands/Malvinas War], 1983) (Rattenbach B., 1983)	113
	In ARA the Bouchard	116
	May 14	117
	May 15 (Vv. Aa. Historical Book Bouchard 1982a:467)	117
	May 16 (Vv. Aa. War Diary Bouchard 1982c)	117
	Night from May 17 to May 18, Day of the Argentine Navy	120
	The British Continental Operations: The Perspective of the Parties Involved	121
	Meanwhile, the Commandos…	133
	Operation Mikado	134
	Operation Mikado as Described by a British "Historian"	137
	Epilogue	140
	References	141

12	**The Patrol Continues (From May 23 to May 27)**	143
	The Domestic and International Context and the Hostilities (IRI, 1994) (Vv. Aa., *Historia de la Fuerza Aérea Argentina* [History of the Argentine Air Force], 1998) (Vv. Aa., informe oficial del Ejército Argentino, *Conflicto Malvinas* [Official Argentine Army report on the Falklands/Malvinas War], 1983) (Rattenbach B., 1983)	143
	In the ARA *Bouchard*	145
13	**The Last Patrol (From May 31 to June 6)**	147
	The Domestic and International Context and the Hostilities (IRI, 1994) (Vv. Aa., *Historia de la Fuerza Aérea Argentina* [History *of the Argentine Air Force*], 1998) (Vv. Aa., informe oficial del Ejército Argentino, *Conflicto* Malvinas [Official Argentine Army Report on the Falklands/Malvinas War], 1983) (Rattenbach B., 1983)	149
	In the ARA *Bouchard*	152
14	**The Return to Puerto Belgrano After the Defeat**	153

Appendix A: List of Commanding Officers 157

Appendix B: Voyages of the Destroyer ARA *Bouchard* Under the Argentine Flag 159

Appendix C: Captain Barcena's "Farewell Address" to his Crew 169

Appendix D: List of Crewmembers 173

Epilogue: An Undeserved End 187

Bibliography 191

Chapter 1
Characteristics of the Destroyer ARA *Bouchard*

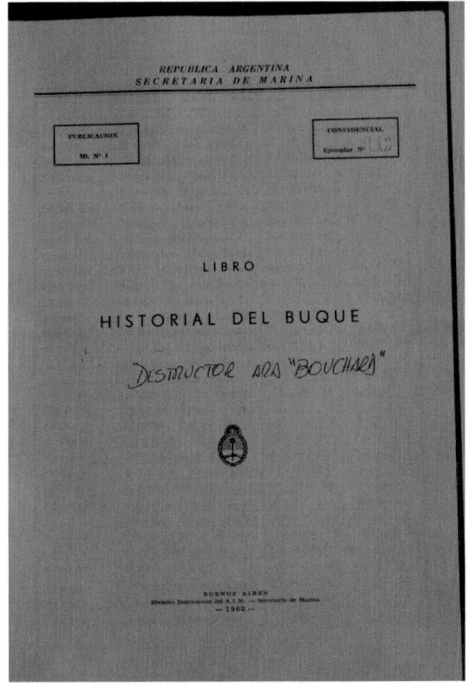

Cover of the historical book of the destroyer ARA Bouchard (Confidential).

Abstract The technical characteristics of the ship are described, as well as its propulsion plant, weapons systems and hull. This is to inform expert readers, naval enthusiasts and all the people who approach military literature for the first time, about the warship and its capabilities.

1 Characteristics of the Destroyer ARA *Bouchard*

Naval history and heritage command. https://www.history.navy.mil/content/history/nhhc/

The destroyer ARA *Bouchard* was built in the Federal Shipbuilding and Drydock Company Shipyard, in New York City, United States. It was launched on July 4, 1944, undoubtedly a very special day for the country. It was delivered to Argentina on July 1, 1972, and arrived to the country on November 17, of that same year.

The weight of the ship is known as its "displacement". When empty, it is called its "light displacement". Ships in *Bouchard's* class had a light displacement of 2857 tons. They had a minimum displacement of 2926 tons in order to operate and maintain an adequate stability and, when fully loaded (with everything necessary to navigate and operate safely), its displacement was 3225 tons.

Displacement (weight)	2926 ton
Light displacement (empty)	2857 ton
Maximum displacement (fully loaded)	3225 ton

Its freedom of action with regard to water and fuel was relative since with a 300 ton decrease in weight due to a reduction in the amounts of water, fuel, munitions and food supplies, it reached its minimum operational displacement. Certainly, this was a significant limitation that forced it to replenish frequently these types of units.

Its draught[1] at maximum load was 14 feet, $1^3/_4$ inches (4.31 m). Its draught under minimum operational conditions, once the 300 tons mentioned in the previous paragraph were consumed, was 13 feet, $2^1/_4$ inches (4.02 m). Here we can also appreciate that the change in draught between the maximum and minimum loads was very small.

The overall length of the ship was 376 feet, 6 inches (114.76 m). Its beam at waterline was 40 feet, $9^3/_4$ inches (12.42 m) and its maximum beam was 41 feet, $^3/_4$ inches (12.51 m).

The ship's moulded depth[2] at the main frame was 23 feet (7.01 m). Its propellers ended 4 feet, $7^3/_8$ inches (1.45 m) behind the keel[3] and the sonar transducer (the antenna), a piece of equipment designed to detect submarines, measured 5 feet, $5^1/_4$ inches (1.67 m).

Draught (maximun depth reached at the keel)	14 ft $1^3/_4$ (4.31 m)
Overall length	376′ 6″ (114.76 m)
Beam at the waterline	40′ $9^3/_4$″ (12.42 m)
Maximum beam at the main deck	41′$^3/_4$″ (12.51 m)
Ship's moulded depth (between the keel and the main deck	2′ (7.01 m)

The ships of this class had 210 frames, a type of rib that gives the shape to the ship and on which the hull is attached, the external shape that we see when looking at the ship. By design, these frames were spaced 21 inches (0.53 cm) apart.

| 210 frames | Spaced 21″ (0.53 m) |

In its interior, there were tanks containing, amongst others, 495 tons of fuel oil, which fed the boiler burners that generated the necessary steam[4]; 21 tons of JP5,

---
[1] The maximum depth reached by the hull.
[2] The measurement between the keel and the main deck.
[3] The lowest part of the hull.
[4] Distilled water specially treated to be used in boilers of steam-powered ships.

aviation fuel to supply the helicopters; 11 tons of lubrication oils, for the ship's endless array of propulsion mechanisms; 94 tons of water to feed the boilers; and 39.8 tons of water for general purposes, for the crew's consumption. This totalled a liquid bulk of 660.8 tons. It is important to mention that the tanks were only filled to 95% capacity, because the ship's movement caused the contents to slosh through the venting tubes.

Fuel oil	495 ton
Air fuel	21 ton
Lubrication oils	11 ton
Feed water (for the boilers)	94 ton
Fresh water (for general purposes)	39.8 ton
Bulk total liquid	660.8 ton

Its operational range, at an efficient 12 knots, which allows a propelled object to reach the greatest distance with all its fuel, was 3990 miles (7388.12 km).

Cruise speed	12 knots.
Maximum speed	32 knots (59.25 km/h)
Maximum range (at cruise speed)	3990 miles (7388.12 km)

The bridge was 28 feet, $10^{1}/_{2}$ inches (8.8 m) above the waterline and 104 feet, 4 inches (31.8 m) from the bow.

Machinery

The ship had a complex propulsion system. It included two propulsion units with steam turbines, each outputting 30,000 hp at full load, i.e., giving it a total of 60,000 horsepower. This allowed it, originally, to reach a maximum speed of 32 knots (59.25 km/h), which is a significant speed for a ship, even today. Each propulsion unit powered a propeller shaft, meaning that it had two four-bladed propellers, generally made from bronze or steel.

Its four boilers, manufactured by M Babcock & Wilcox, had separate ovens and reheating controls, closed wick draught, and a single funnel for both ovens. The pressures and temperatures output by these machines were impressive; the operational pressure was 634 lb/in^2 (44.57 kg/cm^2).

The low pressure turbine condenser recovered the evaporated water in the boilers, which the high and low pressure turbines used as a fluid to propel the rotors. However, it was also necessary for the ship to have a distiller, called an evaporator. This distiller took water from the sea and evaporated it. The vapour was then condensed and distilled water produced, which was used in the boilers sending the water to the feeder tanks. Subsequently, part of the water was remineralised to be fit for human consumption and sent to the service water tanks. These were low pressure, single band and submerged tube evaporators (there were two units, manufactured by Griscom & Russell), and according to the manual they produced 16,000 gallons (60.5 m^3).

In addition, the ship had two main and two auxiliary generators. The mains were driven by 1200 rpm vapour turbines generating 500 KW AC, 450 V of voltage, and 50 KW of 120 V of DC. On the other hand, the auxiliaries generated 100 KW of 450 V AC and the CC that they generated was for their own operation.

Main engines (two steam turbines)	30,000 hp each (60,000 hp total)
Shafts and propellers (two)	Four-bladed
Boilers (four)	(M Babcock & Wilcox)
Sea water distiller	16,000 gallons (60.5 m^3) (Griscom & Russell)
Generators: main (two) Auxiliaries (two)	500 kW AC 450 V 50 kW 120 V DC 100 kW 450 V AC

Naval history and heritage command. https://www.history.navy.mil/content/history/nhhc/

Elements for Deck Operations

The ship had two Baldt bower anchors, each weighing 4003.6 lb (1816 kg). They were attached to the ship by anchor chains, the links of which were $1^1/_4$ inches (3.175 cm) thick. Chain sections were linked together by shackles. In *Bouchard's* case, and generally in ships of this type, each section of links is 11 feet, $11^3/_{10}$ inches, (26.5 m) in length.

The ship had 17 chain shackles, eight on the port anchor and nine on the starboard anchor. To raise the anchors, it had two vertical drum capstans, powered by a 30 hp electric motor.

Tugs were used for its approach to port. In addition to these manoeuvres, it had tow ropes made from synthetic fibres (nylon) with an 8 inch circumference and $2^1/_2$ inch diameter (203 and 64 mm, respectively). Two of these ropes were 183 feet, $8^7/_{10}$ inches, (56 m) long, while a third was shorter, 147 feet, $7^7/_{10}$ inches (45 m). To remain safely in port, it had six berthing ropes, these were 5 inches in circumference with a diameter of $1^6/_{10}$ inches (127 and 40 mm, respectively), with a total of 1774 feet, $7^8/_{10}$ inches (540 m) berthing ropes.

For tugging and berthing operations, it used not only the two anchor capstans, but the ship also had two horizontal drum winches, powered by electric motors, that brought a great deal of versatility to rope operations, which were joined by great efforts from the deck crew working manually on these operations.

It also had smaller boats, like the 20 foot, 8 inch (6.30 m), 5 foot, $10^9/_{10}$ inch (1.80 m) beam, and 6 foot, $6^3/_4$ inch (1.20 m) moulded depth draught launch with plastic hull and sides. This vessel weighted around 4409.2 lb (2000 kg) and was propelled by a four-stroke 75 hp engine.

Later, in Argentina, a 15 foot, 5 inch (4.70 m) draught, and 2204.6 lb (1000 kg) capacity inflatable Zodiac boat was added, with a Jonson 40 hp outboard motor. In the event that the unit had to be abandoned, it had 22 Firestone self-inflating rafts, with capacity for 15 people each.

When operations had to be carried out with torpedoes on-deck, in the middle of the ship near the torpedo tubes, there was a manual boom a little over 21 feet, 3 inches (6.5 m) long, which had a maximum load of approximately one ton. In addition, it had other davits for launch manoeuvring, accommodation ladder, shipwreck rescue, and torpedo operations.

Another crucial element for operation, both in port and at sea, is the rudder. A system of hydraulic pumps propelled by electrical motors moved the rudder blade (which is submerged and makes the necessary course changes). These ships had two pumps that could work independently or together, manufactured by Waterbury.

Anchors (Hall type) (two)	4003.6 lb (1816 kg) Baldt Bower
Cables (two $1''¼$ thick Chains)	$11'11^3/_{10}''$ length (26.5 m) each shackle
Port anchor length	8 shackles
Starboard anchor length	9 shackles

(continued)

(continued)

Capstan (two)	2 (electric motors)
Towing ropes (two)	8" circumference 183'8$^7/_{10}$" (56 m) long
Berthing ropes (six)	5" circumference 1774' (540 m) total long
Boats (two)	20'8" (6.30m) 75 hp 15'5" (4.70m) 40 hp
Survival rafts	22
Manual boom (for torpedoes operations)	21'3" (6.5 m) length
Rudder blades (two)	Hydraulics pumps (waterbury)

Other Elements

The ship had a cold room, with two independent refrigeration circuits powered by electric motors. Ventilation was provided by fixed ducts and the air was circulated by electric motors. The ventilation system was supplemented with equipment that preheated the air, to heat the liveable areas using steam heat exchangers. Some areas, like the one used after the installation of the Exocet missile system, were cooled with air conditioners. It also had what are known as "spotlights", large and very powerful directional lights that have several uses (for combat, visual communication during the day or night, searching for objects at sea or in the air, direct approaches, etc.) and were placed on the signal bridge (above the bridge). Three lights were manufactured by Westinghouse and one by General Electric.

Artillery

The main battery had three 5 inch (127 mm) twin turrets called "dual-purpose", because they were versatile enough to be used to engage naval, air and land targets. It was controlled by a fire-control system,[5] the MK 37, which included an MK 1-A fire control table, which calculated all the ballistic corrections to be made in order to hit the target; an MK 6 stable element, which offered a constant horizontal reference plane to balance the ship's motions produced by its movement and the hydroclimatic conditions; an MK 25 radar, a specially adapted fire control radar, only used in combat (to the point that today being "lit up" by this type or radar is considered a threat or aggressive action), and an MK 5 target designation system. In addition, the ship had

---

[5] In naval jargon, "fire-control" includes the systems that provide the necessary adjustments to correctly fire a shot, i.e., that control the shooting of the ship's main artillery guns.

three magazines,[6] one below each turret. In total, it had 2305 artillery shells[7] and 2314 projectiles.

Later in Argentina, the ship was fitted with a quadruple assembly of Aeroespatiale MM 38 Exocet missiles.

Main battery (three)	3 5″ twin turrets (dual purpose)
Machine guns (two)	12.7 mm
Fire-control system	MK 37
Fire control table	MK 1-A
Fire control radar	MK 25
Gun direction system system	MK 5
Shells (main battery total storage)	2314
SSM missiles (four)	Aeroespatiale Exocet MM38

Anti-submarine Weapons

The ship had a number of different weapons and systems for anti-submarine warfare, such as torpedoes, hedgehogs, a Fanfare noisemaker, and a depth charge thrower.

- *Torpedoes*: It featured two triple torpedo mounts MK 32, Mod. 5, which were used to launch battery-powered MK 44 torpedoes. It could carry 30 torpedoes, 6 of which were installed in the tubes. Accessory to the launchers, it had a Worthington four-stage high-pressure compressor, which propelled the torpedo from the tube into the sea. Then, the torpedo autonomously propelled itself towards the target using the energy from its batteries.
- *Hedgehogs*: It had two MK 11, Mod. 0 mounts. They were a type of horizontally placed projectiles, which were launched in volleys and, depending on the configuration given to their mounting, formed a sort of discreet sized circle. However, if the submarine was within that circle, it would be hit with one of these primitive but lethal projectiles.
- *Fanfare*: It was designed to produce noise and sound at different frequencies, to confuse smart torpedoes launched by a submarine.

---

[6] Ammunition storage.
[7] Sheaths with gunpowder.

Anti-submarine Weapons

- *Depth charge throwers*: During the 1979 repairs, a depth charge rack was installed. It was mechanical and manually activated. It was placed port side, at the stern. The bombs installed were six old MK 9 depth charges.

Torpedo tubes Launchers (two)	MK32 Mod. 5
Torpedoes MK 44 and A 244 S	30 (6 in the tubes)
Hedgehogs Launchers (two)	MK 11 Mod 0
ASW decoy	Fanfare
Depth charge throwers (six)	MK 9 depth charges

Sensors

Air warning radar (one)	SPS 40
Surface warning radar (one)	SPS 10
Navegation radar (one)	Decca 1110
Sonar (one)	SQS 29
Electronic Survelliance Measures (one)	WLR 1
Searchligts (four)	Above the bridge (for combat and visual communications)

Aircrafts

Helicopter (optional) (one)	AI–03 Alouette III

Alouette helicopter belonging to the cruiser ARA General Belgrano on the flight deck before taking off to get the Commanding and Chief Operating Officer

Chapter 2
Borie II, Campaign in the Pacific Ocean (WWII), in the Korean War, in the Vietnam War, in the Mediterranean (July to December, 1956), Miscellaneous, Other Minor Actions

Abstract *Borie II* and its participation in the Pacific Ocean campaign, Iwo Jima, Okinawa and kamikaze actions, the passing of President Franklin Delano Roosevelt and the events in Tokyo's metropolitan area. The atomic bombing of Hiroshima and Nagasaki.

Nav source naval history photographic history of the US Navy. https://www.navsource.org/archives/05idx.htm

Campaign in the Pacific Ocean

The campaign in the Philippines began on October 10, 1944, with air raids on Okinawa, Formosa and Luzon. Between October 14 and 26 of the same year, the United States landed its forces and large scale naval battles took place, like the landing and huge battle at Leyte Gulf. During this engagement, the Japanese naval forces were rebuffed, with great losses on both sides. Later on, there were landings in Mindoro, on December 15, 1944, and the Lingayen Gulf (Luzon), on January 9; finally, the Allied troops also landed at Palawan, on February 28. *Borie II*'s contribution to this campaign started on January 24, with the beginning of the bombardment of Iwo Jima. In February of 1945, a conference in Yalta was held to discuss the situation of the world. Two decisions were made there regarding the Pacific area: to capture both Iwo Jima and Okinawa.

Iwo Jima

"The Americans had to take control of Iwo Jima at all costs as it was a crucial base for its bombers en route to Japan" (Vv. Aa. 1965a: 427). Iwo Jima is an island of flat land, not very high and not very extensive, of around 5.6 × 3.1 miles (9 × 5 km), with a small volcano in the extreme south-west, with beautiful vegetation and black sand beaches (Vv. Aa. 1965a: 427; Bartley 1954: 4, 5).

The objective sought by capturing Iwo Jima (Vv. Aa. 1949: 18), was to have bases to launch attacks by air on the Japanese metropolitan area (Bartley 1954: 23), support the air and naval blockade of Japan, enable the invasion of the metropolitan islands and maintain military pressure on Japan. Admiral Nimitz and his Staff knew that it was not going to be an easy task, and their experiences in Tarawa, Kwajalein, Eniwetok, Saipan, Guam and Peleliu, led them to believe that the resistance would be fierce, which turned out to be true (Morrison 1960: 13; Martinez de Campos y Serrano 1956: 261).

On November 24, 1944, this strategic Japanese position was bombed, under the suspicion that it was the base for Japanese B29 bombers, which were supported by P38 fighters, together with the 5th Cruiser Division and six destroyers (Morrison 1960: 11). From that moment until the landing, Iwo Jima suffered, like no other position, an unceasing and significant bombardment to soften coastal defences (Bartley 1954: 39). Tons of air-dropped bombs and ship fired shells devastated the Japanese facilities and forces (Morrison 1960: 13).

Japan had over 5000 Army men, supported by artillery and machine guns with 120 mm artillery pieces for coastal defence and 25 mm anti-aircraft weapons, operated by 2000 men from the Japanese Navy, under the command of Admiral Toshinosuke Ichimaru. On the day of the Allies landing, February 19, 1945, the total defence forces numbered, at least, 21,000 men (Morrison 1960: 14; Bartley 1954: 5; Vv. Aa. 1949: 19; Bartley 1954: 51). Task Force 58 (TF) was under commanded by Vice-Admiral Mitscher, aboard the *Bunker Hill* aircraft carrier (Carrero Blanco 1957: 259). This force belonged to the Fifth Fleet, commanded by Admiral Spruance, based in Indianapolis.

Borie belonged to Task Force 58.3, which included two aircraft carriers, one light aircraft carrier, two battleships, five cruisers of different types and sizes, and fourteen destroyers, among others. In command of this Task Force was Rear-Admiral Sherman, who also counted with the presence of the Task Force 58 Commander, since one of the subordinate ships the *Bunker Hill* aircraft carrier (Morrison 1960: 383; Bartley 1954: 40).

While the actions on Iwo Jima continued with fierce intensity, since the defenders resisted the Allied invasion to their last breath, on February 25 the Task Force headed towards the so-called Japanese metropolitan area, to shell Nagoya and Tokyo (Vv. Aa. 1965a: 436). The inclement weather made the journey difficult, especially for the smaller ships like the destroyers. The waves swept over the decks and standing was difficult on *Borie*. The violent and constant movements prevented all activities on-board and, for several days, the food ration was limited to canned meats and whatever hot drinks the overburdened cooks were able to prepare, while risking accidents. The same situation was experienced by the other destroyers.

Admiral Mitscher ordered, at 12:15 on February 25, that all operations be cancelled, when the Force was a mere 190 miles from south-eastern Tokyo. Due to the bad weather forecast for February 26, which would prevent operations, the Admiral decided to head towards Nagoya, a target for attacks. On the way, they sunk several small Japanese boats that tried to attack the fleet. Task Force 58.3, to which *Borie* belonged, was attacked at 00:30 on February 26, by one of these Japanese pickets. The weapon's firing greatly damaged the equipment of one of the destroyers, killing one of its men and wounding two others. The Japanese vessel almost crashed with *Porterfield,* and the destroyer *Stockham* was ordered to approach and destroy it. The destroyer fired its 40 mm anti-aircraft guns and was able to severely damage the enemy. It was later lost in the night, but in conditions that were utterly hard to bear: the sinking of that vessel was a matter of minutes (Morrison 1960: 58).

Due to the damage, the Force decided to reduce its speed to 12 knots and, because of the delay, the Task Force Commander decided to cancel the attack on Nagoya. It is likely that the crew of the small Japanese boat never knew that their heroic actions prevented a ferocious attack on the city of Nagoya (Morrison 1960: 58).

The events at sea continued on: shelling the Iwo Jima coast, the answering fire from the island's batteries, submarine attacks, ships from the Japanese Fleet that had to be rebuffed. The defenders did everything in their power to halt the conquest. They even resorted to the support of logistics convoys, that were unable to arrive in time due to the artillery and zealous encirclement carried out by the United States Navy. Meanwhile, the marines conquered beaches, opening the way for the torturous advance.

On March 5, in the face of the massive American onslaught, the Japanese survivors mustered in the north of the Island. By March 18, only 800 soldiers were left alive and, by the 23, practically none remained (Vv. Aa. 1965b: 12–11; Bartley 1954: 189). At 18:00 on March 16, the island of Iwo Jima was conclusively conquered with the surrender of the remaining pockets of resistance. The cost had been exceedingly high: the marines lost 3885 men and the final tally was over 6000 KIAs and 17,000 wounded. This was the beginning of the end of the Japanese Empire (Bartley 1954: 191).

Okinawa

The taking of Okinawa was the hardest in the whole Pacific campaign. According to historians, the operation code-named 'Iceberg' (Nichols and Shaw 1955: 12) was the most audacious and complex one carried out until today (Vv. Aa. 1965a: 441). However, the considerable effort was worth the results. The island had excellent anchorages for the Pacific Fleet, and ideal locations to build aerodromes and airfields, as well as favourable places to concentrate logistics and forces for future landings. As expected, the Japanese defence was desperate and fierce (Vv. Aa. 1949:19). In fact, the deployments that began in October 1944, included an amphibious assault with the participation of over 1300 ships (Nichols and Shaw 1955: 63) on April 1, 1945, and finally ended on June 21, of the same year.

The first attack was under the command of Admiral Mitscher and carried out by his Task Force, which included nine aircraft carriers, five battleships, eight escort carriers, four heavy cruisers, seven light cruisers, three anti-aircraft cruisers and 58 destroyers, one of which was *Borie II*. On October 10, 1944, they launched an all-day attack that greatly damaged the Japanese defences. The defending forces received 541 tons of bombs, 652 rockets and 21 torpedoes. They also lost airplanes, both on land and in dogfights, cargo ships, a minelaying submarine, and hundreds of tons of rice, ammunition in several calibres, etc. They would then have some respite until January 1945 (Vv. Aa. 1965b: 20).

At first, it seemed like the 287,000 invaders were met with over 77,000 Japanese defenders. However, it was later determined that there were less than 55,000 (Morrison 1960: 90), who, given the size of the island of Okinawa, occupied every square yard of land. The whole of the III Amphibious Corps of the United States Marine Corps was engaged in the occupation, many of whom were veterans from previous landings on neighbouring archipelagos (Morrison 1960: 88).

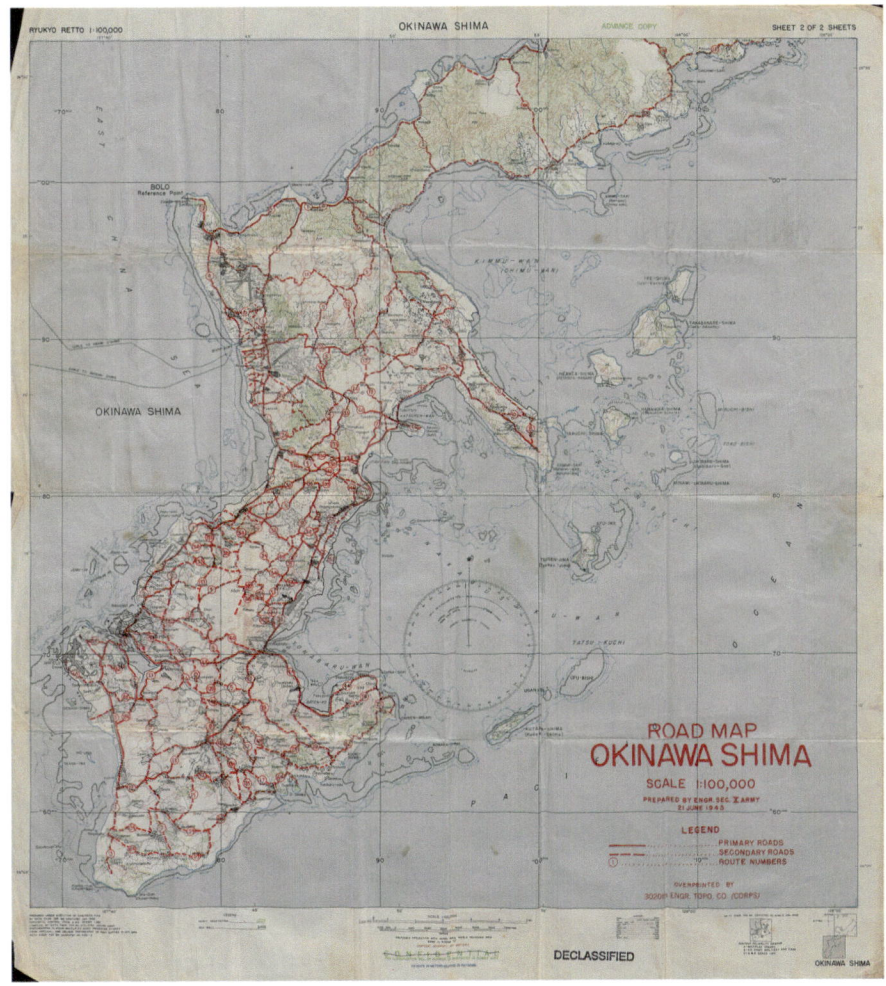

Kamikaze Actions

Japan, in addition to concentrating all possible air forces in the East China Sea, considered the training and fine-tuning of the kamikazes' tactics to be of the greatest import. The first kamikaze attacks took place on October 20 and 21, 1944, during the Allied invasion of Leyte, although they were unsuccessful. However, attacks on October 25 resulted in the sinking of a carrier, and three other ships took damage.

The decision had been made to fight until the last breath, and the young pilots had to immolate themselves to defend their country (Nichols and Shaw 1955: 82), besides learning and practising how to cause the greatest devastation possible, the greatest damage, while impacting against enemy ships (Vv. Aa. 1965b: 121–129). The different types of vessels that were to be attacked and their weak points were carefully studied. The sacrifice should not be in vain. Airplane manufacture in Japan diminished every day due to the Allied bombing, from 1900 in January to 1260 in February 1945.

Taking part as a kamikaze was on a voluntary basis. In fact, the number of volunteers was so overwhelming that they had to draw lots to decide who would sacrifice themselves and who would pilot the escorting fighters. A kamikaze unit consisted of five airplanes, three kamikazes and two escorts. The targets, in order of importance, were: (1) aircraft carriers, (2) battleships and cruisers, and (3) destroyers and logistics or auxiliary ships. The fighters, in addition to escorting and covering the kamikazes, were to assess the damages caused and suggest tactical changes. For example, when attacking aircraft carriers, they suggested that the attacks be carried out on the elevator doors so that, should the ship not be sunk, it would be left out of service (Vv. Aa. 1965b: 20).

Initially, they approached from a very low altitude to avoid being detected by radar. For this reason, radar pickets were added,[1] that singled out a destroyer stationed at a considerable distance so that early warnings could be given. The results were mediocre since they were unable to inflict damage because of their low speed. Therefore, the tactics were changed and they increased their altitude by 1312 or 1640 ft (400 or 500 m), from where they crashed into the doors of the aircraft carriers or the magazines on battleships and large vessels (Vv. Aa. 1965b:121–129).

The last suicide attack was the one by Admiral Ugaki, head of the kamikazes. Together with 23 other kamikazes, on August 15, 1945, he unsuccessfully attacked the Allied Fleet. After a spirited and pain filled speech, he boarded his airplane and died together with his men, trying to prevent the inevitable. That same day, Admiral Ohnishi, the inventor of the kamikaze's tactics, performed harakiri after leaving a heartfelt letter where he stated his admiration for the kamikaze pilots and asked that his agony not be shortened, since his pain would pay, in part, his debt to his country (Vv. Aa. 1965b: 121–122). For Japan, that was the main area of contention, decisive for the defence of the Japanese metropolitan area, and so the greatest possible effort was expended.

---

[1] Vessel stationed at a certain distance to detect possible enemy attacks with its radar, i.e., to act as an early warning system for possible attacks.

Nav source naval history photographic history of the US Navy. https://www.navsource.org/archives/05idx.htm

The Fight Continues in the Pacific

With Admirals Toyoda and Ugaki commanding the Fleet and Air Force, their objective was the Allied logistics and cargo ships. The Japanese Admiralty understood that the only path to delaying defeat, or revert the trend seen until then, was to disrupt the Allies' logistics.

On March 14, under the command of Admiral Mitscher, Task Force 58 (which included *Borie*) left Ulithi heading north (Vv. Aa. 1965b: 121–127), to attack the Kyushu aerodromes and prevent the feared Japanese aircraft from taking off. The counterattack was swift, and on March 18, TF 58.4 received the greatest damage caused by Ugaki's aircraft (Nichols and Shaw 1955: 44). On March 19, a merciless and relentless naval battle took place, with dozens of ships, aircraft carriers, battleships, heavy and light cruisers, and destroyers, including *Borie*. In this battle, which took place on the inland sea between Kure and Kobe, the kamikazes deployed heavily and intensely, and inflicted severe damages (Morrison 1960: 94/95).

As a consequence of the Quebec (Canada) Conference of September 1944, a British Expeditionary Force joined the Pacific Allied Fleet on March 15, 1945. This Force was under the aegis of the Pacific Fleet, which was commanded by Admiral

Nimitz, until the end of conflict (Morrison 1960: 105). The Admiral welcomed the Force and assigned it to the Sakishima Gunto area, between Formosa and Okinawa.

There were no lack of storms and typhoons that, allied with the defending forces, caused significant damage and delays to over 600 ships that sailed the waters near Okinawa (for example, the weather endured from March 25 to 30, 1945) (Carrero Blanco 1957: 262–263; Morrison 1960: 11). Once the inclement weather was overcome, the TFs 58.1, 58.3 and 58.4 attacked the areas of resistance on the island.

The coastal bombardment was supported by minesweepers that, in accordance with their motto: "the first to arrive, the last to leave", had to sweep moored[2] and drifting mines that caused severe damage to the ships nearing the coast to fire on targets without being in range of coastal defence artillery, which was put in place by the defenders. In addition to the mines, the suicide boats (a surface type of kamikaze) were the most significant dangers to an attack on the coast.

On April 7, airplanes sunk *Yamato* (Nichols and Shaw 1955: 85), the largest battleship in the world, which had a displacement of over 72,000 tones and a main battery consisting of nine 460 mm guns with a range of 137,795 feet (42,000 m); it was the pride and joy of the Imperial Navy. The battleship was heading to Okinawa to resist the Allied advance, when TF 58 intercepted it and its carriers launched the torpedo and bombing attacks that, at 14:20, sunk the battleship and a large part of the Task Group (TG) of the operation called "Ten-Go" (Martinez del Campo y Serrano 1956: 264, 268–269; Carrero Blanco 1957: 264).

Roosevelt Passes Away

The sunrise was bright and clear on April 13. The news of the death of the President of the United States, Franklin Delano Roosevelt, was heard through the speakers of every ship. The Commander in Chief of the United States Armed Forces had died from a cerebral haemorrhage. By order of the Secretary of the Navy, James V. Forrestal, a religious service was held in honour of the deceased President aboard every vessel and on every naval station on April 15 (Morrison 1960: 231). This event was the cause of much woe and distress amongst the crews and higher command.

The mass attacks by kamikazes, called kikusui or floating chrysanthemum, caused significant material losses and casualties. The Allied forces were attacked by over 1900 kamikazes, with different levels of success (Morrison 1960: 233). It was because of this kikusui that the role of the destroyers was crucial when they deployed with radar pickets. They were to position themselves at a certain distance from the Force, facing towards the attack vector, and raise the alarm and offer resistance when the radar picket detected the presence of air or seaborne attackers. It was confirmed that the defensive actions of the destroyers was far superior to the quality of information

---

[2] Mines suspended below the surface of the water by means of an attached weight that lies on the seabed.

provided by the Force's sensors. A new concept took hold in Japan's defensive strategy: "A plane for a ship, a boat for a ship, a man for ten enemies or a tank" (Nichols and Shaw 1955: 49).

On May 4, the flagship, the aircraft carrier *Bunker Hill*, was attacked by a kamikaze, leaving it on fire and killing several Staff Officers and NCOs (Morrison 1960: 264). One hour later, a destroyer transferred Admiral Mitscher and his Staff to *Enterprise*. The fire could not be controlled and left a tally of 353 dead, 43 missing and 264 wounded. After several destroyers helped extinguish the fire, *Bunker Hill* was forced to return to Bremerton for repairs; it was one of TF 58's most damaged ships. From *Borie II's* bridge, they were silent witnesses to the events.

On May 12 and 13, part of TF 58, including *Borie*, headed to the Kyushu and Shikoku area. On May 14, the flagship, which was now *Enterprise*, was attacked by a kamikaze. This time, the damages and fire were controlled in a mere half-hour, leaving 13 dead and 68 wounded. Once again, the Commanding Officer had to change ships and board *Randolph*, with his whole Staff (Morrison 1960: 264). Between June 3 and 7, the last kikusui (kamikaze) attacks were received. These were a complete failure, since they inflicted neither damages nor casualties (Morrison 1960: 274).

The invasion continued in all the archipelagos surrounding the Japanese metropolitan area. Borneo was very easy to take, since the resistance faced by the Allied forces was minimal. The landings at Tarakan, Brunei Bay and Balikpapan were simple after the events at Okinawa (Vv. Aa. 1949: 20).

Between June 18 and 21, 1945, any organised resistance was ended and the invading forces were devoted to reducing the last pockets of resistance. On June 21, at 13:05 h, the taking of Okinawa was finished and, on June 22, at 10:00 h, a ceremony was held to celebrate the achievement and to say farewell to the soldiers lost in action (Nichols and Shaw 1955: 256–257).

Nav source naval history photographic history of the US Navy. https://www.navsource.org/archives/05idx.htm

The Forces Go for Tokyo

Between July 1 and August 15, large scale air raids were carried out on Japan's metropolitan islands, with the main targets being Tokyo, Hokkaido, Honshu, Kure, and Nagoya. These attacks were in advance of the invasion that had been planned for November 1945, in the south of Kyushu. From July 1, 1,300,000 tons of bombs were dropped on Japan's metropolitan area (Carrero Blanco 1957: 272). On the last day of July 1945, a huge typhoon hit where TF 58 was stationed, and which included *Borie*. Admiral Halsey, in command of the Force, chose to withdraw from the path of the inclement weather to avoid additional damage.

Admiral Nimitz ordered the Force to head towards the north of Honshu, since intelligence reported a mustering of bombers and kamikazes that would attack the bases of the B-29s in the Mariana Islands. From July 9, *Borie* participated in attacks on the islands of Japan's archipelagos. On August 9, devastating attacks were conducted north of Honshu, at least 251 airplanes were destroyed by the Allied attack and another 141 were damaged. Thus, the Japanese attack on Saipan was quashed.

No kamikaze had gotten near an aircraft carrier during the attack. However, one of them was able to attack a destroyer stationed on the radar picket, 50 miles southeast of the Task Force position. The destroyer attacked was *Borie*, whose CO, Commander Noah Adair, saw the enemy airplane approaching from starboard at 14:56. His eyes could not believe what they were seeing and, from the bridge wing, he gave the desperate and forceful order: "Hard-a-port!" He knew the consequences this attack would have on the weak superstructure. The weapons systems did not have the chance to redirect their fire towards the attacker. Before the ship could be manoeuvred, the superstructure was impacted between the main battery fire control and the mast, and a massive fire broke out immediately. The bridge could not be entered. The Quartermaster took his place on the servomotor, aft, above the rudder's motor, together with a telephone operator who received the headings from the on-duty officer. The whole ship dove wholeheartedly into the task of extinguishing the fire, which could not be allowed to reach the magazines, since that would mean the complete loss of the ship. Sympathetic hands looked for the wounded amongst the warped metal that had been the fire-control system. For those men, the air-sea battle had finished; the battle against the fire had just begun.

After two hours of fighting, the damage control team managed to control the fire and save the ship. However, 48 men lost their lives, between those KIA and MIA, and 66 were injured to different degrees. With grimy faces, burnt hands and frayed uniforms, they gathered at the stern, while the damage control teams[3] finished the task of extinguishing the last fire hotspots. A general formation was called, to determine those who were missing. The faces showed the anguish of those who were searching for a crewmate in the dark interior corridors, in the hopes of finding him, and the sadness of knowing that he had been on-duty at or under the fire-control. The desperate cries of team members could be heard, of the colleagues that couldn't accept their loss. The Division Chiefs gave their report to the Executive Officer, and he reported to the Commanding Officer; a routine that this time brought terrible news. A significant part of the crew had been lost. It could be replaced, but it would leave a deep hole in the hearts of those who had, until then, shared the Pacific Campaign. This might have been the last successful kamikaze attack of the war, perhaps a parallel to the old *Borie I*.

The End of the War in the Pacific

On August 6, the first atomic bomb fell on Hiroshima, dropped by a B29 known as *Enola Gay*, commanded by Coronel Paul Tibbets. The bomb was made with enriched uranium (Vv. Aa. 1965a: 469). The plane left Tinian at 02:45, at 09:11 it was over the city of Hiroshima, and at 09:15, at 31,600 ft, it dropped the bomb that would change history. The *Enola Gay* landed at Tinian at 14:58, with "no issues to report". The

---

[3] In naval jargon, it is the team made up of ship personnel, of any specialty, that works to deeply know a part of the ship and the equipment they have available to fight any unfortunate event (fires, flooding, collisions, etc.), and every day has different drills to ensure that, when the time comes, they can react automatically and in an organised fashion to any event.

result of this attack was a toll of 71,379 dead, 19,691 gravely injured and 171,000 people left without a home, this does not include the later health catastrophes caused by the enriched uranium spread during the explosion. President Truman described the strike as "a great event in history" (Morrison 1960: 344; Carrero Blanco 1957: 276–277).

Before sunrise on August 9, Russia declared war on Japan (Martinez del Campo y Serrano 1956: 271), and Premier Suzuki tried to convince the Emperor of urgently accepting the Potsdam Declaration. While the cabinet was debating, news of the second bomb dropped on Nagasaki arrived. This time, the bomb was made from plutonium, and even more devastating than the one from New Mexico. The original target of the bombing had been the city of Kokura, but the dense cloud cover prevented it from doing so. The target was changed to Nagasaki, which was also covered by clouds, so they had to navigate with the help of radar. The aim was off by 3.1 miles (5 km), but the destruction was significant (Vv. Aa. 1965a: 469).

While Japan offered its unconditional surrender on August 10, *Borie* headed towards Saipan, searching for support to be able to continue towards Pearl Harbor and then on to California, where it would enter dry-dock in Hunter's Point for major repairs on September 10. On August 14, Japan's surrender was accepted. It was signed aboard the battleship *Missouri*, in Tokyo Bay, on September 2, 1945 (Vv. Aa. 1965a: 20–471; Carrero Blanco 1957: 277).

Borie II in the Korean War

Abstract *Borie II* in the Korean War. The deployment of the UN organised forces. The battles. The desperate rescue of civilians. The endless bombings.

Borie II became a part of the Korean War on September 6, 1950. However, the war had started on Sunday, June 25, when the Army of North Korea launched the first attack and invaded South Korea (Karig et al. 1952: 41), encountering scarcely any resistance (Cagle and Manson 1957: 3; Field 1962: 39). North Korea took Chuncheon and Kaesong, and the only response was the evacuation of the people. Communist history states that the first attack was conducted by South Korea. However, this is false, since it was the North Korean Army that, armed with Russian-made equipment and large reserves, initiated a surprising and devastating attack. With great secrecy and stealth, they took the South Korean forces by surprise, forcing them to withdraw as quickly as possible to avoid being massacred.

On June 27, President Harry Truman (Cagle and Manson 1957: 28) ordered his forces to support South Korea, whose own forces were overwhelmed by the communist advance. He also ordered the Seventh Fleet to protect Taiwan from a likely Chinese invasion (Karig et al. 1952: 42; Field 1962:41). Truman's response was said to be in the national interest, since he was accused of being too lax regarding communist actions, which at the time were very active at every latitude.

On July 7, 1950, the National Security Council of the United Nations published its third resolution, wherein it condemned the attack and advised UN Member States to support South Korea (Cagle and Manson 1957: 29). With the assistance provided, the Army of South Korea was able to reorganise itself and stop the unexpected advance, at just 19 miles (30 km) from Seoul. The arrival of an increasing number of US Air Force Squadrons allowed the withdrawal and evacuation to be safer and ensured that the airspace was not wholly controlled by North Korea's Yak-9s. The airfields, which until then had been attacked unopposed, began defending themselves, and the mounting enemy losses started to worry the attackers, although their persistence remained unfaltering (https://www.monografias.com/trabajos13/monodos/monodos.shtml).

The response was swift and, as soon as weather conditions allowed, the United States forces attacked all kinds of targets of opportunity, like troop concentrations, ammunition and fuel depots, bridges, transport columns, etc. This advance also caused losses to the attackers, several B-26 s amongst them (https://www.monografias.com/trabajos13/monodos/monodos.shtml).

On July 1, 1950, Task Force 77 (Karig et al. 1952: 58; Field 1962: 56), which would include *Borie II*, left Tokyo heading towards Pyongyang, on the west coast of Korea. It was a combined United States and British fleet, the attack objectives of which were airfields, bridges, railroads, roads, and everything that would support North Korea's war effort (Karig et al. 1952:37).

Despite the delay, the response was overwhelming and decisive. The advances could not be stopped; they were carried out at night and with force. In a few weeks, almost the whole of the Korean peninsula was in the hands of the invading armies. The speed of the advance was estimated at 3.7 mph (6 km/h). The UN focused its efforts in preparing a response to the invasion of the port of Pusan, which became a hive of activity with the constant arrival of US and Japanese troops; they would be responsible for providing a fierce and powerful answer to the invasion. The enemy's march forward was stopped, but the situation came to a standstill as the UN forces were unable to advance (https://www.monografias.com/trabajos13/monodos/monodos.shtml). The countries taking part in the operation were Australia, Belgium, Canada, Colombia, Ethiopia, the Philippines, France, Greece, the Netherlands, New Zealand, Luxembourg, the United Kingdom, South Africa, Turkey, and Thailand.

A few days before the arrival of *Borie* in the operational zone, a ferocious attack on the Pohang airfield forced the UN forces to be evacuated by sea, since they would have been annihilated by the numerous North Korean soldiers had they remained. This airfield was retaken on August 20, with great losses on both sides.

General Douglas MacArthur was responsible for devising the strategy to make the invaders withdraw to the 38° parallel north. To this end, the Marine Corps landed to the north of the fronts where battle was joined, to cut off the supply lines, thus the communist forces were unable to receive logistical support and were forced to withdraw. The operation was code-named "Operation Chromite" (Field 1962: 181), and its execution was approved on August 28, 1950, by the UN's Joint Chiefs of Staff.

By September 6, *Borie* was already in Korean waters as a part of Task Force 77 (Cagle and Manson 1957: 514). The landings began on the 15th (Karig et al. 1952: 159) and, that same afternoon, the US Fleet was ordered by the UN to start bombarding Incheon. By mid-afternoon, the troops disembarked, without encountering much resistance. By midnight, the three objectives set by the plan had been met. As stated by General Almond (Karig et al. 1952: 105), Incheon was the worst possible place for an amphibious landing, but the only one where the destruction of the enemy could be ensured.

There were 250 vessels that participated in the war, including the battleship *Missouri*, two aircraft carriers, cruisers, destroyers, cargo ships, and minesweepers. On their arrival, the seas had been completely mined with Russian mines (Cagle and Manson 1957: 121), laid by hand by small fishing boats and junks. These led to human and material losses and a huge endeavour from the minesweepers (Cagle and Manson 1957: 122; Karig et al. 1952: 285; Field 1962: 231). In a short time, the mission seemed to have been achieved and the UN had reached the 38° parallel north. In spite of having given the ultimatum, a warning was issued that if the UN crossed the parallel, China would support North Korea (Cagle and Manson 1957: 109), an event which materialized on October 10, 1950.

During the night, China sent soldiers and equipment to Korea, without being noticed by the UN forces (Field 1962: 259). Shortly, North Korea had over 180,000 men at its disposal, which was surprising, since the belief was that they had no more than 60,000. Later, it was determined that 300,000 men had faced 230,000 UN troops. This gave a significant advantage and superiority to the North Korean forces, which had to be matched by the intense participation of the Air Force, which attacked bridges, factories, supply transports, and everything that supplied the troops.

On the night of October 29, 27,000 men landed in an orderly fashion[4] and without resistance at Riwon. Despite the lack of resistance, *Borie* was protecting the force by patrolling the outer perimeter of the operation (Karig et al. 1952: 333). Between the mines, which had caused large losses, and the threat from the air that could come from the north, the ship was seething with tension. The destroyer, under the command of Merle F. Bowman, had participated in operations almost two months before which guaranteed that the crew was well trained, in view of the compelling circumstances, to react appositely to any situation. That night, the tension was at its peak since the rest of the ships were tasked with the landing, and attention had been focused mainly on the submerged enemy, the mines. The rest of TF 77 was at the mercy of *Borie's* performance (Cagle and Manson 1957: 109). By evening on the 31st, 50,000 men had already landed and *Borie* continued patrolling (Karig et al. 1952: 334).

Initially, the air battle was highly unequal. The MiG-15s were superior to the F-80s, but the US pilots were able to compensate their technological inferiority with their intense training. The situation would have been different had the fighters been piloted by the Russians, who trained the Chinese, since they were at the same level as the American pilots. Also, the MiGs were faster, better armed, and could take more

---

[4] Without resistance or opposition, in a normal way, without the presence of enemies struggling against the landing.

punishment than the F-80s. The United States put their F-84 Thunderjets and the renowned F-86 Sabres into play. Later, in 1951, Truman relieved MacArthur from command for having proposed a nuclear attack on China, for having talked about Taiwan's intervention in the war, and for having attitudes that could almost be termed disrespectful; this complicated the President's standing.

By the end of November 1950, almost all of the objectives assigned to the Air Force had been destroyed or significantly impacted, but this did not seem to affect the Chinese troops who continued their advance and forced the UN forces to withdraw to the 38° parallel north. By December 15, the Korean climate showed its face. With temperatures of −34.6 °F (−37 °C) at night and 5 °F (−15 °C) during the day, the battles were far harsher. The Chinese troops advanced on all fronts. Pyongyang had to be evacuated, and everything was destroyed as the forces retreated. The forces headed towards Hungnam, where transports awaited both civilians and servicemen, since it was their only chance to remain alive (Cagle and Manson 1957: 165). The Forces and civilians were protected by the fierce resistance of the 1st Marine Corps Division and the Air Force's aircraft, which dropped bombs and fired their machine guns, without truly inflicting real damage on the Chinese forces.

A wall of fire was provided by the ships and the aircrafts aboard delayed the fall, preventing the untold massacre of civilians and servicemen (Cagle and Manson 1957: 186). *Borie II* aimed its guns at maximum range, as did the rest of the Fleet, and together with the battleship *Missouri*, heavy cruisers, and destroyers like *Forest Royal, Norries, Englis, Lind, Hank, and Massey*, they emptied their magazines in a slow movement off the coast. Inside the ship, the smell of gunpowder flooded the passageways and no one was startled anymore by the sudden shocks on the superstructure and deck at each volley. At that point, naval bombardment had become a routine, and the men did not alter their lives, showers, lunches or meetings because of the violent shuddering of the main battery, as it completely demolished targets invisible to the crew, which were assigned to Task Force 77 with exacting precision by Admiral Roscoe and his Staff, who were guided in turn by the flight of airplanes acting as spotters (Cagle and Manson 1957: 186; Karig et al. 1952: 434).

The fall of night did not halt the action. *Missouri* provided light to the battlefield with enormous spotlights, and the rest of the Task Force participated in the bombardment that seemed unable to even put a dent in the Chinese and Korean forces that multiplied in-front of the very eyes of the defenders who were delaying the enemies' advance until the operation could be completed (Cagle and Manson 1957: 187). In the end, 105,000 men, 91,000 refugees, 17,000 vehicles and 350,000 tons of materials were rescued (Field 1962: 259, 289, 296, 312; Karig et al. 1952: 430). At that point, the UN had already deployed 350,000 men and they had to face 485,000 men under the command of Lin Biao and 12 North Korean Divisions. In addition, the UN forces had to face guerrilla fighters that attacked the areas under their control. The UN forces reached 850,000 in number.

The border would remain almost fixed, repeatedly changing hands between the North and South, until July 27, 1953 (Field 1962: 408), when peace was negotiated, 37 months and 2 days after the beginning of the conflict. The financial cost for the

United States was of 20 billion dollars (Cagle and Manson 1957: 490; Field 1962: 446).

As stated by Truman, the war had a specific and defined goal, returning to the previous *status quo*, and it was considered to have been achieved. The toll was over 1 million Koreans and 44,000 Allied and American troops. Other sources list the total casualties to 9.2 million: 5 million from South Korean and the rest from China and North Korea.

Nav source naval history photographic history of the US Navy. https://www.navsource.org/archives/05idx.htm

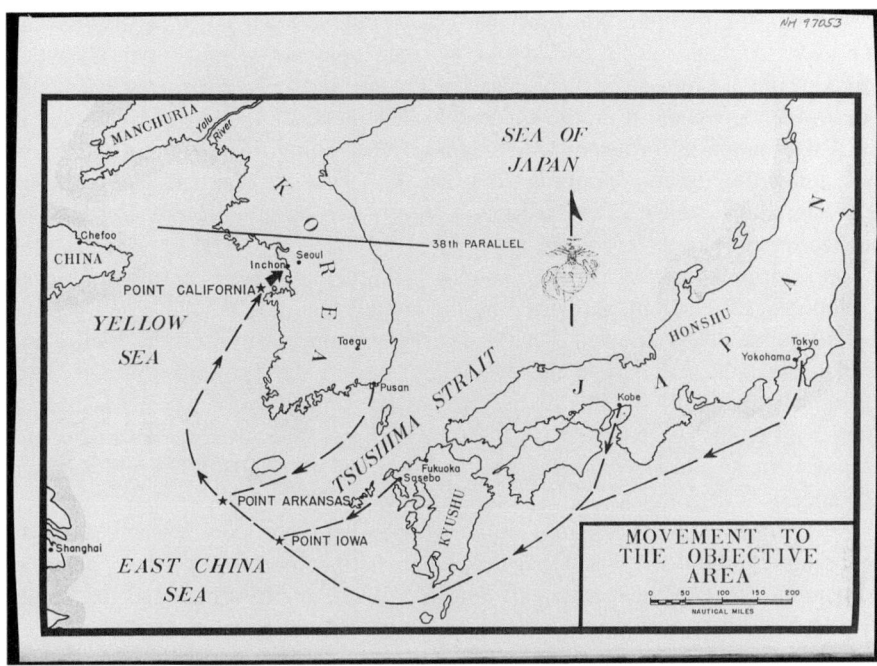

Vietnam War

Abstract Vietnam, another test for *Borie II*. Beginning of the conflict. *Borie II*'s participation.

Nav source naval history photographic history of the US Navy. https://www.navsource.org/archives/05idx.htm

Although the Vietnam War took place between 1959 and 1975, its origins date back to 1945. After the Second World War, the countries of the so-called French Indochina did not want to be recolonised by France, and therefore sought the chance to become independent from the anti-culture league which they had been forced to join. This league was formed by Cochinchina, Cambodia, Annam, Tonkin, and Laos. Thus, and within the context of the Cold War, the formal governments, supported by the Western bloc, were checkmated and overthrown by irregular forces supported by the Sino-Soviet bloc.

The identifiable parties were (to simplify a highly complex event), on one side: the Republic of Vietnam, supported by the United States, Australia, South Korea, the Philippines, New Zealand, Thailand, all of whom sent forces into battle; and Germany, Iran, Morocco, the United Kingdom, and Switzerland, who offered logistical support. In addition, other countries, like Taiwan and Spain, offered assistance in terms of teams of observers (in the case of Spain, this was a team of doctors assigned to treat collateral damage in the civilian population and offer general medical assistance).

The Democratic Republic of Vietnam was on the other side. It was backed by the direct actions of the Viet Cong or National Liberation Front, which acted as an insurgent force in the territory of South Vietnam, and by China and the Soviet Socialist Republics, who provided weapons, logistics and training support.

Beginning of the Conflict

Nav source naval history photographic history of the US Navy. https://www.navsource.org/archives/05idx.htm

To the north of the South China Sea, there is a gulf called the Gulf of Tonkin, where the Government of the United States created the ideal situation to enter the war.

On August 2, 1964, (some authors state that the event occurred on August 4), the destroyer *USS Maddox* (DD 731), a sister ship to *Borie II*, was patrolling the gulf's waters. It was on a secret electronic warfare mission to support the defensive actions of South Vietnam (Plan 34—Alpha, guided by the American Central Intelligence Agency, the CIA). To this end, it intercepted three North Vietnam patrol ships, reported a supposed attack by torpedoes (which caused no damage or consequences) and fired three volleys from the main battery targeting the patrol ships, severely damaging them. This event came to be known as the Gulf of Tonkin Incident and was enough for President Lindon B. Johnson to have legal grounds to involve the United States in one of the least popular and most resisted wars by the American people.

On August 7, the United States Congress passed the H.J. Res. 1145, known as the Southeast Asia Resolution, which gave President Johnson the power to conduct military operations in the region and declare war. The Ticonderoga and Constellation carrier groups were sent to the South China Sea. Anecdotically, we can also mention that the Vietnamese Navy Day is celebrated on August 5, as "a group of torpedo boats chased and ousted the destroyer *USS Maddox* from Vietnam's territorial waters, which was the first victory over the American Navy".

Nav source naval history photographic history of the US Navy. https://www.navsource.org/archives/05idx.htm

Borie II's **Participation**

In February 1968, *Borie II* was sent to the Gulf of Tonkin to escort an aircraft carrier group. Its mission was to be stationed as picket radar and support the aircrafts that, day and night, took off from the carriers to bomb the Viet Cong's supply lines.

It was then sent south to provide fire support for land troops. There, the guns of its main battery fired 7000 volleys on targets in Phan Thiet (a paradisiacal beach in central Vietnam, which would be used by American troops as a resting place for the combat front) and the mythical Mekong Delta.

This would be its last combat operations under the United States flag, since it was recalled in early 1969 to return to routine peace time tasks, and it became a training vessel for the United States Navy Reserve, until June 1972, when it was definitely retired from service.

Naval history and heritage command. https://www.history.navy.mil/content/history/nhhc/

Borie II in the Mediterranean (July to December, 1956)

Abstract *Borie II* in the Mediterranean (from July to December, 1956). Cruising Europe. The Arab–Israeli conflict. The UN's intervention. Evacuation of American citizens from the conflict area.

Nav source naval history photographic history of the US Navy. https://www.navsource.org/archives/05idx.htm

Borie did five tours in Europe and the Mediterranean. During the last tour, between July 28 and December 4, 1956, it participated in the evacuation of American citizens and members of the United Nations from the Gaza Strip, Egypt and Haifa (Israel).

Until May 14, 1948, British forces occupied Palestine and, as it had been decided at the UN in December 1947, two states were to be formed: one would be Arab (Palestine) and the other Jewish. There would also be an international zone in the city of Jerusalem, controlled by the United Nations. However, as soon as the British forces left the country, the first Arab–Israeli war broke out, which lasted until January 1949. As a result, Israel was able to gain far more territory than originally foreseen by the UN. The ultra-nationalist Egyptian President, Gamal Abdel Nasser, provoked a confrontation with England and France because of his nationalization of the Suez Canal, in July 1956, with the aim of using its income to finance the Aswan Dam. Soon after the action was implemented, he prohibited Israeli ships from passing through the canal. On October 29, 1956, because of this situation and the fear that English and French oil shipments would fall under the same measures, these countries, with Israeli support, started the second Arab–Israeli war, which lasted until November 1956. At that time, *Borie II* was amidst its fifth patrol of the Mediterranean, which had started in July 1956 and ended in December of that same year.

This war, which was not supported by the United States, forced the intervention of the UN. The Security Council demanded the immediate withdrawal of the invading countries forces and the canal was placed under United Nations surveillance. *Borie II* played an important role in the evacuation of American citizens who were in the Gaza Strip, Egypt and Haifa. This situation was disadvantageous to the West, since it exposed a significant rift to the Soviet bloc, who seized the chance to position itself favourably with the nascent Pan-Arabism, which considered the West to be on Israel's side.

Miscellaneous, Other Minor Actions

Abstract *Borie II*'s other miscellaneous and minor actions until its delivery to Argentina. The successful recovery of the capsule of project "Mercury" carrying Ham, the chimpanzee. Its retrofitting. Rescue of Cuban rafters and Jamaican fishermen. The Cuban Missile Crisis. Rescue of an F-8 pilot who failed to land and fell into the sea, and was saved by an officer of the destroyer.

In the previous chapters, the main actions that *Borie II* participated in were described, in greater or lesser detail. The ship was an active participant in some of the most significant events of the time.

With the end of the Second World War, the ship was repaired and joined the Atlantic Fleet, where it remained for a significant period of time, with the sole interruption of its involvement in the Korean War. At the end of that war, it returned to the Mediterranean and served five tours, during one of which it carried out the aforementioned evacuation in the Gaza Strip.

It successfully recovered the nose cone of the "Mercury" project and the monkey, named Ham, which had been sent into space. Project "Mercury" was a rushed response from the United States to the initial advantage gained by the Union of Soviet Socialist Republics (USSR) when they sent Yuri Gagarin into space, beating John Glenn who, on February 20, 1962, was the first American to go to space. The data and experience learnt from Mercury Redstone 2, the first suborbital flight with a living being on board, were crucial to Glenn's later achievement. For this reason, *Borie* was of great importance at this stage of the project. The launch was carried out on January 31, 1961.

The ship also supported the monitoring and surveillance tasks carried out by the Polaris ballistic missile submarines, *George Washington Carver* (SSBN 656) and *Robert E. Lee* (SSBN 601). In 1961, together with several other destroyers in its class, it underwent a process of modernisation, called FRAM (Fleet Rehabilitation and Modernization), to improve its performance and extend its service life.

In 1962, in addition to saving nine Cuban "rafters" and three Jamaican fishermen, it took part in the resolution of the missile crisis, when the USSR intended to install missiles in Cuba. In this crisis, called the Cuban Missile Crisis, the ship participated in the fierce encirclement of the island, preventing the ships transporting the weapon system parts from entering. The crisis developed between October 14 and November 20, 1962, and the end result was Russia withdrawing the nuclear missiles installed in Cuba and, in return, the United States withdrew its missiles from Turkey, and a direct communication channel between Washington and Moscow was installed, which became known as the "red telephone". Although the crisis was a consequence of a series of sensitive situations, somehow the discovery of the installation of a

Soviet missile base in Cuba (by an American U-2 spy plane) caused a deep sense of vulnerability in the United States Government and this, together with the defeat at the Bay of Pigs, led to a large loss of prestige in the face of a small, poor, and technologically backward Cuba.

Later, acting as an escort to the aircraft carrier CVA 38 *Shangri-La*, *Borie*'s crew observed that an F-8 did not manage to land correctly and was rushing into the sea. The ship manoeuvred both to approach the wrecked aircraft and to protect it from the sea's buffeting. During the operation, a Midshipman saw that the pilot was in dire straits and that his life was in danger. Without hesitation, he dove into the sea, rescuing the pilot alive from the wreckage.

Further on, the ship participated in the Vietnam War, which has already been described in Chap. 5. Once again in American waters, and considering it obsolete for the United States Navy, *Borie* was assigned to the Navy Reserve, where it became a training vessel until it was decommissioned from the US Navy Vessel Register.

References

Campaign in the Philippines

Bartley W. (1954). Iwo Jima, amphibious epic. Historical Branch G-3 Division Headquarters U. S. Marine Corps, Washington.

Carrero Blanco L. (1957). Historia de la Segunda Guerra Mundial: la guerra aeronaval en el Mediterráneo y en el Pacífico. Ediciones Idea, Madrid.

Martinez del Campo y Serrano C. (1956). Historia de la Segunda Guerra Mundial. Las campañas del Pacífico y de extremo Oriente 1941–1945. Ediciones Idea, Madrid.

Morrison S. E. (1960). History of United States Naval Operation in World War II. Brown and Company, Boston.

Nichols C. S., Shaw H. I. (1955). Okinawa: victory in the Pacific. Historical Branch G-3 Division Headquarters U. S. Marine Corps, Washington.

Vv. Aa. (1949). Desarrollo estratégico de la guerra naval en el Pacífico 1941–1945. Escuela de Guerra Naval de Argentina, Buenos Aires.

Vv. Aa. (1965). Gran crónica de la Segunda Guerra Mundial: de Stalingrado a Hiroshima. Selecciones del Readers Digest, New York.

Vv. Aa. (1965). La Segunda Guerra Mundial. Editorial Codex. Buenos Aires..

Borie II in the Korean War

Cagle M. and Manson F. (1957). The Sea War in Korea. United States Naval Institute. Annapolis.

Field J. (1962). History of United States Naval Operations—Korea. Government Printing Office. Washington.

Karig W., Cagle M., Manson F. (1952). Battle report, the war in Korea. Rinehart and Company Inc. New York.

Marti C. L. https://www.monografias.com/trabajos13/monodos/monodos.shtml

Chapter 3
Hipólito Bouchard: His Origins and Arrival in the Country

Picture of Captain Hipólito Bouchard

Abstract Hipólito Bouchard. His origins and arrival in Argentina. There follows a brief biography of the Argentine hero after whom the ship received its name. The first time he saw action at the Battle of San Nicolás. Afterwards, he served as a grenadier under General San Martín. His return to the sea. War as a privateer. The journey around the world announcing Argentina's independence and fighting the Spanish. End of the campaign and return to Valparaíso. The tragic end of his life.

Undoubtedly, the name given to the ship bestowed a certain spirit. In fact, on each page of this account and through the description of our forgotten hero's life, Bouchard's traits will be identified in the behaviour displayed by the destroyer. According to Bartolomé Mitre, Bouchard was a "tall, athletically and solidly built man, who could resist fatigue with impunity. He was dark-skinned, with thick raven-coloured hair and harsh, slanted, black, piercing eyes; everything about him revealed a fiery temperament" (Mitre 1968).

André Paul Bouchard, the eldest son of André Louis Bouchard and Anne Marie Therese Brunet, was born on January 15, 1780, on the seaside in Bormes-les-Mimosas, a city in the south of France (Lajous and Pereira Liate 1967: 9). Then the family settled permanently in Saint Tropez, where they had another four children, two girls and two boys (Lajous and Pereira Liate 1967: 9). His father manufactured corks and was able to achieve a somewhat secure financial position, but he died unexpectedly when Andre Paul was just 20 years old. He therefore had to manage the family business until his mother remarried. The financial disruptions and family discontent that this caused led him to leave Saint Tropez and to enlist in the Napoleonic Navy (Lajous and Pereira Liate 1967: 10).

In Saint Tropez, they still talked about the atrocities carried out by Spanish troops when they invaded the area, and of the heroic defence undertaken by a local named Suffren. Bouchard grew up hearing stories of valiant battles and probably accumulating resentment towards Spain, the source of his fellow countrymen's sorrows (Ratto 1961: 14, 15).

In 1802, after being part of the Napoleonic Navy, he journeyed to the United States, where he pursued maritime trade and completed his studies on navigation and seamanship to become a ship officer (Lajous and Pereira Liate 1967: 10). It is important to state that the date of his arrival in Argentina is a mystery to this day. Some historians believe it was close to the English invasions. Others think that it was in 1810, since they relate him with his countrymen Azopardo and Hubac, with whom he collaborated to build the first national squadron (Lajous and Pereira Liate 1967: 10). Another historian places him in 1809, on board a French privateer, and believes that he decided to stay and be a part of the first national squadron when the revolution sparked (Piccirilli and Gianello 1963: 74). What is certain, however, is that Bouchard was in Buenos Aires in 1810 and that he was a highly active participant in the organization of this squadron, whose figurehead was none other than Francisco de Gurruchaga, who was a former Frigate Lieutenant,[1] veteran of Trafalgar, and a National Congressman for Salta.

Bouchard expended huge efforts to secure money, supplies and the most important resource for a warship: its crew and officers. The few who had previous experience were abroad or in the Army (Ratto 1961: 15). However, they needed to keep the Paraná River unobstructed and face the enemy that was going ashore along the Argentine coastline, stealing livestock and causing pillages, keeping the population on tenterhooks, and preventing the forces from Entre Ríos, who were engaged in the Banda Oriental, from receiving supplies (Piccirilli and Gianello 1963: 74). General Belgrano's defeat in Paraguay emphasized even more the need for the prompt organization of a National Fleet.

He was only 30 years old when, in command of the *25 de Mayo,* and together with Azopardo on the *Invencible* and Hubac on the *Americana*, they set sail on February 10, 1811, towards the Paraná River. The national government had issued orders to seek "victory or death" in the appointed task. The ships cast off and set sail with a crowd at their back under a merciless sun, and left the coast on the path to glory.

The First Action: San Nicolás de los Arroyos

The cast-off of the national ships did not go unnoticed to Commander Jacinto de Romarate, who commanded the Spanish squadron at Montevideo, and he rapidly pursued them. The Argentine vessels, aware of the situation, decided to put up a fight near San Nicolás de los Arroyos.

The expectations for the inexperienced crews were very important; they distributed artillery pieces from the *Americana* on land to surprise the Spanish squadron. Bouchard and Azopardo manoeuvred and anchored their ships to present their broadsides to have a greater field of fire. Hubac positioned his ship further upriver, under the protection of the flagship, to which it had relinquished most of its armament.

Forming for combat with their fledgling crews was very difficult. Not only were they unknowledgeable regarding the terminology used, but it was the first time that many of them were to be a part of real action, and they had had almost no opportunity to train and drill. Everything had to be ordered specifically and the lack of preparation required constant guidance by those in command. The reckless firing from the men on land put the Spanish squadron on alert, and they decided to take precautions. The battle had just begun when the men Bouchard commanded, untrained and poorly integrated into a combat team, fell prey to fear. In spite of the captain's efforts, disorganisation spread. Holding a sabre in his hands, Bouchard tried to hold them together and push them towards the front lines. Eventually, many fled in fear.

The outcome was a catastrophic defeat. Azopardo was captured and sent to an extremely harsh prison in Africa. The ships taken as prizes by the Spaniards headed

---

[1] Translator's note: The Frigate Lieutenant is a rank roughly equivalent to a Sub-lieutenant in the Royal Navy or a Lieutenant Junior Grade in the US Navy.

towards Montevideo, while Hubac, Bouchard, and the crewmembers who managed to escape returned by land to Buenos Aires, where a War Council awaited them. The Council determined that Bouchard's actions were in line with the decisions a commanding officer should take. Although the result showed a complete lack of moral cohesion, experience, and doctrine, these qualities could not be quickly learnt in the brief time available to create the squadron and set sail, especially considering that the combat was unequal both in numbers and experience, facing a centenary and professional navy. The decision acquitted Bouchard from all charges, but sentenced several of his men for fleeing, despite the captain's efforts to hold them back.

Later, other actions had Bouchard in critical roles, like the defence of the Buenos Aires port, which was attacked by the Montevideo based fleet. The city, which was defended by only small vessels, found in Bouchard a fierce protector and in Gurruchaga once again the organiser of a squadron that did not finished assembling itself (Ratto 1961: 20, 21). After several unfortunate measures, the Buenos Aires Defensive Fleet was sent to the Riachuelo River, to deliver the ships and their men on leave to the Army's care. As a result, Bouchard enlisted in the Mounted Grenadiers Regiment, together with many others.

The Triumvirate's lack of strategic vision, together with a focus placed excessively on the continent itself, caused the country to suffer 10 years of intermittent blockades during its first years as a new nation (Ratto 1961: 23).

Bouchard: Grenadier

In April 1812, Bouchard enlisted as a grenadier, a corps being organised in Retiro by José de San Martín, who had recently arrived from Europe. He was given the rank of Second Lieutenant of the 1st Company, which was under the command of Captain José Zapiola. His virtues quickly came to the attention of San Martín himself, who proposed that Bouchard be promoted to Lieutenant in charge of the 1st Company, 1st Squadron.

In the Battle of San Lorenzo (February 3, 1813), Bouchard stole the Spanish war flag, also taking the bannerman's life, as San Martín wrote in his own report of the battle as soon as the combat had finished. Four months later, he was promoted to Captain of the 1st Company, 3rd Squadron (Lajous and Pereira Liate 1967: 62, 63).

After Belgrano's defeat, San Martín took command of the Army of the North and assigned Bouchard as support to the Senior Staff, headquartered in Tucumán, as he reorganised and disciplined the Army of the North.

Political intrigue interfered with military action. Alvear, the nephew of Supreme Director Posadas, was openly confronted with San Martín. During the Siege of Montevideo, Alvear was appointed leader of the sieging forces (which had been in charge of Rondeau), and received all the honours. Afterwards, when Rondeau was in command of the Army of the North after San Martín's withdrawal, Alvear once again tried to be appointed leader of the campaign. However, this was prevented thanks to a mutiny, in which apparently Bouchard had active participation, forcing

Alvear to return to Buenos Aires as soon as he had arrived in Córdoba. Eventually, Posadas resigned as Supreme Director and Alvear replaced him.

Return to Sea

In 1813, two months after marrying Miss Norberta Merlo, the National Constituent Assembly granted Bouchard Argentine citizenship. They had their first daughter that same year. He was still commissioned as a Captain in the Grenadiers and, on January 9, 1815, he was placed in command of the Buenos Aires port, since the previous person in charge had fallen ill.

Meanwhile, San Martín was working strenuously in Mendoza to prepare for the famous heroic deed. The General saw the need to wear down the Spanish Forces and trade from the Pacific Ocean and, at the same time, to incite unrest in the Native Peoples to introduce them to the revolutionary ideals. For this reason, he considered corsairing as the most effective path towards reaching his goals.

In 1815, thanks to his nautical expertise, he was placed in command of the frigate *María Josefa* (Ratto 1961: 26). On April 14, 1815, he entered the Navy with the same rank he had in the Grenadiers. However, on April 17, he requested that his situation be reconsidered. Two months later, in July 1815, he was once again on the rolls as an "attaché" of the regiment. These events drove him to leave the Army and return to sea and privateering, in October 1815 (Martí 1967: 70).

War as a Privateer

Brown and Bouchard were preparing to open the privateering front of the war in the Pacific. Brown sailed aboard the *Hércules*, together with his brother-in-law, Captain Guillermo Chitty, on the brigantine *Trinidad*. They sailed on September 15, 1815, with the objective of meeting on Mocha Island (Piccirilli and Gianello 1963: 78).

On the other hand, thanks to funding from Dr. Vicente Anastasio Echevarría, *Halcón* was prepared so that it could sail for eventful and fruitful privateering in the Pacific, under Bouchard's command. *Halcón* would set sail together with the frigate *Constitución*, commanded by Oliver Russell, which was funded by Chilean refugees (Father Julian Uribe among them). Unfortunately, the *Constitución* was shipwrecked in a storm off of Cape Horn—although some people suggest that this was caused by the excessive amounts of victuals that were on board, since they had been generously provisioned by Chilean refugees.

On September 21, Bouchard received his orders from the government (Lajous and Pereira Liate 1967:105). On October 27, both commands were headed south to meet as it had been agreed. The endeavour was not easy for Bouchard: a mutiny, which he quelled bluntly, was followed by 14 days of storms, and the disappearance of the *Constitución*, of which no trace was ever found.

They separated on December 31, and Brown headed towards the Juan Fernández Islands to free Chilean prisoners. They met again on January 14, 1816, to coordinate details for the bold attack on the Peruvian port of El Callao, on January 20 and 21. There, in spite of severe casualties, they captured several important prizes and they gave warning to the bastion about the Spanish naval power in the Americas. Although the crews of the previously captured ships had issued warnings, the reinforcements and measures taken were not enough to prevent serious damage to the port, fear spreading to the authorities and locals, and substantial financial rewards for the sacrifice and valour of the privateers, even though 24 men from the national squadron lost their lives in the attack.

Soon afterwards, the Battle of Guayaquil followed, on February 9, 1816, where Brown was taken prisoner. In response, Bouchard and Brown's brother, Miguel Brown, threatened to unleash a devastating bombardment over the city, but fortunately they could negotiate the release of the prisoners. The privateers met on San Carlos Island, in the Galapagos Archipelago, and decided to head their separate ways. Bouchard, aboard the frigate *Consecuencia*, rechristened *Argentina*, one of the prizes from El Callao, began the journey to return to the country. He arrived in port on July 18, 1816, and was promoted to Sergeant Mayor in the Navy.

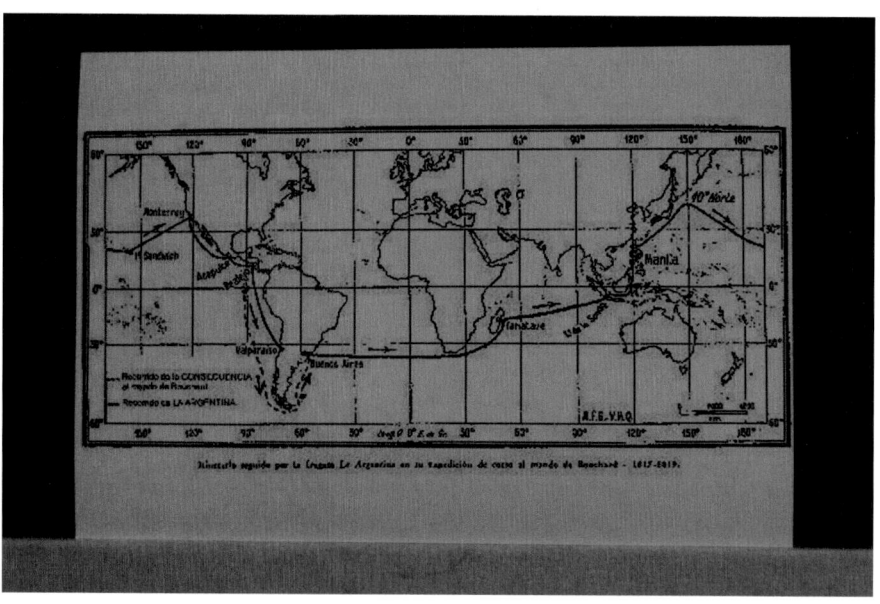

Hipólito Bouchard privateering around the world

Argentina in the World (1817–1819)

On June 27, 1817, when his wife was about to give birth to his second and last daughter, Bouchard set sail towards Barragán cove, where he finished the preparations for privateering. The previous night, some sailors emboldened by alcohol had caused an insurrection. It was finally subdued by the Naval Infantry on board, leaving two dead and four wounded, who had to be transferred.

On July 9, 1817, a year after the Argentina's Declaration of Independence, Bouchard sailed from Barragán cove heading towards Madagascar (Ratto 1961:36, 37). Forty days later, on September 4, 1817, and after many events full of risk and emotion (like a fire at sea), he cast anchors at Tamatave, on the island of Madagascar. Once there, at the request of an English privateer, he prevented four English and French ships from loading shipments of slaves. He stayed for ten days, until he was relieved by an English warship (Ratto 1961: 38, 39).

Since there was no Spanish ship in the area due to the privateers of other countries, he set sail for Java, passing through the Sunda Strait. This cruel crossing exacted the life of more than one sailor, victims of scurvy, until they finally reached Java. A few days later, despite the fact that the disease had not run its course, he went to sea to continue seeking Spanish ships to capture (Mitre 1968:59).

On December 7, in the Makassar Strait, amidst exasperating calm seas, the crew was exhausted and distressed by the lack of results, when, at midday, the lookout reported seeing five ships approaching. They were the bloodthirsty and brutal Malayan pirates, who were quietly rowing closer. The largest of the ships, advancing with the vigorous rowing of 10 oars, launched the attack, having left the other pirate vessels behind; its men were hidden under a thatch shelter and were utterly merciless.

Bouchard, who could not manoeuver and whose crew was in no fit condition due to their sickness, decided to make them pay dearly for their audacity and, fetching their weapons, they prepared to repel boardings. As soon as the ship came alongside, the Naval Infantry officer launched himself upon the attacker's bow with a group armed with pistols and cutlasses. Nevertheless, they were not fighting the inexperienced, but seasoned and merciless killers. After an hour and a half of hand-to-hand combat, the captain, seeing that he would not be victorious over the crew of *Argentina*, stabbed himself and dove into the sea, with five other men from his crew. The rest of the crew members stopped fighting and were bound while trying to inflict damage to their triumphant opponents. After a council of officials, and considering the abhorrent actions perpetrated (like the unprovoked massacring of the whole defenceless and surrendered crew of a Portuguese merchant ship), the decision was made to remove the pirate ship's masts and bring the younger members aboard, and then fire the cannons on the ship, with the pirates on board. Cries of "Allah" were heard as the ship received the cannon fire and was sunk. The four other pirate ships, silent witnesses to the events, fled as fast as their oars would take them.

The journey continued towards the island of Luzon. At the end of January 1818, they patrolled the Manila Strait, which at the time was the centre for Spanish colonial power in Malaysia. As a strange connection, during the Second World War, the destroyer *Borie II*, the Argentine destroyer ARA *Bouchard*, proudly sailed these same waters, participating in the Allies' difficult struggle in reconquering the Pacific's archipelagos, occupied by the Japanese.

For two months and under the very noses of the Spaniards, Bouchard captured 16 merchant ships, confiscated their cargos, and sunk them unashamedly. Even though there were superior forces in port, they did not attempt to attack him. Searching for other routes that the galleons were taking, he sailed north of the island and, amidst calm seas, sighted a brigantine which, upon seeing *Argentina* and knowing the resolve of its Commanding Officer, lowered boats and headed to the shallows of Santa Cruz port. There, Bouchard sent three boats, armed and with boarding complements, to capture the vessel. Somers, his esteemed officer of the Naval Infantry, unwisely surpassed the other boats. As a result, he and 14 of his subordinates were killed, some speared while in the water. An enraged Bouchard then captured a smaller boat, took the brigantine, and routed the defenders on land who significantly outnumbered him, but could not match his resolve and daring. Thus he avenged his dear and courageous subordinate. He crewed the brigantine and sailed in convoy, the latter with a small Argentine garrison. A few days later, and soon after having captured a schooner, a furious storm destroyed the vessels sailing with the *Argentina*. Bouchard entered San Ildefonso port to wait for them. After 15 days, he assumed the loss and decided to seek new prey. He initially headed towards Guangzhou (China), but strong storms and a new epidemic dissuaded him to change destination to the Sandwich Islands. These picturesque islands had been historically dominated by minor rulers with barbarous and bloody practices. However, 30 years before they had been pacified, socialised and united into a single kingdom by King Kamehameha, who called himself Peter the Great of the South Seas (Mitre 1968: 65).

On August 18, 1818, Bouchard anchored in Kealakekua Bay, in the Island of Hawaii, which was the capital of the kingdom at the time. There he saw the corvette *Chacabuco*, which had flown an Argentine privateering flag and, with a mutinied crew, had committed piracy in Chile and Peru. Upon reaching the bay, the mutineers sold the ship to the sovereign. Some of the men stayed to live on the neighbouring islands while others took ship to Guangzhou. When Bouchard became aware of the situation, he decided to negotiate with Kamehameha for the return of the ship and the surrender of the mutineers, so that they may receive their just punishment. After arduous negotiations, the King decided to return the ship and surrender the mutinied sailors, in exchange for being reimbursed for the ship's cost and paid for the incurred expenses. On August 20, 1818, a treaty for peace, war and trade was signed, which recognised Argentina's independence; this was the first time that a sovereign nation recognised Argentina as a free and sovereign country. After presenting gifts, which were profusely appreciated by the King, the kingdom of Sandwich became the first power in recognising the independence of the Argentine people.

Eight days later, the recovered corvette was ready to sail in convoy with *Argentina*. Due to Bouchard's insistence in wanting to recover the mutineers, and the king's fear, it was decided to deliver the supplies for the future cruise and the mutineers at another island of the kingdom. The provisions and over 20 men were delivered on two separate islands. However, since the leaders of the mutiny were on a different island governed by an independent king, an emissary was sent to demand the surrender of the men. The King accepted, and the men were sent before the council of officials, gathered specially for this event. The leader and instigator was sentenced to die by the firing squad, but the King let him escape that night. An irate Bouchard threatened to respond with force, but the King responded arrogantly. Nevertheless, seeing that preparations continued on the Argentine ships and in the face of an imminent attack, the prisoner was delivered to be shot.

Then, with the Argentine flag flying high, the ship headed towards Monterrey, Alta California, where it anchored on November 22, 1818. Unfortunately, the community had been warned by an American vessel that had been in the Sandwich Islands with them, as the officers had heard some *Argentina's* crewmembers commenting on their Commanding Officer's intentions. These officers arrived in California before the Argentines, where they sold a military cargo (cannons, gunpowder and ammunition) to the Governor of Monterrey, who also requested reinforcements from further inland. The city set up the artillery pieces, reinforced its men, and safely stored its treasure and shipments of valuables, which were to be shipped to Europe.

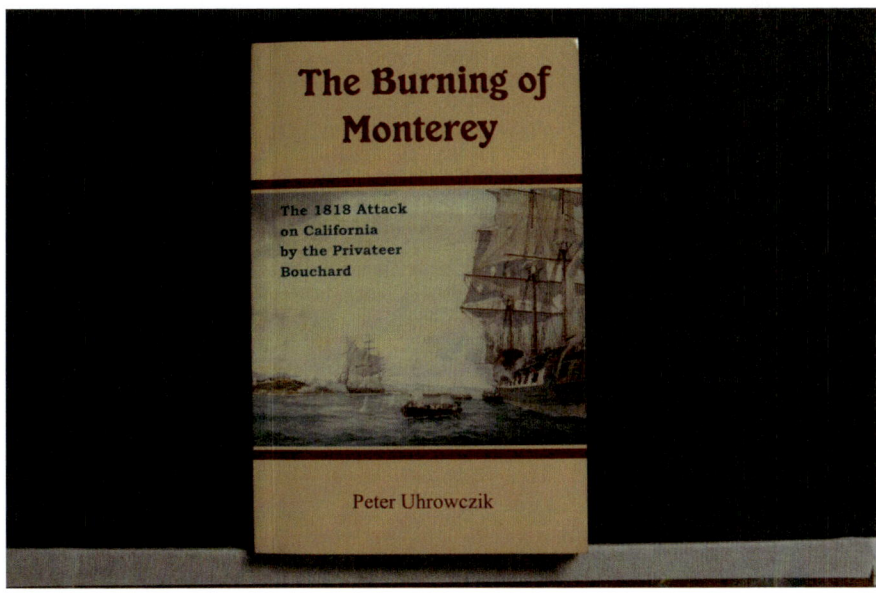

Book published in California, United States, recounting the actions of the privateer Hipólito Bouchard in Monterrey

Bouchard's plan was to send *Chacabuco* flying American colours to the port and, once it had arrived, *Argentina* would enter under the Argentine flag and capture the "helpless" enclave, almost without a fight. But events unfolded very differently. Calm seas left *Chacabuco* at the foot of the fortress and *Argentina* unable to enter due to the current, even when smaller boats tried to tow it.

On November 23, having being discovered, *Chacabuco* raised the national flag and readied for the unequal battle. Bouchard, aboard *Argentina*, looked on in fury as the fortress' cannons destroyed the rigging, massacred his men, and painted the deck bloody red. After the 19th cannon shot, everything was lost and they decided to lower the flag. Thanks to a breeze, *Argentina* was able to approach and to cover the corvette with fire to prevent it from being devastated. Bouchard then sent a messenger to ask the Governor to let him remove the corvette to save his men, but a large ransom was demanded in exchange.

By nightfall, Bouchard was able to bide the necessary time to execute his plan. While the defenders were celebrating frantically, Bouchard sent all his boats to fetch all the men that were still able to fight in battle. The wounded were left behind and, with their complaints, prevented the defenders from realising what was happening.

At sunrise on November 24, 200 hundred armed men landed, fighting against almost 400 cavalrymen and taking the fortress and the city. For 6 days, the Argentine flag waved on the fortress' flagpole. The temples and houses were respected and left untouched, but all the artillery pieces, prisons and royal stores were destroyed. In addition, they loaded some silver bars they found in a barn and some bronze artillery pieces. To this day, this event is commemorated in Monterrey by raising an Argentine flag, and it is known as the "pirate day". They were known as the black frigate and the small frigate (Lajous and Pereira Liate 1967: 216).

On November 29, after repairing the corvette, Bouchard returned to sea, to repeat these events to the south, in the ports of San Juan and Santa Barbara, among others. On January 25, 1819, in Mexico, he blockaded San Juan, Acapulco and Sonsonate. The latter offered more resistance, due to the presence of veterans. However, Bouchard's fame motivated the defenders to quickly withdraw.

After inflicting severe damage on Spanish trade in the north Pacific, destroying each segment of their power on the coast and at sea, his name was feared, and his deeds were legend. However, Central America was still left undefeated, and Spain maintained its power in the area, which still deserved respect and caution. The port of Realejo in Nicaragua became the most attractive target, and the ships turned their bows to bear in that direction. It was a very well protected port, both due to its natural geography, as well as its ramparts, which had been built to safeguard the port from cruel pirate attacks. It was very well known in the Hispanic world for its shipyards, rich neighbouring regions and active trade. Thanks to the information Bouchard learnt in Sonsonate, he was aware that there were four loaded ships. He planned the attack for April 2, and decided to capture the ships with smaller boats, which he commanded himself. However, one got lost in the darkness and the wait was in vain. At daybreak, they were detected by the lookout, giving warning about the Argentine privateer. The attack started with a heavy exchange of fire, which intermingled with the light of the nearby volcano. The intensity of the exchange gradually lessened as vessels were captured and the defenders retreated speedily. The owners of the ships and shipments offered Bouchard a significant amount of money to recover them, but the answer was the setting on fire and sinking of two of them, and the capture of the other two. Meanwhile, a Spanish barquentine fired over 10 cannon shots on

Chacabuco, which were resolutely answered. A few days later, it was sighted again, but left upon seeing the Argentine Fleet.

When he returned to where his ships were anchored, Bouchard was surprised to see that *Argentina* had raised its anchors to pursue a ship flying the Spanish colours, and that the only men remaining on *Chacabuco* were inexperienced and green, since the best men were in Realejo dealing with the ships taken as prizes. Then, they were attacked by the barquentine. Bouchard decided to put up a fight and, due to his skill and determination, was able to sweep away the bridge of the barquentine with precise fusillade. However, three of his men were killed and others seriously injured. When he readied to receive the boarding, he saw that the ship lowered its Spanish flag and raised a Chilean flag. Fury flooded his veins to see so much blood pointlessly shed. He then requested that the Commanding Officer of the barquentine send a surgeon to tend to the wounded, but they left without offering help. Upon returning to *Argentina* with a prize, it was declared that it belonged to the Chilean ship and was returned. The wounded died without receiving proper care. This was the last and regrettable battle of the cruiser *Argentina*.

Ending of the Campaign and Return to Valparaiso

On July 9, 1819, exactly two years after leaving Barragán cove, Bouchard anchored in Valparaiso, where he met the Chilean squadron under the command of Admiral Cochrane. *Argentina* was the last to arrive, as *Chacabuco* and the prizes had outpaced them. The fatigue after two years of fighting prevented him from noticing that the country's flag was not waving on the flagpoles. Upon arrival, his ships were confiscated and the crew placed under guard.

On the night of July 9, two officers approached Bouchard, aggressively unsheathed their swords, and issued orders given by Admiral Cochrane: they were to leave the ship at his disposal. All the crew and officers were detained and transferred to *San Martín*, without the due formalities necessary in these cases (for example, taking a detailed inventory of the property aboard the ships, which were completely stripped). After this shameful display, *Argentina* had no sails, smaller boats, nor a rudder. Cochrane, true to form, kept everything that had the slightest value, the silver bars, captured jewellery, money, etc.

Those who should have exerted pressure in order to free him felt that their hands were tied. On the one hand San Martín, because a larger goal, the freedom of Peru, depended on the support of the squadron under Cochrane's command. The government of Chile, on the other hand, had no one else to take command of this squadron and did not want to lose such a skilled admiral, even though his inordinate greed for money was known to all. After being unjustly imprisoned for almost five months, Bouchard was finally released due to the insistence of Coronel Tomás Guido, then a National Congressman of the United Provinces and the Argentine representative before the Chilean government, as well as due to the pressure of his charterer and financier, Dr. Vicente Anastasio Echevarría.

After several proceedings, the tribunal acknowledged that he had been imprisoned under inconsistent charges, put an end to his unjust captivity, and awarded him $50,000 as compensation, a figure that was unfair and insufficient, since Cochrane and his accomplices had divested him of a far larger amount. A few days before his release, Necochea and some grenadiers decided to compensate for this injustice, boarded *Argentina* and raised the national flag.

On returning to *Argentina*, a deep existential angst and profound rage took root in his hardened heart. Nothing remained of that brave ship, it had no arms, masts, yards or sails, and its holds laid empty, it had been turned into a pontoon. All its officers and crewmembers were on other ships or had enlisted in the Liberation Army. Bouchard felt deeply alone, but motivated to show of what he was capable of.

Bouchard went to sea two months later, on August 20, 1820, under Cochrane's orders, shipping around 500 grenadiers and hunters (Ratto 1961: 63). In December 1820, once the previous operation had ended, he requested permission from San Martín to return to Argentina, but the General requested that he stay with Cochrane to harass the El Callao fortress. At this time, his relationship with Echevarría deteriorated irrecoverably when he accused him of not caring for and maintaining his family while he was abroad, and of not sharing the bounties from the prizes and what was given by the government for his privateering and later services. Relations between San Martín and Cochrane also deteriorated, due to the violent capturing of Lima's funds and spoils, later stored in the ships at Ancon roadstead. Eventually, this episode resulted in San Martín expelling him from Peru and deciding to create his own squadron, under the command of Admiral Guise and Blanco Encalada as second-in-command, and with several English officers who left Cochrane's command. Cochrane, in defiance of his orders, kept heading north to violently capture the Spanish ships that had surrendered to the Guayaquil patriotic government. On his return, he met in El Callao with the new Peruvian squadron and with Bouchard, Commanding Officer of its flagship, the frigate *Prueba*. Old scores resurfaced, Cochrane demanded payment of the unpaid debts for his services, as if the stealing of the funds had not being enough. The Minister Guido refused to continue the conversations. Cochrane threateningly anchored his squadron in the island of San Lorenzo, near El Callao. Bouchard received orders to be alert for any possible sneak attack. However, no order was necessary, since everything was at the ready. At night, Cochrane set sail and entered the port to board *Prueba*. The darkness bursted into light with the cannons from *Prueba*. The beacons of the artillerymen were lit, and were soon to claim a very high price for their enemy's audacity. Cochrane, who knew Bouchard's resolve, left and sailed towards Chile.

Bouchard continued in the service of the Peruvian Navy, on an expedition to Guayaquil. After Guise's death, Bouchard took command of the Peruvian Squadron on January 19, 1829. Two months later, the frigate *Presidente*, formerly *Prueba*, caught on fire and its magazine exploded, being decommissioned from service.

A Tragic End

Bouchard finally left the service, after participating in almost every battle on the Peruvian coast from 1820 until 1829. Some documents indicate that he was on leave until 1833. The Peruvian National Congress awarded him an estate in San Javier and San José de Nazca, in recognition of his indefatigable efforts in defending the highest ideals of the cause for independence (Lajous and Pereira Liate 1967: 293).

An event that was never fully explained ended with the death of the South American hero on January 4, 1837, perpetrated by a group of his workers. Without knowing his second daughter, without having returned to Argentina, and without being able to die as every hero deserves, far from his affections and enduring the pain of oblivion, one of the greatest heroes of our history passed away.

References

Lajous F. and Pereira Liate C. (1967). Hipólito Bouchard marino al servicio de la independencia argentina y Americana. Departamento de Estudios Históricos Navales. Buenos Aires.

Martí P. (1967). Hipólito Bouchard: marino al servicio de la independencia. Departamento de Estudios Históricos Navales. Buenos Aires.

Mitre B. (1968). El crucero de La Argentina 1817–1819, episodios de la revolución. EUDEBA. Buenos Aires.

Piccirilli R. and Gianello L. (1963). Biografías Navales. Departamento de Estudios Históricos Navales. Buenos Aires.

Ratto H. (1961). Capitán de navío Hipólito Bouchard. Departamento de Estudios Históricos Navales. Buenos Aires.

Chapter 4
Condition of the Destroyer ARA *Bouchard*

> Ship's Generals
> Author: Eugenio Luis Facchin
> Credits: Eduardo López (photographer)

Abstract Situation of the destroyer ARA *Bouchard* at the beginning of the war. Crew and material. Its own tactical procedures. Available intelligence.

Crew and Materials (Bárcena, 1982)

As regards the crew, when setting sail for the Malvinas Operation, 40% of the complement had never been a part of this type of unit, and 5% came from other assignments and were called to complete the complement. Only one of the Senior Staff Officers had previously been on this assignment, the rest were new and many of them had never even shipped on this type of vessel (Vv. Aa. 1983: 121). In addition, the crew had not been able to attend any of the training courses on all areas of knowledge available at the Navy's education centres, which would have provided the crewmembers with the basic expertise necessary. The Senior Officers were forced to transmit these

---

Data provided by the report made by the Commanding Officer of the destroyer ARA Bouchard, our own and our enemy's tactical procedures, virtues and defects, page 86 ff.

skills to their subordinates and vice versa. Moreover, constant drills were carried out on board to improve the response to potential combat situations.

As the voyage progressed, mechanism and system failures gradually increased. From April 16 onwards, the ship sailed almost 78 days without interruption, with its capabilities noticeably diminished (Vv. Aa. 1983: 123). A test was conducted on June 14, upon arrival in Ushuaia, to verify the crew's ability to survive in the case of sinking. The results showed that the MK 3 (Vv. Aa. 1983: 134) life rafts did not inflate correctly, despite having been checked in October 1981 (less than a year before). Additionally, some of the life rafts could not be removed from their covers and it would have been very difficult for them to work properly in extreme conditions. Eventually, it was decided to replace them with container-type life rafts, such as those seen on all ships nowadays.[1] This prompted writing a note, on June 23, 1982, requesting their replacement and describing the test conducted (characterised by DEBU, ATE No. 41/82 "Reserved").

In the aforementioned note, it was also suggested to allocate cold weather uniforms for the units operating in the area, like the ones supplied to fast attack crafts and other units in the region. The warm clothes the ship had were appropriate for the Bahía Blanca area and a few degrees of latitude further south, but weather conditions in Ushuaia were truly harsh to endure, especially for the men who had duties outside the ship during their watch. This same issue was faced by the stationed ships, generally fleet ocean tugs,[2] which were assigned watches for one or two months (even three, when the relief malfunctioned), and did not receive the correct uniforms, since the south was not their usual posting. In any case, the accountant aboard *Bouchard* was skilful, ingenious and creative, and managed to ensure that every crewmember had the minimum items necessary not to have to suffer the inclement weather conditions; he was even able to procure some accessories that were the envy of the other units (like thermoses, which allowed them to drink *mate* during the long hours at battle stations, while they waited for a gong to announce who they were to face).

The same situation applied to the rationing, which was meticulously calculated for the different areas, so as to avoid both excess and lack of calories, since operating in adverse weather conditions required a large number of calories. On the other hand, combat portions were not taken into account by the authorities, and so, on several occasions, *Bouchard* only had polenta and stews. The cooks and waiters creatively garnished the meals, with the valuable help of the supply officers, to stave off any complaints. Even today, many of the crews fondly miss the plentiful and delicious meals aboard the *Bouchard*.

In addition, there was an almost complete lack of logistical capabilities in Ushuaia, despite the efforts expended by the Base's personnel to improve this issue. The destroyers depended on the Puerto Belgrano[3] Naval Base and the mobility provided by Naval Aviation, which transported personnel and replacement parts to the area in order to overcome the site's weaknesses (Vv. Aa. 1983: 137).

---

[1] Liferafts made in the United States with a capacity for 15 people.

[2] A fleet ocean tug is a towing ship, a small vessel with reduced dimensions, a fleet auxiliary.

[3] Translator's Note: Puerto Belgrano is a naval base about 250 miles southwest of Buenos Aires.

The distilled water to feed the boilers was a critical operating element, because the ships required both fuel and distilled water to function. The Ushuaia Base lacked water and storage capacity, which somehow complicated operations. The enemy was not only at sea, there were also oversights that stood in the way of the operations of the Argentine Forces (Vv. Aa. 1982). It is important to remember that, at the time, most of the Sea Fleet was propelled by steam turbines, a crucial factor for provisioning.

Replacement parts were another important factor. The logistical management for this type of ship was copied from the one used by the United States. The ship had immediate and frequent use parts aboard and these were managed by the ship's accountant, who had to keep careful record of the replacements and replenishments on ledgers specific for this purpose. Furthermore, on land there was another large warehouse holding larger and less frequently used parts. In the case of TF 79.3, every part, except from those already on board, had to be brought from Puerto Belgrano.

Berthing at the Puerto Belgrano Naval Base a few days before setting sail for war

Bouchard's Tactical Procedures

In a chance engagement with a British submarine, it became evident that there was no Limit Angle of Attack, i.e., due to their speed and weapons, the British could attack from any point, without limitation (Bárcena 1983). Moreover, the Torpedo Danger Zone was so large that the ships belonging to the Task Group could not cover it. In addition, the kinematics was such that they faced the British who had a submerged speed of 25 knots, with a speed of 12–14 knots with the tanker, and 17 without it.

The weapons' reach was just as unequal: 15,000 yards for the British torpedoes and a maximum of 4500 for the A 244 S torpedoes, which had been recently added and were experiencing serious difficulties when actually launching the shot. These weapons were added on April 16, 1982, i.e., after the war had already started, with no training or formal instruction for the operators on board, who manned them on a mount with portable equipment. They also had the well-known MK 44s, with a range of 1000 yards, but they were not up to the task.

As regards the sensors, the destroyer had a sonar (SQS 44 with a frequency of 10 kilocycles) that under favourable conditions for the bathythermographic tracks had a maximum range of 7000 yards (however, it was shown that the predicted range never exceeded 3000 or 4000 yards). The British, on the other hand, could hear hydrophone noise from the Task Group at 50,000 yards. This distance increased the whole theatre of operations, since they had smooth satellite information from the Americans and the valuable intelligence and kinematic information supplied by the Chileans.

With the sinking of the cruiser ARA *Belgrano*, the Task Group lost their only helicopter, which was lightweight and had no anti-submarine capabilities. All possible measures were employed to avoid an attack or minimize its potential damages, within the serious technological restrictions that they were under. These were the result of combat experience shared with friendly navies during joint exercises, or based on the experiences acquired by Navy personnel assigned to various courses abroad. As regards anti-aircraft defence, the destroyer had 40 mm and 125 mm guns, designed for naval combat and land targets, but they would not be useful during an engagement with British Aerospace Sea Harriers.

Installation of the anti-surface MM38 missiles was completed, and the teams who had to launch them were drilled to increase their performance, yielding excellent results. The Exocet was developed by the French company Aerospatiale, and was a launch and forget type missile: all the target's coordinates are loaded on the ship and once launched it is automatically guided to the target and flies using different profiles depending on the circumstances. The missile is launched once the target's information is loaded: orientation and distance from the target. The launcher's sensors (in this case, the ship itself) provide this data. After two seconds of acceleration provided by the Cóndor rocket booster, the other rocket motor (Helios) engages for 150 s, while the missile flies at low altitude. During this cruising trajectory, the missile is guided by an inertial system: based on the data set at launch, the approximate position of the target is calculated. Once the missile is within 6 miles (10 km) of the anticipated position of the target, a monopulse tactical homing head is turned on. The target is then acquired by the weapon's own systems and the final phase of the attack begins at one of three preselected altitudes (these are chosen depending on the sea's weather conditions in the target area). The Exocet MM38 has a range of 26 miles (42 km). Once the war was over, the Commanding Officer discovered that the control equipment was not properly adjusted and, probably, when launching the weapons, two per target as stipulated, the effect would not have been as expected:

there would have been firing errors or, simply, the missiles would have been headed straight into the sea.

Anchored in "El Rincón", Bahía Blanca estuary

Intelligence

The intelligence available to the Naval Operations Command was limited and the intelligence at the disposal of the ship was public in nature, from specialised publications, magazines and reports. While it was neither profuse nor of great quality, it was sufficient for the ship's tasks and the decision level that was addressed by the ship's command, which was at a lower tactical level.

It can be speculated, from the outcome of the events, that there was an adequate level of intelligence, but they did not have, like the British, the support of satellites and field intelligence of the United States, Chile and the inhabitants of the islands, a modest yet efficient contribution to the final deployment and progression of the operations.

Once the conflict ended, certain events and operations conducted by Naval Intelligence were made public, like Operation "Algeciras", where a group of Argentine Naval Intelligence agents were about to blow all the ships stationed at the Rock of Gibraltar. When these facts became known, it was evident that the actions undertaken by intelligence were important, even with their limited budget and support, and that they had great imagination and courage. Perhaps in time we will learn more on the subject; for instance, why the destroyers were in front of Río Grande precisely on the nights when two frustrated attempts were made to destroy the Super Étendard naval fighter and attack squadron.

References

Bárcena W. (1982). Report by the Commanding Officer of the destroyer ARA Bouchard. Buenos Aires.
Bárcena W. (1983). Statements to the war actions review board. Puerto Belgrano.
Vv. Aa. (1982). DEBU Office, CMT N° 13/82 "Secret" operation report annex VIII-1. Puerto Belgrano.
Vv. Aa. (1983). South Atlantic operations report. File 12 destroyer ARA Bouchard. Puerto Belgrano.

Chapter 5
Background and Outbreak of the Falklands/Malvinas War

Abstract Having read various sources on the subject, both from Argentina and from Great Britain, I have come to the conclusion that the Falklands/Malvinas War was the greatest intelligence operation conducted by Britain since the Second World War. England was driven by the requirements of a domestic policy, a dilapidated Royal Navy and a draconian reduction in military expenditures. Argentina, by a ruling Military Committee that lacked legitimacy and was hounded by charges of human rights violations, in conjunction with popular sentiment regarding the Falklands/Malvinas' issue. It all converged in a favourable basis to persuade Argentines that a military solution was advisable. Seizing the Falklands/Malvinas by force inexorably turned Argentina into the aggressor, transformed Britain's armed forces into a nonexpendable asset, and rescued the British Government from the criticism to which it was exposed as a result of its ineptitude. Although the foregoing is a bare outline of an intricate web of interactions and associations between the two countries, which is well worth a far more comprehensive examination, it will suffice to provide the framework for the following chronological account, documented from official records and renown research centres.

Pertinent Historical Background (Vv. Aa., IRI, 1994) (Rattenbach B., 1983)

1820. In November, the Government proclaimed, in Buenos Aires, its sovereignty over the Falklands/Malvinas. In the following years, land on the islands was granted to many Argentines for grazing cattle and other purposes.

1823. Pablo Areguatí was appointed Commandant of the islands.

1825. Great Britain and Argentina signed a Treaty of Friendship, Commerce and Navigation. Neither party raised any objection concerning the Falklands/Malvinas.

1829. Luis Vernet was appointed Political and Military Commandant. On June 10 of that year, Great Britain issued its first protest regarding that appointment.

1831. In view of the ruthless predation of pinnipeds conducted by the crews of American ships, which nearly drove them to the brink of extinction, Vernet ordered to sequester three American ships for breaching the laws governing both fishing and the hunting of sea lions. Later that year, the American schooner *Lexington* laid waste Puerto Luis on East Falkland (Isla Soledad) and imprisoned all its inhabitants in reprisal for the capture of their countrymen.

1832. In October, the Argentine corvette *Sarandí*, commanded by José María Pinedo, reached the islands. Pinedo became the Governor after overcoming some impediments.

1833. On January 2, soldiers brought by the British warship *Clio* landed, seized the islands, and hustled Pinedo and the Argentine settlers on board the *Sarandí* and dispatched them back to the mainland. On January 15, the Argentine Government complained to the British *chargé d'affaires* in Buenos Aires, thus beginning a long series of Argentine notes of protest that continued until 1888, when the national Government announced that Argentine rights were not undermined by the British de facto possession of the islands.

1946. After the founding of the United Nations (UN), Argentina submitted its objections regarding the Falklands/Malvinas' issue in Resolution No. 66 (I) during the UN's first session.

1960. The Decolonisation Committee continued its work up to the issuance of Resolution No. 1514/60, which granted independence to colonised peoples and territories.

1964. At the First Special Inter-American Conference, Latin America decided to support Argentina's claim to the Falklands/Malvinas.

1965. The UN passed Resolution No. 2065 urging the Governments of Argentina and Great Britain to undertake negotiations on the Falklands/Malvinas.

1967. UN Resolution No. 2353 stated that colonial rule was incompatible with the organisation's purposes and principles.

1970. Resolution No. 2621 declared that the persistence of colonial rule constituted a crime that breached the UN Charter.

1971. A joint declaration was signed concerning communications between the islands and the mainland. Flights were launched between the Falklands/Malvinas and the Argentine mainland. Argentine state-owned enterprises established branches on the islands. Among them were two state airlines, namely LADE (Líneas Aéreas del Estado) and Aerolíneas Argentinas (the flag carrier); a shipping line, Transportes Navales; and two state oil and gas enterprises, YPF and Gas del Estado. This led to an unexpected interaction. That very year, British geologists discovered indications of vast hydrocarbon reserves surrounding the islands.

1974. The UN passed Resolution No. 3160, quoting its prior resolutions referring to the Falklands/Malvinas' issue and urging both Governments to speed negotiations to settle the dispute peacefully.

1976 and 1977. A number of incidents occurred and several meetings were held to focus the negotiations according to the UN's resolutions.

1979. In March, Margaret Thatcher became British Prime Minister.

1980. In September, a secret meeting lasting several days was held in Buenos Aires between the British Minister of State for Foreign Affairs, Nicholas Ridley, and Argentine authorities. It was agreed that Britain would relinquish sovereignty over the Falklands/Malvinas and the surrounding waters, but would retain South Georgia and South Sandwich islands, since the arguments on sovereignty raised by Argentina were not yet accepted by England. In order to avoid disrupting the islanders' lives, it was agreed that Argentina would lease the Falklands/Malvinas to the United Kingdom for 99 years. The treaty conditions would be reviewed every ten years.

1981. However, a number of obstacles coalesced to impede solving the dispute: negotiations in New York City failed; on the Falklands/Malvinas, the most radical anti-Argentine groups won the local elections; both Houses of the British Parliament urged the Government to maintain the Royal Navy's presence in the South Atlantic to support the islanders' wishes and to guard British interests over the islands.

1982. In February, in the course of a new round of negotiations in New York City, the British delegation stated that they had not assessed the Argentine proposal, which deeply disappointed the Argentine committee. This snub directed to the Argentine delegation constituted nothing less than an open defiance and a provocation, a deliberate humiliation intended only to elicit a response from the Argentine Government. Said response was materialised a few months later, thus evidencing Great Britain's gross lack of expertise in handling such weighty international negotiations.

The Davidoff Incident

Constantino Davidoff, a well-known Argentine scrap merchant who had conducted several important deals with the British, received suggestions from English acquaintances proposing him to salvage equipment from abandoned whaling stations on South Georgia Island. These interactions dated back to 1978 (Vv. Aa., *Historia de la Fuerza Aérea Argentina* [History of the Argentine Air Force], 1998).

His keen business instinct was stimulated at once by the proposal. He talked to friends with some degree of influence in England and got in touch with the South Georgian authorities. Towards the end of 1981, once he had complied with a series of requirements, he signed a contract at the British Embassy in Buenos Aires (BBC.com, 2010), undertaking to pay USD 270,000 to the Scottish owners of the whaling stations, Salvensen Ltd., based in Edinburgh, for the right to salvage all the metal scrap present at one of its whaling stations on the South Georgia islands. Stripping that forsaken whaling station would have been the most profitable business deal of his career. The premises were packed with valuable materials and the shelves in its storerooms were filled with wood, metals and other items.[1]

After hiring 41 workers, Davidoff needed a ship he could charter to load the salvaged materials and transport them to Buenos Aires. The vessel that he managed to acquire at a modest price and suitably equipped was the ARA *Buen Suceso*, a cargo ship which belonged to the Comando de Transportes Navales, an office of the Argentine Navy devoted to promote activities in Patagonia.

---

[1] Personal interview with Constantino Davidoff, 2012.

The cargo ship's maximum displacement was 3900 tons; it had three holds and accommodations for one hundred passengers. It had been built in 1950 at a shipyard in Halifax, Nova Scotia (Canada), and had ample cargo space, up to 172,000 cubic feet of bulk cargo and up to 5000 cubic feet of freezer space in its holds and between decks. Also, it was well equipped with deck gear and had excellent manoeuvrability (Vv. Aa., Histarmar 2021).

Davidoff sailed to South Georgia aboard the Argentine Navy icebreaker, the ARA *Almirante Irizar*, and landed in Leith Harbour on South Georgia on December 20, 1981, to inspect the premises together with a team of technicians and Captain Trombetta, the Joint Commander for the Antarctic. Both men arrived with many objectives to achieve. On the one hand, to assess the feasibility of the business venture, and, on the other hand, to draft a report to plan the actions constituting the so-called Operation "Alpha", the purpose of which was for a team of elite commandos to seize the South Georgia Islands (Vv. Aa., Argentine Ministry of Defence, 2012). The aim of the journey was to assist Davidoff in planning the operation of stripping structures and machinery at several whaling stations.

During the first days of 1982, an intelligence team was assembled at the Argentine Naval Operations Command whose mission was to plan the operations. The ruling Military Committee held a meeting on January 12 to discuss possible military operations in the event that the talks with London fell through. The Military Committee appointed three military commanders: an Army General, an Air Force Brigadier and a Navy Admiral to that end. The plan drafted was named "Outline Plan of Campaign" and, together with another document named "National Strategic Directive No. 1/82", were reported only to the Commander in Chief of each of the three branches of the Armed Forces, the President, and the Minister of Foreign Affairs. The level of secrecy was so high that both documents were handwritten to avoid using any mechanical or electronic means in order to preclude any sort of discovery by British spies. Eventually, the plan was disclosed on January 26, and the outbreak of hostilities was scheduled for the middle of March.

On January 29, the Navy Transport Service (STN) carried a load of fuel, gas, machine oil and general cargo to Port Stanley (currently Puerto Argentino), which was to be distributed among the town's inhabitants. The committee and the STN representative seized the opportunity to draw up an intelligence plan according to the requirements set by the Naval Intelligence Service (SIN).

On February 2, the team preparing the outline plan concluded that it was unadvisable to continue developing Operation "Alpha", and even suggested that Davidoff's voyage to South Georgia be postponed, since such a trip would disrupt the negotiations currently underway. The Argentine Military Committee still harboured hopes that the British would be more willing to continue the negotiations. The Military Committee was unaware that the British cabinet had long ago decided to manoeuvre the Argentines into a situation that would prompt them to make the worst decision, thus turning them into the aggressors.

On February 16, the drafting of the Landing Force Operations Plan began. The Navy submitted to the committee its own operations plan in support of the overall plan.

On February 26 and 27, 1982 the representatives of Argentina and Great Britain met in New York City. However, the talks failed in view of London's indifference to address the issue with the seriousness it deserved, while the Kelpers'[2] influence was increasingly significant. It is speculated that London was prompting the islanders to make a hue and cry so that the Government could thwart Argentina's claims more effectively by persuasively brandishing the argument of self-determination, thus protecting the interests of the FIC (Falkland Islands Company), which feared losing its economic prerogatives on the islands.

At the beginning of March, the Outline Campaign Plan was approved and the Commander of Transportes Navales returned to the Falklands/Malvinas to finalise an intelligence plan in response to new requirements that had arisen in the development of the plan.

Davidoff sailed from Buenos Aires on March 11, 1982 on board of the *Buen Suceso* together with his 39-man crew and 80 tons of cargo (equipment, tools and consumables to disassemble the facilities and load the precious cargo onto the old ship). On March 18, the work crew landed at Leith Harbour to begin scrapping without delay. At the same time, the polar cargo ship ARA *Bahía Paraíso* sailed from Buenos Aires, bound for the South Orkney Islands to complete the final stage of the Antarctic Campaign.

---

[2] The inhabitants of the islands. The nickname refers to an algae widely spread in the area. Nevertheless, this term is considered derogatory in the islands due to its negative connotations, and the islanders call themselves *Falkland Islanders* or *Falklanders*.

On March 19, the British Government raised a pointless objection, claiming that the proper procedures had not been followed to conduct the scrapping operation, and, therefore, the presence of the Argentine party was unlawful. However, Davidoff had requested and duly obtained all permits demanded both by the British Embassy at Buenos Aires as well as the island authorities. This is yet another piece of evidence to prove the British conspiracy intended to elicit Argentina's indignation and force it to resort to force. On March 20, the HMS *Endurance*, anchored in the harbour of Puerto Argentino (Port Stanley), promptly set sail for South Georgia to forcibly evict the Argentine party from the island.

On March 22, the British media began calling Davidoff's presence on South Georgia an "Argentine invasion" of the island.

On March 23, the ARA *Bahía Paraíso*, anchored at the Argentine Orcadas Antarctic base, was ordered to sail for South Georgia to prevent the HMS *Endurance* from expelling the Argentine crew.

On the March 24, in response to a notice received from the British the previous day, a Special Forces team was ordered to deploy to Mar del Plata to board the submarine ARA *Santa Fe* and sail for Leith Harbour in order to protect the Argentine citizens there. A 13-tactical diver's squad landed at Leith Harbour, while helicopters from the ARA *Bahía Paraíso* patrolled the area. There, the *Bahia Paraíso* encountered the HMS *Endurance*, which had departed Puerto Argentino (Port Stanley) on March 20. Also, the RRS *John Biscoe* left Montevideo, Uruguay, bound for the Falklands/Malvinas.

On March 25, the RRS *Bransfield* sailed from Punta Arenas, Chile, toward the Falklands/Malvinas.

On March 26, the Military Committee decided to occupy Falklands/Malvinas between April 1 and 3, and to send a corvette, the ARA *Guerrico*, carrying a unit of Argentine Naval Infantry to occupy South Georgia. Eventually, the vessel sailed on March 29. On the same day, the polar cargo ship ARA *Bahía Paraíso* dropped off 14 poorly armed men to defend the scrapping crew from any British attack.

Chapter 6
The Days Before the War (Vv. Aa. Logbook 1982)

Trunk containing the war flag of the destroyer ARA Bouchard

Abstract The domestic and international context and hostilities. The days before the war. February 3, 1982. Its first sailing of the year (day of setting sail). February 16: course to Ushuaia. The first basic manoeuvres on March 4 and 5. Training continues from March 17–19. From March 20–25: "Operativo Cimarrón VII" with the Uruguayan Navy and manoeuvres with the aircraft carrier ARA *25 de Mayo*. From March 29 to April 7: heading to war unawares.

Sailing on the outskirts of Río Grande

The Domestic and International Context and the Hostilities (Vv. Aa., IRI, 1994) (Vv. Aa., *Historia de la Fuerza Aérea Argentina* [History of the Argentine Air Force], 1998) (Vv. Aa., informe oficial del Ejército Argentino, *Conflicto Malvinas* [Official Argentine Army report on the Falklands/Malvinas War], 1983) (Rattenbach B., 1983)

On March 28, the Argentine landing expedition set sail. The submarine ARA *Santa Fe* carried 13 tactical divers who were in charge of marking the beach where the landing would take place. The landing troop numbering over 400 soldiers was aboard the landing craft ARA *Cabo San Antonio* and the destroyer ARA *Santísima Trinidad*. The icebreaker ARA *Almirante Irízar* remained in the background ready to offer support if needed. However, weather conditions in the South Atlantic were very hostile and forced to postpone the landing.

By now, both Britain and the United States were well aware that Argentina had chosen the military option. In fact, Britain decided then to dispatch nuclear submarines to the South Atlantic.

On March 30, the Military Committee decided that the date to recover the Falklands/Malvinas would be April 2 at midnight. On the opposite side of the ocean, while planning, the British Admiralty realised that additional forces would be needed, so several more Royal Navy ships as well as a number of merchant vessels were committed to the campaign. Moreover, in anticipation of Argentina's imminent attempt to reconquer the islands, Great Britain ordered the destroyer HMS Antrim and several additional ships to head for South Georgia in support of the HMS *Endurance*.

On April 1, the President of the United States, Ronald Reagan, got in touch with General Fortunato Galtieri, who held the positions of President of Argentina and Commander in Chief of the Argentine Army, to try to dissuade him from launching the military campaign. According to a media version, that day the nuclear submarines HMS *Spartan* and HMS *Splendid* set sail from England.

On April 2 at 6 a.m., Argentine troops landed both at Puerto Argentino (Port Stanley) and at Darwin. They had been ordered to reclaim the islands while avoiding bloodshed, refraining from harming the civilian population and their property, and without causing any British casualties. Nonetheless, when Argentine soldiers arrived at the residence of the Governor, Rex Hunt, a confrontation broke out during which Lieutenant Commander Giachino was killed. That afternoon after the British surrender, the Governor, his family and the 66 royal marines in charge of guarding them were flown out to Montevideo, the capital of Uruguay. Shortly thereafter, the United Kingdom withdrew its diplomatic staff from Argentina.

On April 3, the corvette ARA *Guerrico*, supported by the polar cargo ship ARA *Bahía Paraíso*, reclaimed Grytviken. British forces surrendered at 1 p.m. after withstanding the Argentine assault heroically and causing great damage to Argentine equipment and killing a crewman of the corvette.

The United Kingdom broke off all diplomatic relations with Argentina, appointed Switzerland the representative of British interests and warned that it would apply economic sanctions. Argentina followed suit regarding the United Kingdom. The Security Council of the United Nations passed Resolution No. 502 demanding an immediate ceasefire and the withdrawal of Argentine troops.

Argentine Navy and Air Force aircrafts were tasked with ferrying soldiers and supplies to the islands. At the same time, on the mainland they redeployed personnel from their peacetime locations to reinforce southern contingents of troops, and to relieve troops that departed to the Falklands/Malvinas through the Chilean border. That same day, Britain launched the so-called "Corporate" Operation and the Task Force ships sailed from Portsmouth. On April 4, Argentina responded by flying massive numbers of soldiers to the Falklands/Malvinas in order to fortify and defend them from the British riposte.

On April 4, the United States granted Great Britain the use of their Wideawake air station on Ascension Island.

On April 5, the European Community penalised Argentina with economic sanctions in reprisal for the attack on the islands. Argentina stopped all payments to Britain. Canada and Austria suspended shipments of warfare materials to Argentina. Peru was the first Latin American country to openly espouse its support of the Argentine cause.

On April 6, the President of the United States, Ronald Reagan, named General Alexander Haig to mediate between the belligerents. Nicaragua followed Peru's lead in declaring its complete support for Argentina.

On April 7, Argentina announced the creation of the South Atlantic Theatre of Operations (Spanish TOAS) while Britain established the so-called maritime exclusion zone which spanned 200 nautical miles around the islands.

Whereas in the international arena France, Belgium, Holland and the Federal Republic of Germany were banning the sale of weapons to Argentina, General Haig flew from Washington DC to London to convene with Prime Minister Thatcher. However, he was met by a British Government adamant and unwilling to consider any negotiated solution. Indeed, Britain never even envisaged the possibility to arrive to any solution, since the war was developing favourably for British interests and this embodied the very solution to their problems. Moreover, Great Britain could rely on material support from the United States, who had supplied them with equipment and satellite intelligence. The British were thus in a position to anticipate Argentine moves.

A ceremony took place at the Town Hall in Puerto Argentino (Port Stanley) to establish the Argentine military rule, with the presence of an ample entourage of dignitaries who had flown in from the mainland.

On April 8, an air shuttle service began between the Argentine mainland and the Falklands/Malvinas to transport troops and supplies. Argentine Foreign Minister, Costa Méndez, returned from Washington DC and announced to the press that the threat of war was remote. But the American Ambassador in Buenos Aires informed via cable that the Argentine Foreign Ministry was unable to placate the Argentine Navy, who accused the US of supplying satellite images to Britain, thus obliterating the element of surprise from the force's moves toward the Falklands/Malvinas.

On April 9, the British ocean liner SS *Canberra* set sail from Southampton swarming with troops, many of whom were Special Forces. SS *Canberra* was a passenger ship 820 feet in length and displacing 49,000 tons that could transport up to 1,500 passengers. The British Ambassador in Santiago de Chile announced that the Chilean Air Force was willing to receive British aircraft in emergency to land in Chile, and, if it was so decided, to execute British bomb raids against Buenos Aires from Chilean air bases. The United States offered Britain its premises on Ascension Island as support for military operations. Meanwhile, the Argentine Government set forth the basis for the negotiations, among which was the indication that sovereignty over the Falklands/Malvinas would not be negotiated.

On April 10, the American Secretary of State, Alexander Haig, visited Buenos Aires offering to initiate a mediation, in order to find a negotiated solution to the conflict. Galtieri, who had attended University in the United States and boasted of his close friendship with many extremely influential American generals, received Haig under the impression that the United States would support the Argentine position to arrive at a negotiated solution. Later, when Galtieri addressed a multitude gathered in Plaza de Mayo, in front of the Government House, he said: "If they want to come, let them come. We will face them in battle," which must have been music to British ears. In England, Margaret Thatcher thanked the United States for letting Britain use Ascension Island, thanked West Germany, France and other European countries for their support, and announced that the British fleet was underway toward the Falklands/Malvinas.

On April 11, the Argentine Armed Forces began organising and fortifying its defences on the islands, deploying the 5th Naval Infantry battalion and the Army's 10th Mechanised Brigade. At the same time, the British submarines HMS *Splendid* and HMS *Spartan* were already approaching the Falklands/Malvinas. From Rome, Pope John Paul II implored both countries to avoid bloodshed. It should be noted that Haig's negotiations had failed from the standpoint of persuading the parties to reach an agreement, whereas they had been a brilliant success if measured by the standard of delaying Argentine initiatives long enough for the British to prepare adequately for war.

On April 12, with the assistance of the submarine HMS *Conqueror*, Operation "Paraquat" began, the purpose of which was to recover the South Georgia Islands. The HMS *Antrim*, HMS *Plymouth* and the logistics ship RFA *Tidespring* set sail from Ascension Island bound to the South Georgias carrying a company of commandos.

Additionally, Argentine submarine ARA *San Luis* was patrolling its assigned beat north of Falkland Sound (San Carlos strait), while the ARA *Santiago del Estero*, which was out of commission, was being secretly towed to Puerto Belgrano as a ruse. For its part, the ARA *Santa Fe* was preparing to transport a group of commandos to reinforce Argentine units deployed to South Georgia. The ships of the Ocean Fleet[1] that had participated in the reconquest of the islands, belonging to Task Forces 20 and 40, arrived at the Puerto Belgrano Naval Base.

---

[1] Translator's Note: The Ocean Fleet (Flota de Mar - FLOMAR) is one of the four branches of the Argentine Navy, next to Naval Infantry, Naval Aviation and the Submarine Fleet.

The ship *Córdoba*, belonging to an Argentine state-owned shipping company called ELMA, abandoned its attempt to sail to the islands from the Patagonian port of Puerto Deseado for fear of being attacked by British submarines, thus averting the possible loss of its valuable cargo: aluminium panels destined to lengthen the runway (which would have allowed stationing Argentine fighter jets on the islands), artillery and more than 2,000 tons of ammunition. As from that moment, only ships carrying fuel, rations and clothing would cross. Finally, from April 18 to 20, cargo aeroplanes hauled 900 tons of such supplies to the port of Comodoro Rivadavia on the Patagonian shore, and then flew from there to the Falklands/Malvinas.

The Argentine Foreign Minister met with the Soviet Ambassador. There has been much speculation on the outcome of that meeting, on which support the Soviet Union offered Argentina and the real help obtained. But the truth is that those of us who were stationed on the front didn't notice that there was any external help whatsoever, except for all the moral support we received from all Latin America (with the exception of Chile), and the supplies sent by our brothers from Peru.

Alexander Haig reported to the Argentine Foreign Minister that Britain was unyielding in its position as regards reaching a negotiated solution. Sweden, for its part, decided not to adhere to the embargo levied on Argentine exports, and Panama announced its support for the Argentine cause.

On April 13, two Argentine Coast Guard cutters, *Islas Malvinas* and *Río Iguazu*, arrived at the Falklands/Malvinas to join its defence. One of them had to be towed by the other, since it had consumed all its fuel battling the heavy storm it encountered during the crossing.

On April 14, while the British Task Force met with the HMS *Endurance* to begin operations in South Georgia, the Argentine Foreign Minister called Haig to ask him to confirm the press versions on whether the United States would provide full support to England. In the course of the war, it was proven that the US had provided England with state-of-the-art warfare materials, such as Sidewinder L air-to-air missiles, which wreaked havoc among the Argentine Air Force, as well as technical-logistic support and intelligence. In hindsight, the collected public announcements from Haig, Reagan and other American officials allow us to conclude that those talks were not intended to settle the conflict, but instead to stall for time so Britain would be properly prepared and secure a victory.

While Haig was flying from London to Buenos Aires, Margaret Thatcher received the approval of Parliament to move forward with waging war. The political climate adverse to the Government was starting to shift in its favour, and patriotic fervour was beginning to awaken. Winning the war was all that was needed to attain the desired objectives, and it seemed that it was going to be very easy to accomplish. Argentine media started revealing Haig's true role and his evident lack of impartiality, which could no longer be disguised behind his neutral mediator masquerade. Nonetheless the Commander of the South Atlantic Theatre of Operations, Vice-Admiral Lombardo, informed the servicemen assembled at Puerto Belgrano that the Government was still seeking a compromised settlement.

On April 15, the President of the United States, Ronald Reagan, phoned Galtieri to reassure him that his aim was to achieve a peaceful solution to the conflict. Meanwhile, the British Task Force was still near Ascension, and the Argentine Ocean Fleet set sail from Puerto Belgrano toward the Falklands/Malvinas. Undoubtedly, peace on the South Atlantic was beginning to falter. In view of the situation and the failure of the talks, the Argentine Government started considering whether to invoke the Inter-American Treaty of Reciprocal Assistance (commonly known as the Rio Treaty or TIAR as its acronym in Spanish), a mutual cooperation in defence and security matters treaty, which considers that any armed attack by any State against any American State must be considered an attack on all of the signatory States.

February 3, 1982: First Voyage of the Year

The ship, with the full complement that would participate in the conflict almost wholly mustered, sailed from Puerto Belgrano during the morning to test the engines. It returned to port after a short test manoeuvre—to configure systems, work teams, etc. They could not even leave the channel, as the forward engine reported issues and they were forced to stop. The destroyer anchored near the port's access channel and a launch was lowered to fetch the replacement part. A few minutes later, it was reported that the launch's motor was having problems; it was mid-way between the ship and the port. It was assisted by a pilot boat that was berthed alongside one of the buoys in the access channel. It was later determined that they could enter port with the assistance of a tug. Although the men of the Navy were used to working in adverse conditions, the ship's first voyage did not inspire confidence in its fledgling crew.

February 16: Destination, Ushuaia

The ship sailed towards Ushuaia using only its forward engine, since the aft engine had broken down the moment they weighed anchor. When they arrived alongside marker 03,[2] almost at the edge of the Bahía Blanca estuary, the decision was made to return to port and the ship anchored at Punta Ancla, after 20:30 h. Once again, breakdowns prevented the ship from accomplishing the plans.

It was helped into Puerto Belgrano by the tugs on the following day, entering at 09:20. Dejected and disappointed, the crewmembers undertook their everyday tasks while the engine room staff redoubled their efforts to improve the performance of the ancient mechanisms. Despite their efforts, the journey to Ushuaia was thwarted.

---

[2] Translator's note: The lateral markers define the edges of a navigable channel and they are most commonly used when entering or leaving harbours.

March 4 and 5: The First Basic Drills

Starboard of the tanker ARA Punta Médanos for replenishment

The ship sailed towards the El Rincón area a little before midday, having undergone some small and final repairs. Each department seized the opportunity to establish roles, battle stations and mechanisms, and to test every system they were unable to assess while in port. The bridge teams worked on basic issues, performing drills such as sailing in channels, practising man overboard manoeuvres, and assessing the ship's response to different possible manoeuvres, etc. The Commanding Officer himself tried to commune with and feel the ship as an extension of his body, so that in the face of any situation, he would be able to issue the right orders: not a degree over bearing, not a knot below speed. Whoever could not do this from the start would not be able to do so when the circumstances become pressing and adverse.

The day passed without major breakdowns and, slowly, drill after drill, the teams consolidated their relationships. In addition, significant progress was made thanks to the training dummy (who they affectionately dubbed "Charly" or "Carlitos"), who acted as the man overboard and was cast into the sea from different areas of the ship so that they could rescue him. This exercise allowed the bridge team to acquire skills that would be highly useful later on.

During the second day, they underwent drills without warning: battle stations, man overboard, sailing from secondary stations (very useful when the bridge disappears due to enemy action, as was the case with the fleet ocean tug *Sobral*), abandon ship, artillery, and other minor but equally important drills to solidify the operating and work teams.

Although breakdowns still happened one after the other in the different systems of the ship, the complement had started to familiarise themselves with each one and were able to solve them quickly and efficiently. The ship had almost become a warship, with everything this entails.

March 17 to 19: The Drills Continue

Drills and breakdowns continued aboard the ship. The port side shaft had to be stopped due to an issue with a pump. However, despite the malfunctions, the drills became increasingly more complex, without neglecting the basics: boats were lowered; the ship was sailed from secondary stations; different manoeuvring posts were practiced, like battle stations and others. On the 17th, they were forced to navigate from the secondary station due to electrical issues. They anchored at night and, together with the aircraft carrier and other destroyers, they begun manoeuvres at 08:00 h on the 18th to start the yearly training. Different exercises were conducted that day: manoeuvres with helicopters, sailing in formation with the aircraft carrier and other destroyers, smaller vessels were lowered and raised, etc. The Commanding Officer was also transferred to the aircraft carrier and back. It was an exciting day, filled with new experiences for a crew that was almost completely new and inexperienced.

The following day, the ship sailed the whole night and entered port after 10:00 h; they were delayed by the ARA *Cabo San Antonio*, which was leaving port to start its annual exercises.

March 20 to 25: "Operation Cimarrón VII" With the Uruguayan Navy and Aircraft Carrier Exercises

In the afternoon of March 20, the ship sailed to hold the "Cimarrón" exercises with an Uruguayan destroyer. The afternoon was peaceful, with a pleasant temperature, some clouds and a little wind. While they sailed the channel, they took the opportunity to fine-tune their roles for anti-submarine combat or abandoning ship. Once they left the channel, they sailed in formation, with *Bouchard* as guide and the Uruguayan ship stationed behind (a position in a ship formation). In this way, the planned exercises begun.

During the night of the 20th, the formation encountered a group of destroyers that were returning to port after several days on manoeuvres. Later, at first light, the exercises with the Argentine submarine ARA *Santa Fe* began, with the submarine taking on the role of enemy to the reduced joint Fleet. The manoeuvres were very basic: they watched the submarine raise and lower different attachments, and they tried to identify the echoes they heard on their sensors, training the operators with these observations. After this training, the submarine was attacked, while it conducted basic manoeuvres so that the operators would not lose their target. The exercises lasted the whole day and continued into the night. The hours of darkness were leveraged to develop anti-submarine attacks, with the generous forbearance of those who were submerged, rendering the task easier to perform. The teams of the different duty shifts took advantage of this training, and day by day the professional attitude of the ship increased.

The night of the 21st was used to sail in formation, with the Uruguayan ship as guide. During the morning, they manoeuvred and approached each other, passing within 49–66 feet (15–20 m).[3] This is used to transfer light loads, people, and even fuel using the rigging and specially designed equipment. In this case, the occasion was used to honour the Uruguayan vessel, as a show of gratitude for its participation and in respect for the flag it flew.

In the afternoon, other anti-submarine exercises were conducted with ARA *Santa Fe*, increasing the difficulty of the manoeuvres to demand more from the operators of both destroyers. After 18:00 h, the ships that participated in the joint exercises berthed at the Mar del Plata Naval Base.

On March 22 and 23, the ship remained at port and the crew was able to visit the city of Mar del Plata, where they took the opportunity to fraternise playing football and doing other activities. Of course, as any good host, the crew of *Bouchard* let their opponents win. They visited the Sierra de los Padres hills and went shopping in the city centre; they also could not miss the chance to buy hundreds of *alfajores* (a local confectionary) to store in the lockers of both ships once they returned to port.

They set sail on the 23rd, past 18:00 h. After weighing anchors, they went on port and starboard watches (6&6), a way of dividing watches in a combat zone in which the ship's crew has a six hour watch followed by six hours of rest. Thus they are highly alert for combat and any response is immediate. On its return, the ship joined the destroyers *Py* and *Piedrabuena*, with the aircraft carrier *25 de Mayo* as the nucleus of the formation. They conducted firing runs and transferring light loads exercises, exchanging cakes and wine so that the crews might enjoy them. Later, taking the rescue position, it sailed in support of the flight operations lead by the aircraft carrier during day and night, where the skills of the naval pilots could be appreciated in the landing operations.

On March 25, the ship sailed to port to supply, arriving past 10:00h.

---

[3] Translator's note: This manoeuver, frequently performed on the open sea, is called *pasaje al habla* in Spanish (literally, "passing with a speaking-distance"). In this manoeuvre, two or more ships approach and sail very closely for a time (respecting all relevant security measures), allowing them to speak directly from bridge to bridge. This is generally complemented with the transfer of small loads, personnel, or liquid loads (water and fuel).

From March 29 to April 7: To War, Unawares

With over 2,500 miles sailed, the ship left Puerto Belgrano at 06:20 on March 29, with only the docks lights illuminating its departure. Only the Commanding Officer, the Executive Officer and the Chief Operating Officer knew the real reason for their voyage.

The weather was better than average for the season: 63 °F (17 °C), 20 knot wind, with a downward trend, coming from the north-northeast. ARA *Bouchard* had left the channel by 09:15 *h* and was sailing in formation with the destroyer *Py*. During the morning, the artillery and engines were fine-tuned and minor repairs were undertaken for the latter. The Executive Officer and the Chief Operating Officer briefed the Senior Staff on the situation and the mission of Task Group 20.0, which consisted of the aircraft carrier *25 de Mayo*, and the destroyers *Seguí*, *Py* and *Bouchard*. (Gardiner 1982) They explained, by way of information only, that Task Group 40.0, made up of the landing ship *San Antonio*, English type 42 destroyers *Hércules* and *Santísima Trinidad*, as well as the icebreaker *Irízar*, would be in charge of transporting, supporting and guarding the Naval Infantry and Army troops that would capture the islands, currently hosting 40 British Marines.

In late afternoon, the ship stationed itself for rescue operations alongside the aircraft carrier *25 de Mayo*, which lasted until 19:00 h. Despite the flight operations being forestalled, the destroyers took different positions in the formation, which had the V2—as the aircraft carrier was designated—as the formation guide and nucleus.

On March 30, the ship sailed alternatively positioned as the aircraft carrier rescue or in the screen until 16:00 h, when *Bouchard* received orders to no longer follow the aircraft carrier's manoeuvres. As a consequence of an engine malfunction, it was separated from the rest of the group for a brief period. On its return, the destroyer rejoined the formation on orders from the Officer in Tactical Command (OTC).

Fuel replenishment was convenient for the destroyers, and on March 31, the tanker *Punta Médanos* was to act as the supplying ship. *Bouchard* was the first in line. In order to practise, they stopped the manoeuver and engaged the emergency systems, which were used in the case of an imminent attack during replenishment. There were no issues with the procedure. However, when only 10 tons were still left to load and due to the violent motion of the seas, the hose cut off and the distance line was lost, which was crucial for the manoeuvre. (Gardiner 1982) *Bouchard* covered the rescue stations so that *Py* could act. The tanker suffered serious damage to its fuel transfer system, surpassing the breakdowns suffered by the destroyers. Therefore, they had to wait for the indefatigable crewmembers to conduct repairs before continuing. In a matter of minutes, the repairs were finished and the manoeuver could proceed.

On April 1, the destroyers were stationed patrolling areas designated A (Alpha) and B (Bravo). These areas were located to the north of the Falklands/Malvinas Islands, and their mission was to prevent any ship from nearing the islands, south of the 50th parallel south, while the operation to recover the archipelago was taking place.

The last contact with the V2 was at 00:30 h and the ship headed east-southeast to the patrol area. The actions began early. At 08:50, *Py* reported an unknown ship 10 miles to the southeast. Artillery was prepared and hatches battened down, combat could be felt in the air. The contact was the Polish fishing vessel *Mielmo*, who had not responded to hailing and was headed to Puerto Argentino (Por Stanley), where it was later reported that its mother vessel was located. Seeing the destroyer, the fishing ship stopped its engines. It was ordered to remain north of the 50th parallel S, until it would be given notice to manoeuvre freely. Some hours later, when the destroyer was away from the fishing vessel, they were ordered to once again intercept the ship since it was again headed to the Falklands/Malvinas. Once they intercepted it, the order was given again and, this time, they seemed to understand the seriousness of the situation. At nightfall, the *Mielmo* insisted on the need to reach port due to a lack of water on board. A zodiac with crew was sent to verify the truth of the information and to try and solve the situation. Midshipmen Rey Álvarez and Borgogno were assigned the task. On their return, a few yards from the ship, the zodiac's motor malfunctioned and stopped, and they experienced some tense moments, because the seas were rough and it was dark. However, they were able to row and rejoin the ship without further issues. (Gardiner 1982) At 23:00 h, a new contact interrupted the night's calm, as *Py* reported the presence of another ship. Half an hour later, they returned to patrolling the B area.

On April 2, the ships were carrying out control activities from very early in the morning. In addition to investigating the Polish fishing vessel *Mielmo*, at 01:40 h *Py* ordered *Bouchard* to investigate a contact which was quickly lost. That night, the electromagnetic propagation allowed reaching incredible distances. *Bouchard's* radar detected land 102 miles away. It was the north of the Falklands/Malvinas, but they were unable to recognise the exact area on their charts. The ships continued patrolling for the rest of the day. The fishing vessel was authorised to replenish from other ships further up north. *Bouchard* was ordered to patrol another area, designated D (Delta), always north of Falklands/Malvinas. While the ships of the TG 20.0 kept a fierce lock north of the islands, actions were developing at a frantic pace. Partial knowledge of current events was attained through operational channels. In addition, news reached them about two men seriously wounded and the raising of the Argentine flag on the Falklands/Malvinas at 11:25 h. (Gardiner 1982).

There were few operational options on April 3, and the reduced visibility caused the crew to be immersed in tedium, which was only disturbed by the news arriving from the continent bringing updates about the events happening on the islands. Great happiness and deep sadness were engendered simultaneously, because the Chief Engineer was a colleague of Captain Giachino, first KIA and first hero of the war.

The ship requested fuel replenishment, they were on their seventh day of sailing and they had only been replenished once. After midday, *Punta Médanos* delivered almost 160 tons of fuel oil. Once this was completed, port and starboard watch was ordered and it acted as a rescue destroyer for *Py's* replenishing manoeuvre. Having concluded this, they formed up with *Punta Médanos* as the capital ship to be protected. The ships went dark and sailed without lights, in what is called "stealth navigation". The general bearing was north-northwest.

The formation continued its return to Puerto Belgrano, bearing north-northwest, and was joined by the destroyer *Piedrabuena*. On April 5, they sailed with port and starboard watches and conducted passing manoeuvres[4] and discrete communication exercises, the latter with flags and lights. The following day's activities were similar, taking advantage of the fact that they were sailing in radio silence to practice discrete communications.

In the first minutes of April 7, the final day of the voyage, the Recalada lighthouse was sighted on the way towards Bahía Blanca. The communication restrictions were lifted and contact was made with the YPF (Fiscal Oilfields) tanker *Campo Durán*. At daybreak, the destroyers *Py* and *Piedrabuena* approached *Campo Durán* to replenish. There were two reasons for this: the first was to replenish the ships, which had last received fuel three days before, the second and more important one was to verify the viability of and conditions for replenishing from that tanker. The Navy had installed the rigging and necessary elements on the tanker to be able to supply any vessel in the Fleet, to assist the worn down *Punta Médanos*. The manoeuvre finished successfully at 17:30 h. Although the oil tanker was not designed for these tasks, it did them with sufficient aplomb to warrant being greenlit for operations.

The ship berthed in Puerto Belgrano as the day was ending. Just as when it set sail, the only light was provided by the weak lights on the dock and the ones on the board-side ship. However, it was clear that something had changed. It was a hub of frantic activity, trucks and other vehicles were constantly coming and going, the crane for nautical services was moving gangway ladders and defences, and the general workshops' crane was busy with items that could not be identified in the gloom. Everything had changed and Puerto Belgrano would no longer be the same.

References

Gardiner M. (1982). "Crónica de Malvinas". Personal diary. Puerto Belgrano.
Vv. Aa. (1982). Logbook of the destroyer ARA *Bouchard*. Buenos Aires.

---

[4] Translator's note: See comment below about the so-called *pasaje al habla*.

Chapter 7
We're at War

Abstract The domestic and international context and the hostilities. We're already at war! From April 16 to 27. Actions undertaken north of the islands to prevent interferences from affecting the landing.

The Domestic and International Context and the Hostilities (Vv. Aa., IRI, 1994) (Vv. Aa., *Historia de la Fuerza Aérea Argentina* [History of the Argentine Air Force], 1998) (Vv. Aa., informe oficial del Ejército Argentino, *Conflicto Malvinas* [Official Argentine Army Report on the Falklands/Malvinas War], 1983) (Rattenbach B., 1983)

On April 16, whilst Royal Navy aircraft carriers still lingered at Ascension, Argentina was steadily building up its strength on the islands. Argentine Air Force Hercules transport planes shuttled busily back and forth between the Falklands/Malvinas and the mainland ferrying Army and Naval Infantry troops. Also, despite Haig's patent partiality, Argentine negotiators persisted in their vain efforts to achieve a compromise peace.

On April 17, Haig submitted to Argentina a five-point proposal envisaging a joint administration of the Falklands/Malvinas, the immediate withdrawal of troops from both sides, and the beginning of negotiations intended to resolve the conflict in the short term. The Argentine Foreign Minister, Costa Méndez, declined the proposal by Haig, who was forced to report the bad news to the British Foreign Secretary, Francis Pym. Meanwhile, in the United States there were growing concerns that Argentina would invoke the TIAR, and that the Soviet Union would ship a vast arsenal to Argentina in exchange for cereals.

Conversely, Argentina requested the United States to send LANDSAT satellite images on April 21 and 23. However, after considering that this would translate as a major political gesture, even if there was nothing relevant to show, the US decided not to provide these images. It is believed that this request was intended to test confidence and solidarity, instead of responding to any actual operational need.

On April 18, as a way of exerting diplomatic pressure in light of the repeated failures of Haig's mediation, the British Task Force set sail from Ascension. The vanguard of the flotilla was composed of the destroyers HMS *Brilliant*, HMS *Glasgow* and HMS *Sheffield*. In addition, Victor tanker aircraft and Vulcan strategic bombers began using Ascension Island as base for landing.

That same day, Argentina dispatched five UH1H helicopters to the Falklands/Malvinas to reinforce the islands and to ferry Infantry soldiers. A team of amateur radio operators, both civilians and Air Force personnel, flew to Puerto Argentino (Port Stanley) to support aerial operations.

On April 19, the cruiser ARA *General Belgrano* was already operating north of Isla de los Estados. That day, Haig received Argentina's official reply to his five-point proposal. The American initiative merely proposed the unilateral withdrawal of Argentine forces, but without assuring any new settlements by Argentines or Argentine sovereignty over the islands. Finally, Argentina invoked the TIAR, and the Organisation of American States voted in favour of summoning the Foreign Ministers.

On April 20, a flotilla split off from the British Task Force and headed for South Georgia to attack the small Argentine force deployed there. A Victor reconnaissance plane flew over South Georgia Island taking pictures.

On April 21, Haig called the British Foreign Secretary, Francis Pym, and the Argentine Foreign Minister, Costa Méndez, and proposed that they meet in person. When they learnt of this initiative, both Margaret Thatcher and the Military Committee gave the same reply: "No talking with the enemy".

On April 22, while Galtieri was paying an official visit to the islands, the group of non-aligned nations declared their support for the Argentine claim.

The following day, April 23, the submarine ARA *Santa Fe* reached South Georgia carrying Special Forces to reinforce the feeble local garrison. Argentina protested before the OAS the presence of British warships near South Georgia, while the British media published several pieces on the possibility for British forces to strike continental Argentine targets before reaching the Falklands/Malvinas. In the end, virtually the entire British Task Force had made ready to depart Ascension.

On April 24, Argentina responded to the British threat to attack any vessel, submarine or aircraft, whether commercial or civilian, interfering with its operations, by warning the UK against breaching international law and that Argentina would repel any attack pursuant to the exercise of its right to self-defence set forth in Article 51 of the United Nations Charter.

That same day, the HMS *Brilliant* arrived in South Georgia, while an Argentine Air Force Hercules flew over the area monitoring British operations. Also, the last substantial Argentine reinforcements reached the Falklands/Malvinas.

On April 25, Britain reported to the UN Security Council that it had landed successfully on South Georgia and had taken complete control of the island. The same day, a squadron of British helicopters attacked the submarine ARA *Santa Fe* on Grytviken, damaging and capturing the vessel. Moreover, whilst Royal Navy ships bombarded the area, Royal Marines and British Special Forces (SAS) disembarked on South Georgia.

On April 26, despite their efforts to resist and in view of Britain's overwhelming weaponry and force superiority, the 189 Argentine soldiers on South Georgia were forced to surrender and were taken prisoners. Some time later, when petty officer Felix Artuso of the Argentine Navy was trying to comply with the British request to remove the ARA *Santa Fe* from the pier, he was murdered by a Royal Marine while operating the systems necessary to move the damaged submarine.

From April 16 to 27

On April 16, at midday, on a brisk cloudy day with gentle northerly wind, the ship sailed together with destroyers *Py* and *Piedrabuena*. The complement was almost complete, but the Chief of Propulsion had been hospitalised due to hepatitis, and had to be was replaced by Ship-of-the-line Lieutenant[1] Piccardi.

As soon as they left the channel, they were greeted by a tug with tow target sleds. The main battery would fire for 30 min to calibrate its systems and so that the operators could receive cursory training. All the bridge work teams and the Combat Information Centre (CIC) took advantage of the training. No watch was kept, there were no people in charge, since no one wanted to miss the opportunity to see and train a combat scenario. Finally, past 19:00 h, the ship was stationed to join the formation and radio silence was established.

On April 17, the formation was already sailing with a general south-southeast bearing at an average of 10 knots (18.5 km/h), and lighthouses kept them apprised of their geographic location. The ships were sailing with port and starboard watches, where the crew is divided in two and all stations are manned, so as to be ready for any contingency. In the afternoon, they conducted combat and damage control exercises, the two most likely contingencies at the time. That night, a short circuit occurred in the fire control system, which was efficiently controlled, but which caused some damage that the specialists had to repair to return it to service. A few minutes later, the gyrocompass malfunctioned and the heading had to be maintained using a magnetic compass, which is a last resort in cases where more advanced technologies fail.

The third day of sailing, April 18, was used to replenish the Task Force. The Fleet's tanker, *Punta Médanos*, began supplying fuel oil at 09:30. As usual, the ships took turns in different roles, acting as the receiving or the rescue ship, while a third ship was the only one that could repel an attack, which in that geography would most probably be from a submarine. They were south of Rawson, approximately 80 miles from the coast.

---

[1] Translator's note: The Ship-of-the-line Lieutenant is a naval rank, roughly equivalent to the rank of Lieutenant in the UK and the US. The name derives from the name of the largest class of warship, as opposed to smaller types of warship (corvettes and frigates).

In the afternoon, they drilled missile launches. Each ship had four MM38-type Exocet missiles (sea-sea), which were useful exclusively for surface targets and had a range under 24.8 miles (40 km). The missiles were made by the French company Aerospatiale, had been installed previously, and had an interface that provided the system with the initial ballistic data in order to shoot efficiently (the Standard Firing Installation). The sequences were repeated over and over again, the keys inserted and removed to begin the drill again. As the days elapsed, the firing sequence and areas of responsibilities became automatic to the system operators and the officers that participated in the missiles' launch. Before sailing, a commission went on board to take measurements and configure settings, as well as to gather data. This commission was composed of officers and NCOs of the highest levels, who had participated in acquiring the weapons, had attended operation and maintenance courses, and had also implemented them in the country.

Long after the conflict had finished, the person in charge of the group confessed to the Commanding Officer that the missile system was not calibrated and that it would have taken many days, which they did not have, to render it operational. This meant that, had they been undergone, most of the launches would have failed. This information was not provided to the Commanding Officer, so that it would not negatively affect the fighting spirit of the crew. There is no doubt that the presence of the missile containers on deck gave the crew a confidence boost, but the professionals on board the *Bouchard* who were fulfilling their mission would have deserved to know the truth to seek operational alternatives in the case of an engagement, and not have to think of them in the midst of combat. In fact, problems are solved by confronting them, not by avoiding them. Every single day, the departments on board had new problems to face, and they were all solved proficiently and professionally (although sometimes by chance), always with the utmost effort.

At 18:30 h, sonar reported contact. Verification was attempted, but there was no other signal that could firmly confirm it or confirm a hostile presence. Although it was dismissed, wariness increased. Had the British or another country's submarines followed the Force's exercises and patrols? In that case, was it possible that a British submarine was in the area only 18 days from the landing? Once the exercises had finished, the Force met 30 miles east of Escondida Island, to sail in formation and under the same radio silence policy active since they had left port.

On April 19, the ships sailed until midday, when they were ordered to anchor near Punta Lobos, in Vera bay; the anchorage was codenamed "Atlas" in the operation plans. Past 16:00 h, cover was provided for a helicopter. The helicopter brought correspondence and then headed towards the destroyer *Piedrabuena*. They sailed at approximately 18:00 h, joined the Force, and continued in formation bearing east-northeast.

On April 20, the destroyer *Hércules D1* became the formation guide. They then began to assess another tool for the war: "chaff", strips of foil that in theory simulate a more intense target than the ship the missile was aimed at, due to the logic used by the automatic guidance system that aims at the greater target. The guide launched the device and the rest watched the results on their radar screens, and some on their binoculars. Not many ships had this type of passive anti-missile defence, and it was the first time many of the crew saw this type of launching. Later, they underwent replenishment at sea for a little over an hour, with *Hércules* acting as the receiving ship and *Bouchard* as the rescue destroyer. After this, *Punta Médanos* became the guide in the formation and the order was given to manoeuvre and replenish during the night. An intense day ended with one of the most dangerous manoeuvres at sea, with the exception of weapons drills.

On April 21, the Force conducted night replenishment. The turn of *Bouchard* was at 05:00 h, when it had already acted as a rescue ship. After the daytime practices, without lights and only a few beams provided by flashlights, the 130 tons the ship received were imbued with a sense of drama that the previous ones lacked. Nevertheless, it was proven that the team in charge of the fuel replenishment was solid and that errors, oversights and failures were minimal, and could be immediately saved by the other members of the group. Everything was foreseen and controlled, from the tiniest adjustments to the need of an immediate cut off because of a potential attack. The ship was assigned a sector on a purely anti-submarine screen, which covered the rest of the day.

In the first minutes of April 22, while the bridge watch were concerned with nautical security or whether the gyrocompass was deviating because of a planet or star, the 00:00–04:00 CIC watch rearranged the vessels from a sector to a circular formation. The Force then travelled to another area of operations. Fog appeared at first light and it was necessary to use whistles to signal and avoid collisions with other ships in the Force or that were sailing in the area. The Executive Officer and department chiefs conducted all sorts of exercises to strengthen the fledgling crew. That day, it was the turn of the artillery drill to go to battle stations as soon as they finished lunch, since combat has no schedule.

At 14:40, the sonar operators detected a new hydrophone noise, which removed the drowsiness from an unfulfilled siesta. The information received by the OCT caused the Force to suddenly change bearing northwards, and *Bouchard*, which detected the contact, was sent to investigate. The azimuth was 160°, they prepared for anti-submarine combat, and the ship headed to the area indicated by the sonar. Nothing was found and, once in formation, everything reverted to the previous situation.

The Force then went on exercises for an air raid. The most complicated part of this type of response is coordinating communication, because of the speed of the attackers and the variables in initial and subsequent attacks. To this end, the Force had to laboriously practice how to assign targets and weapons. However, everyone who knew the technology and weapons they would face in the event of an air raid knew well that any defence would be doomed to fail, unless the enemy made some ill-fated choices. Despite all of the above, the drills were conducted with stubborn professionalism with an, as people say: "C'mon, we've got this!" Thus, the crew's relations were strengthened; the leaders and the skilful stood out from those who only followed orders; there became apparent who was an optimist and who would fall into despair; and the people who would care enough to take a cup of coffee to the men who had missed lunch by 18:00 h distinguished themselves. In essence, matters were crystal clear between team members and nothing was as it had been in February, when they only saw the external traits of the new chief or the new division.

Once antiaircraft simulations were finished, the Force began anti-surface exercises with missiles, where they simulated being attacked by enemy ships, repelling them only with missiles. Once again, the chain of responsibilities and information for a correct anti-surface missile launch was implemented. The exercise was concluded at nightfall, at around 22:20 h, and the ships were ordered to return to their previous positions in the circular screen. Just as the night before, a change in screen was ordered and they started a new surprise anti-surface missile attack exercise, which lasted for the first four hours of April 23. When the latest exercises had finished, they met at Punta Delgada. The change of position put pressure on the engines, which performed above and beyond. They were ordered into a circular formation and *Hércules* was designated as guide. The Force was replenished in the afternoon, with *Bouchard* doing so a few minutes after 16:00 h. In just 45 min, they received over 120 tons of fuel, enough for almost three days sailing. However, the most important point was the inches gained for righting the ship,[2] which is crucial for stability. Later, the formation guide was changed and another day of manoeuvres and exercises was at an end.

The Task Group, consisting of destroyers *Py*, *Piedrabuena*, *Bouchard* and *Seguí*, headed west, with *Py* as formation guide. More combat exercises followed and they sailed without major changes for the rest of April 24, taking advantage to fine-tune internal workings, from combat roles to routines issues regarding the lunch, dinner, and sleep schedules (watch optimisation, distribution of beds and cabins, cleaning, among others). In the afternoon, they received naval message GFHO241248, where the Commanding Officer of TG 79.2 ordered destroyers *Piedrabuena* and *Bouchard* to join TG 79.3. At 14:55, the transfer started in a formation guided by *Piedrabuena*. The ships were divided in sectors, with cleaning and maintenance responsibilities that had to be well defined, and the workloads of which should be distributed correctly to avoid overloads. To this end, each unit's organisation manuals indicated their responsibilities. Subsequent analysis, conducted by the Executive Officer and his department chiefs, allowed assessing this balance should there be a change in the ship, for instance, the number of crewmembers of a department increase to the detriment of another or the addition of systems that overload a department in comparison to the rest (such as installing a missile system, for example).

With small formation changes, they manoeuvred[3] in the morning of April 25. *Bouchard* approached the *Piedrabuena* and the ships were placed alongside at around 49 ft (15 m) distance, sailing at 15 knots. The day was calm and drills within the ship sought the tuning of every role the ship had to play. The peace was broken in the afternoon, when boiler No. 3 broke down, forcing the ship to drop from formation and it could not sail over 4 knots. Once the boiler was brought off line, it could be replaced, and the ship rejoined the ordered formation.

---

[2] Balance of forces, consisting of the distribution of the ship's load that allows it to remain vertical, upright, and compensated, if the distribution is correct. Should it be incorrect, the ship heels and can even capsize in extreme scenarios.

[3] Translator's note: See comment below about the so-called *pasaje al habla*.

In the early hours of April 26, the engines stole the spotlight. The loss of vacuum in the aft engines meant that the port shaft could not propel, leading to the reduction of the revolutions from the other shaft. The formation was maintained with great efforts, and below deck an ever increasing number of helping hands approached to repair the port engine which was completely stalled. With the starboard engine as sole means of propulsion, they continued working on meeting the operational requirements but, due to feeding issues with the boiler, they were forced to stop and restart several times. Past 06:00 h, no engineer was left in his bunk; they were all trying to get *Bouchard* moving.

At dawn, both shafts were propelling and the ship was fully meeting operational requirements. Meanwhile, the engineers trimmed and examined any possibility of future breakdowns that could occur. At midday, the ship began sailing independently. Artillery drills were conducted and a volley of artillery was fired with the main turret, to train on an eventual anti-missile defence. They continued sailing independently until the end of the day.

On April 27, while the ship was sailing to Puerto Deseado, vacuum issues reappeared causing the port side shaft to stop after 01:30. The strenuous efforts of the engine's team brought both back online at around 04:00. They arrived at 06:00 and could recognise Punta Guzmán and the Puerto Deseado lighthouse. A little after 09:00, they anchored in the exterior roadstead. The Coast Guard boat GC 73 approached at approximately 13:00 and 15 crewmembers went ashore. With the right tide, the anchor was raised at 17:30. A few minutes later, due to the same engine issues, the ship was adrift.[4] They could propel with the starboard side and, in a dangerous and tension-filled manoeuver, the Commanding Officer was able to berth at 19:50. With all engines stopped, they performed the proper repairs. Despite having berthed, many hours would have to pass before the temperatures and pressures inside mechanisms and ducts would return to values allowing manoeuvres. The crew went ashore and tried to find solace and fun in a small town crammed with naval officers and soldiers who would cross to the Falklands/Malvinas in a few days.

---

[4] Floating without any propulsion or rudder.

Chapter 8
Operation Algeciras (Vv. Aa., Irizar.Org, 2014) (Nicoletti M., 2000)

A division of Argentine Naval Intelligence in charge of special operations was commissioned to plan and execute an attack on British military targets in mainland Europe, without disclosing Argentine involvement. The purpose was to cause turmoil and uncertainty in Britain by creating the impression that third countries, hostile to Great Britain, were getting involved in a war that should remain restricted to the Falklands/Malvinas, South Georgia and South Sandwich Islands, and the immediate adjoining waters.

The Commander in Chief of the Navy, Admiral Anaya, ordered the operation and kept it secret, without even telling the Argentine President or the heads of the other Armed Forces. Anaya did not disclose the operation to his peers until after the cruiser *ARA General Belgrano* had been sunk by the Royal Navy.

The people chosen to carry out the operation were a Lieutenant Commander in the Amphibious Command (Special Forces) in the Naval Infantry, and three prominent members of the Montoneros, an insurgent organisation under the political ideology introduced by General Juan Domingo Perón. The three men were not living in Argentina at the time, but answered the call eagerly. All the men chosen were expert divers, and one of them had been involved in a Montoneros' attack on the Argentine destroyer *ARA Santísima Trinidad* (sister ship to the *HMS Sheffield*), which was now being repaired in an Argentine shipyard.

Everything was kept in the strictest secrecy. On April 24, 1982, two members of the team travelled to southern Spain, near the Rock of Gibraltar, to assess the operation's feasibility. Even before arriving they had already reported that the operation was feasible. The other two members travelled on a different flight together with the explosives, Italian mines[1] designed for sabotaging ships in port or at anchor, which were sent via diplomatic pouch to the Argentine Navy Attaché in Madrid.

---

[1] Similar Argentine-made mines were available, but their use was ruled out to prevent identification of Argentina as the author of the sabotage. Three mines were sent containing a charge of 55 pounds of TNT concealed inside a buoy.

The former Montoneros travelled with false passports and under assumed names. This would enable them, should they be caught, to allege political motives, thus placing the blame on the guerrilla organisation instead of on Argentina.

The first group was forced to change planes in France, where the passport of one of them was found suspicious by the French authorities. However, after some tense and anxious minutes, they were allowed to travel onward to Spain.

As days went by, they gathered enough information to be able to execute the operation. The target was to be a Royal Navy ship, not a civilian vessel or one belonging to some other country, and previous authorization was required before executing any action. As it transpired from the private conversations held by the former Montoneros, they considered the possibility of dismissing the instructions, acting on their own and then vanishing.

Once in the area of operations, they operated just as they had when they were clandestine guerrilla soldiers in Argentina: they would avoid the authorities, switch locations frequently, avoid crowded places, and stay away from routes and motorways. They would park their explosives-loaded car and shop at establishments where they would go unnoticed.

In Spain, the FIFA World Cup football championship was about to begin (June and July), and security was very tight for fear of attacks by the Basque terrorist organisation ETA.

Although planning had been completed and the operation had been skilfully designed, they waited in vain for the order to execute the attack. Every time they requested authorisation it was denied, since Argentina and Great Britain were still at the negotiating table. On May 2, after the sinking of the cruiser *General Belgrano*, they finally received the go-ahead. Moreover, on May 8, fortune fated that a warship, the *HMS Ariadne*, would dock at Gibraltar. Their sources told them that the ship was scheduled to remain in port for at least three days. The attack was planned for dawn on May 9.

As cover, they had bought a small boat and fishing gear. Weather conditions were suitable, but there was too much light because of a magnificent full moon and a completely clear sky. Consequently, they decided to postpone the operation until the following day.

On the morning of May 10, the chief and one member of the team went to renew the lease on the vehicles, while the others stayed in their lodgings resting before the operation, which was scheduled for 5:00 p.m.

Spanish police suspected the four Argentines and a group of Uruguayans (who they were also watching) of planning to rob a bank. After the Argentines had renewed their vehicle lease, the company phoned the police, who arrested the Lieutenant Commander along with one of the former Montoneros, and then went to pick up the others, who were still at their lodgings, resting.

When they were arrested, the Lieutenant Commander identified himself as an Argentine Navy Officer and claimed that he was conducting espionage against the British on Gibraltar. Top authorities were informed then and the routine police investigation took a completely unexpected turn, especially when the Spanish police discovered the mines in the boot of the car parked at a hotel near the Argentines' lodgings.

The British authorities had already warned the Spanish authorities, since they had intercepted communications and were aware of some details of the situation.

The interaction between the arrested and the policemen was not tense at all; indeed, after arresting the last members, passed noon, they invited the entire police commission to have lunch with them, and the police accepted gladly. After lunch was finished, they organised the return trip. The travel turned into a relaxed transport, with very pleasant conversations—they even stopped by a laundry shop to collect a pair of trousers that a member of the Argentine group had sent to be washed.

Their equipment and explosives were confiscated and the mines were later blown up by the Spanish Army. The only things they were allowed to keep were their diving goggles, which had personalised optical corrections because the divers suffered from short-sightedness and astigmatism—an additional token of the camaraderie that had arisen.

The police flew with them to Madrid, where they changed flights and headed for the Canary Islands. From there, they were allowed to fly back to Buenos Aires without escort.

Spain could not afford such an operation to be executed, since its priority was being admitted to NATO. Nonetheless, the Spanish police hinted that they would have been pleased if such an attack had succeeded in Gibraltar, a Spanish territory usurped by the British.

Thus, an elaborate and ingenious covert operation failed due to the indecisiveness of the Argentine Government top level.

Chapter 9
From Puerto Deseado to the Sinking of *General Belgrano*

Abstract The domestic and international context and the hostilities. Operations since weighing anchors from Puerto Deseado until the sinking of *General Belgrano*. The intense, memorable and emotional hours before the frustrated attack on the British fleet. The attack on the cruiser ARA *General Belgrano*, the explosion of the torpedo below the destroyer, the damage. The subsequent evasion.

The Domestic and International Context and the Hostilities (Vv. Aa., IRI, 1994) (Vv. Aa., *Historia de la Fuerza Aérea Argentina* [History of the Argentine Air Force], 1998) (Vv. Aa., informe oficial del Ejército Argentino, *Conflicto Malvinas* [Official Argentine Army report on the Falklands/Malvinas War], 1983) (Rattenbach B., 1983)

On April 28, Britain reported the enforcement of a so-called maritime exclusion zone around the Falklands/Malvinas with a radius of 200 nautical miles as from 11:00 on the following day. Any ship or aircraft found within the zone, whether civilian or military and regardless of nationality, would be deemed hostile and liable to be attacked.

A number of diplomatic incidents and statements fuelled further the warlike mood. Argentina protested to the European Economic Community on the weapons embargo, while Israel refused a request to suspend the sale of weapons to Argentina. In addition, the OAS Foreign Ministers conference resolved, by 17 votes against 4, in favour of issuing a statement under Article 6 of the TIAR.

On April 29, the United States openly announced its support for Great Britain, imposed economic sanctions on Argentina and deemed terminated its role as mediator in the conflict. Meanwhile, the British Task Force assembled in an area that had been designated as TRALA[1] located some 250 miles northeast of the Falklands/Malvinas, intending to begin operations the following day.

---

[1] Acronym for the Tow, Repair and Logistic Area, located at the rear.

On May 1, the British Task Force arrived in the area of operations. Vulcan Bombers based on Ascension and Harrier bombers deployed on aircraft carriers began bombing Argentine positions. The destroyers HMS *Glamorgan*, HMS *Alacrity* and HMS *Arrow* subjected Argentine positions near Puerto Argentino (Port Stanley) to a barrage of cannon fire. That day, the first aerial dogfights took place and the SAS landed on the shores of the islands.

The Argentine warships sought to envelop the British fleet in a pincers movement. The aircraft carrier ARA *25 de Mayo* approached the British vessels from the north, intending to launch its embarked fighters against the British. Meanwhile, the cruiser ARA *General Belgrano* would approach from the south escorted by two destroyers. The utter lack of wind prevented this planned attack, and the operation was eventually called off in the early hours of the following day.

On May 2, the submarine HMS *Conqueror* sank the cruiser ARA *General Belgrano* and inflicted damage on one of the destroyers escorting it, the ARA *Bouchard*.

In the ARA *Bouchard*

Bouchard sailed past 17:00 *h* on April 28, with only one shaft online. The strenuous efforts of the whole engineering department were not enough to finish the job. Several more hours would have been needed to repair the aft engine, which was responsible for rotating the port shaft. They did not want to remain in port to continue repairs, since they forebode that the pages of glory would be written those days. They were professionals and there were no valid excuses: Argentina had given them *Bouchard* to man, and that is what they were going to do.

They had to wait for the right tide and, when the time came, with a single shaft and a host of unresolved questions regarding its operation, they started another risk-filled manoeuvre. The Commanding Officer slowly and without hesitation pointed out to his Executive Officer which berthing ropes should the crew bring on board one by one. Once the stern was free from any ties, it gradually separated from the dock and, free from all berthing ropes, it began the difficult task of weighing anchors that would take them to combat. The overcast sky hastened the coming of night. Just after 20:00 h, they went on port and starboard watches. After several false starts, both shafts were in operation past 23:00 h. The general heading was southwards and they had to manoeuvre to avoid a merchant ship that was hugging the cost, surely on its way to Ushuaia.

During April 29, *Bouchard* sailed southwards in formation. In the afternoon, it took south-southeast bearing, to head separately to the assigned patrol area. It detected the Isla de los Estados past 21:00 h, and then headed south and anchored almost at midnight in San Antonio bay, close to the rest of the Force. The overcast sky gave a dreary and sad note to the proceedings. In these times, nights were not for sleeping. Once anchored, they lowered a launch and the Commanding Officer went to the cruiser *Belgrano*. The launch returned past three in the morning. The launch's crewmembers had specific requests for the cruiser: an engine salinometer, some punch tape rolls for the cryptographs, etc.

At 07:00 h on the 30th, the Task Force sailed to replenish fuel, which was going to be supplied by the YPF tanker *Puerto Rosales*. Due to the seas conditions, the heading for the replenishment was virtually north. *Piedrabuena* replenished first, with the other ship acting as the rescue ship. Later, at midmorning, *Bouchard* began its own replenishment. Once again, it received almost 120 tons of heavy fuel oil. Shortly after, a new formation guided by *Belgrano* was ordered, and they headed south. At 18:00 *h*, the ships stopped their engines, *Bouchard* lowered its boat, which headed to the cruiser and returned at 19:30. The sector screen was established.[2]

Destroyer ARA Bouchard escorting the cruiser ARA General Belgrano and destroyer ARA Piedrabuena while replenishing the tanker ARA Punta Médanos

On May 1, the Force was between the Isla de los Estados and the Falklands/Malvinas. The sector screen was maintained, covering *Belgrano* from any contingency. However, for the first hours of the day, the guide sailed at 5 knots while *Bouchard*, within its sector, sped at 10 knots. After 08:00, the tanker *Puerto Rosales* started supplying *Bouchard* and then the rest of the force.

At 09:33 h, an unidentified airplane was detected and they went to battle stations. It was never confirmed whether the contact was an Argentine Air Force airplane or a bandit,[3] but an hour later contact was lost and everyone returned to their normal

---

[2] The sector screen is materialised by a circular corona that moves with the nucleus of the formation. Each ship is assigned a specific geographic area where they are to move randomly. The purpose is to prevent submarines from being able to attack the nucleus (the most important ships in the group).

[3] Translator's note: Name given to an enemy aircraft.

duties. However, this alarm caused the manoeuvre to come to an emergency stop, which caused the hoses and distance lines to break and the ships to be dirtied with fuel oil, which later proved to be very troublesome to clean. For many hours, the Deck Chief of *Bouchard* was at the stern cleaning and repairing the hoses, phone lines and distance lines damaged by the emergency. The rest of the department personnel also had a hectic day because of the transfer of the vital fuel. The replenishment finally finished past 13:00. The formation was re-established and the cruiser's helicopter landed on *Bouchard's* deck at 15:00 h. It would take the Commanding Officer and Chief Operating Officer to ARA *Belgrano* for an urgent meeting, where they would remain until 18:30.

The new operation plans and engagement orders clearly showed how close they were to combat. The Commanding Officer gathered his Senior Staff to report the news and orders received, and the Division Chiefs then retransmitted this information to their men. They all knew what was expected of each member of their crew. The initial order, received by naval message 011207, from the South Atlantic Task Force Commander, was to approach in order to gauge the enemy's reaction. This order seemed ridiculous and nonsensical to the Senior Staff, who did not miss the chance to lend their professional contributions. Hours later, the original order was changed to one instructing them to hit targets of opportunity, which was more logical to those who had to actually carry out the operation. This order carried a real combat mission.

Close to 24:00 h on May 1, the crew gathered for a general formation on the signal bridge. The Communications NCO in charge of the watch opened the luxurious chest that held the ship's battle flag; he removed the beautiful light blue and white silk cloth, with a resplendent sun embroidered in gold threads. The flag was only taken out to oversee important formations or to lead a parade. In this case, however, it was to be raised on the ship's military flagpole to behold a crew that was willing to give their very lives, the most valuable gift God had given them, before surrendering the ensign. The crew sung *a cappella* the Argentine National Anthem before a peaceful sea and a wind that unfurled the raised flag with a snap, like a whip punishing the night itself for not allowing the world to contemplate such an intimate and transcendental moment. With the last verses of the anthem, the Chief Artillery Officer and a Midshipman from the department shot their guns, in replacement of the traditional 21-gun salute. The deeply moved crewmembers descended one by one down one of the two rugged ladders that allowed access to the signal bridge. The improvised ceremony deeply impressed their spirits. It was a special ceremony, since they all knew that combat was imminent, that regardless of the years they had spent in the Navy preparing, studying, and drilling, they would face their real empirical test. Each one manned their post: those on duty took up their positions, while those whose turn was to rest six hours quietly retired to their bunks. Everything had been said, the time had come to act. They weren't heroes, they were professionals.

That night, the faithful prayed, the men remembered their families, and some reproached themselves for leaving a task uncompleted or for failing to say something. The cook left the canteen open, so that whoever had the need, could serve himself. There was a single uniting force, regardless of hierarchy: the unbreakable will to fight for what they had been stationed in the South Atlantic. They were not going to forfeit while resources still remained. *Bouchard* was at war and its decks were trod by professionals with the will to fight and scant experience, which would produce valuable veterans for their institution and their country.

From the first hours of May 2, the weather began deteriorating by the hour, the pressure plummeted, the wind increased, the sky became overcast and the seas raged. Everything framed fittingly the tension present on board the Force's three ships. The Force maintained a stubborn 090° bearing east, looking for enemy contacts, until about 04:10 when, after turning north-northwest, it changed again and headed west, i.e., 270°, moving away from the islands and towards the Isla de los Estados.

The Operations Command had decided to abort the mission of finding the enemy, since the lack of wind had prevented the aircraft carrier from reaching the speed necessary for its planes to take off, and the mission was a failure. In addition, they analysed the chance of having been discovered by enemy airplane scouts. The result was the same: the attack was cancelled.

They also knew that the aircraft carrier's engines were not in the finest of conditions, and it had had boiler compartments closed off and offline for years, due to the magnitude of the repairs needed to make them operational. Hence, the Force headed directly to the continent after many hours of approximation. The Task Force Commander had ordered a tactical arrangement that prioritised the defence of the protected cruiser: the destroyer *Piedrabuena* was 8000 yards in-front, while *Bouchard* was to the cruiser's starboard, closer to the islands. This way, *Piedrabuena* would face a possible submarine in the fall back to the continent, and *Bouchard* would be their first line of defence should there be an air raid from the Falklands/Malvinas.

To verify the reach of the hydrophone sensors, at 14:00 h the Commanding Officer of *Bouchard* approached the cruiser until reaching a distance of 4000 yards, where the noise of the cruiser's propellers churning (which was very loud compared to a submarine's propellers) was barely audible. After that disappointing assessment, they returned to their position and the Force took a bearing of 290°. At 16:10, a strong blow to port and a significant heel to starboard made the whole ship shudder. The feeling was the same as when the main 5 inch battery fired a volley. The blow had been very hard. The anti-submarine combat alarm sounded throughout the ship. The bridge ordered full speed ahead, that is to say that the engines were to be powered fully without any gradual ramping procedure; all valves were to be opened so that the steam could flow and the ship would immediately achieve its maximum speed. In addition, sealing condition "Y" was ordered, which was the most severe. The whole ship had to be compartmentalised: all doors and hatches were closed, and all engineers had to stay in their cubicles. There was no more traffic through the ship. If an area was damaged, it would have to be self-sufficient as regards freeing the ship or evacuating. The objective was for the ship not to be lost should it be hit in any one sector.

The ship seen from the periscope of the submarine ARA Santa Fe

There was no doubt, a torpedo had hit them. The bridge and the CIC were trying to issue the correct operational response to the event. They attempted to communicate the news to *Belgrano*, but the communication channels, mute due to the radio silence plan, could not get an answer. From the bridge, the Chief of Communications tried in vain on the marine VHF radio, on channel 16 for emergency and safety. While they began zig-zagging to increase the difficulty for the submarine to fire, the Commanding Officer asked for damage reports from his place on the bridge. In the CIC, they began to search on their radar and, with their electronic countermeasures, they combed through the wavelength spectrum where the submarines, especially the British ones, had their radars. They also attempted to detect a target with the sonar's active pinging, and they looked for any passive hydrophone noise, but nothing was detected on the ancient equipment. The Chief Engineer, who was casually walking on the port side, reported seeing an enormous bubble. There was also an overwhelming smell of explosives outside the ship, which then reached the interiors due to the forced ventilation. Later, the man on watch at the bosun's chair—who was at the ship's stern to offer help should anyone go overboard—confirmed this assertion.

From the signal bridge they were going to great lengths to communicate with the cruiser. The low visibility and distance prevented them from seeing the ship clearly, although they could ascertain that something "strange" was happening. The Chief of Communications ordered the raising of signal flags, lit signs with powerful bulbs, and the use of handheld lighting equipment. The only response they received were three white lights, which had no meaning in any of the active codes, or in any other.

So far, they believed that *Bouchard* had been the target of the submarine attack. The goal of the immediate notice given to the rest of the Force was that, following the operations plan ordered the previous day, the rest of the vessels would move away from the target so that they would not become a target for new attacks. *Piedrabuena* was the only ship to answer. A few minutes later, marking it south-southeast at around 14 miles (23 km), contact with the cruiser was lost.

The ships separated at maximum speed, until reaching approximately 20 miles (32 km) away from the event area. At 17:15, they reversed heading to approach the last confirmed contact location of the cruiser. At 19:00, without finding any trace of the cruiser, they left the search area to meet to a point north of the Isla de los Estados, since the radar search on the supposed place of attack had been completely fruitless.

The inclement weather and the night were harshly foreboding. The Communications Staff was unceasing in their activities: they received messages and tried by all means available on all possible frequencies to establish a line of communication with the cruiser or liferafts. The engineers, in addition to their routine of constant repairs, also had to control water leaks caused by the impact. The bridge's windows had been loosened and the lurches from the sea had cleared the chart-table and damaged the navigation radar repeater, which was left offline. The storm worsened the situation, since the sea struck the bridge uncommonly hard, the windscreen wipers disappeared and the watch officers were soaking wet and had to take refuge in the wheelhouse. Only one person remained on the bridge, to maintain nautical safety and avoid any unfortunate event.

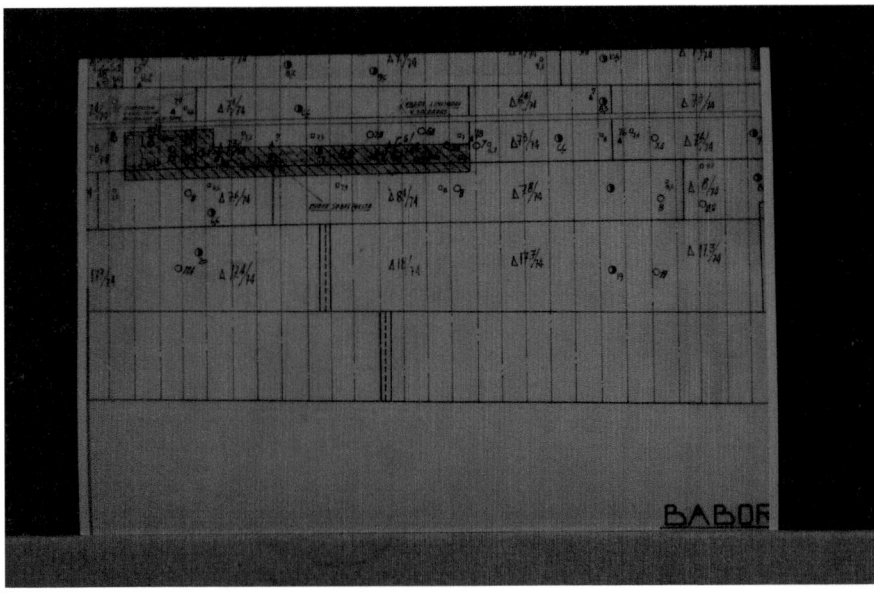

Metal Sheet Change Plan

Entering the dock to change the hull plates (because of the close explosion by the torpedo)

The ship in dry dock for plate changing

The reason for the impact received by *Bouchard* has been much debated. Some theories, later disregarded due to the evidence and statements made by the parties involved, suggested that it had been a product of the echo the hull received as a consequence of one of the explosions the cruiser experienced. However, the facts were different. Three torpedoes were launched at the cruiser. It lost its bow and stern due to the first and second torpedoes, the third hit the cruiser and travelled the 8000 yards that separated *Bouchard* from *Belgrano*. This torpedo, with scarcely any charge left in its batteries, was losing its ability to maintain a stable and adequate depth. Sinking due to the lack of propulsion, it reached *Bouchard's* magnetic influence, which activated its magnetic proximity fuse and caused its cargo to explode, thus creating a great gas bubble. Fortunately for *Bouchard*, this huge gas bubble impacted the port side and led to the upheaval described above. It was this same bubble that the Chief Engineer and the petty officer on watch at the stern would later see, and it was also the origin of the permeating smell of explosives. Besides, the smell perceived by the crew could not have come from the events on the cruiser, since the wind was coming from the north-northwest and the cruiser was to the south-southeast of *Bouchard*.

When they explode, depth charges cause a huge bubble that raises the ship at some point of its length, warping the beam holding the shape of the ship and it can even tear it in two, causing the vessel to sink. There is no need for shards and solid pieces of metal to sink a ship, a huge bubble can do so just as well.

An article published on December 23, 1984, by Walter Pincus, former Lieutenant of the Royal Navy, mentions the weapons that did not work and states that a MK8 torpedo shot by the submarine *Conqueror* hit *Bouchard* without exploding. Furthermore, in an article published by *La Nación* newspaper, on July 20, 2000, the Commanding Officer of *Conqueror*, Christopher Wreford-Brown, claims that he launched three MK8 torpedoes, to overcome any possible calculation error, and that two hit the Argentine cruiser.

The ship was forced to enter dry-dock to change around 161–215 ft^2 (15–20 m^2) of plating, damaged by the event. Nothing could ever make the crew forget the moments endured after the impact.

Chapter 10
General Belgrano Was Sunk!

Abstract The domestic and international context and the hostilities. *General Belgrano* was sunk. The desperate search for shipwrecked men. The first rafts. Gaining distance at night. Beginning rescue operations without being able to stop engines due to the damage. We lose our rescue diver who ends up adrift in a raft with shipwrecked crew. The submarine harries us and maintains its presence. The rescue continues. The ship's own lifejackets are given to the sailors to make them feel protected. Arrival in Ushuaia. Repairs to the damages suffered.

The Domestic and International Context and the Hostilities (Vv. Aa., IRI, 1994) (Vv. Aa., *Historia de la Fuerza Aérea Argentina* [History of the Argentine Air Force], 1998) (Vv. Aa., informe oficial del Ejército Argentino, *Conflicto Malvinas* [Official Argentine Army Report on the Falklands/Malvinas War], 1983) (Rattenbach B., 1983)

On May 3, two British helicopters launched supersonic missiles at the fleet ocean tug ARA *Sobral*, causing severe damage by demolishing its bridge and devastating its lower deck where the radio shack was located. The tug's Commanding Officer died in the attack after giving the order to evacuate all non-essential crewmen (a naval officer, five petty officers and one conscript), to prevent any more casualties. Until it was attacked, the fleet ocean tug had been busy rescuing the Air Force pilots, who had ejected from an obsolete Canberra bomber shot down while carrying out a mission the previous night.

On May 4, two Argentine Navy Super Étendard aircrafts fired AM-39-type Exocet missiles at the destroyer HMS *Sheffield*, inflicting severe damage. As a result, a fire broke out on board and 21 crew members were killed. The Argentine Air Force claimed that the aircraft carrier HMS *Hermes* had also been damaged and, from that day onward, the aerial activity was reduced to at least 50%.

Meanwhile, Air Force aircraft spotted the damaged fleet ocean tug ARA *Sobral*, sailing south of Puerto Deseado on the Patagonian shore, evacuated two severely injured crew members, carried a new Commanding Officer on board, and escorted the vessel to port. During land combat on the Falklands/Malvinas, Argentine troops shot down a Harrier aircraft over Goose Green, and its pilot died due to the impact.

On that same date, Operation "Black Buck II" was launched, which involved ten Victor tanker aircrafts so that two Vulcan bombers could drop their war cargo on the runway of the Puerto Argentino (Port Stanley) airfield, but they did not succeed in causing any damage. In the interim, SAS troops had infiltrated the civilian population to gather and relay precise data on the Argentine defence mechanism.

The aircraft carrier ARA *25 de Mayo* was forced to return to port because of the presence of British nuclear submarines in the area provided with American satellite intelligence, and which rendered the carrier extremely vulnerable.

On the other hand, the British Government stated that it would exercise its power of veto on any UN resolution demanding a ceasefire, unless Argentine forces withdrew unconditionally from the theatre of operations.

On May 5, the fleet ocean tug ARA *Sobral* berthed at Puerto Deseado. The same day, the destroyers ARA *Bouchard* and ARA *Piedrabuena*, together with the fleet ocean tug ARA *Gurruchaga*, arrived at Ushuaia harbour, Tierra del Fuego, transporting 600 survivors from the foundered cruiser ARA *General Belgrano*. For its part, responding to the sinking of the destroyer HMS *Sheffield*, Great Britain renewed its resolve to fight on until the last Argentine was evicted from the Falklands/Malvinas.

After the sinking of the cruiser ARA *General Belgrano* and the destroyer HMS *Sheffield*, diplomatic efforts went into high gear. France pleaded for an immediate ceasefire; Peru and Nicaragua renewed their support for the Argentine cause; the king of Spain offered to mediate; Argentina consented to mediation by the Secretary General of the UN and condemned the blatant American support for Great Britain, which declared that it would disregard any appeals for a ceasefire. The non-aligned countries proclaimed their support for Argentina and asked for a peaceful settlement of the conflict.

Argentine politics expressed their support for the Armed Forces on the war and, despite the deep sorrow for the numerous deaths reported, the general population endorsed the operations and there was an atmosphere of intense patriotic spirit. Back in the United Kingdom, the Government too was now supported by the public opinion that was lacking at the beginning of the actions, as well as the desire to recover the islands and, together with them, the British honour tarnished by Argentina.

In the ARA *Bouchard*

The ship continued bearing north-east until 03:35 h on May 3, when the diminished Task Group commanded by the destroyer *Piedrabuena* headed directly to the area where the shipwreck survivors were believed to be. During the night, they received sporadic signals from the *survival* type communications equipment, which had been placed in the liferafts by the cruiser's radio operators. However, the signals were weak and could not be located with a radio direction finder.[1] They continued bearing 135° until after 08:00 h, when they passed the approximate point where the ship had been sunk. The bridge and CIC team felt vibrations as they sailed the area. That morning, thanks to a notice given by a scouting airplane, they detected a fuel spill that the ship crossed in the dead of night. It was a clear and unambiguous sign confirming that the ship had been sunk, but no one wanted to acknowledge it. The search began, implementing all the techniques that were to be found in search and rescue manuals. Each and every weather data point was analysed and assessed separately, to ascertain the spread of the liferafts, and heading and speeds were adjusted with this information.

---

[1] Taking azimuths (horizontal angles from the north) of radio electrical signals produced by different sources (a radio emitter, radio beacon, radio buoy, etc.) Any radio electrical signal within the range of a radio direction finder can be measured and, with two or more finders at a reasonable distance of separation, the source of those signals can be geographically located.

At 08:00 h, a search called "expanded quadrant with an entry at Latitude 55° 25' S and Longitude 60° 45' W" began.

Piedrabuena established itself as the group's OCT, it directed and controlled all the movements of the small group, which grew with the inclusion of other Navy vessels. At 09:10 h, radio operators reported hearing a very weak signal at 2182 kHz, an emergency frequency. The search was in vain until a report from a Navy scout plane was received and, at 13:30 h, the heading was corrected a few degrees and a liferaft was sighted at 14:10 h.

The ship approached this first sighting with great enthusiasm. The crew on deck had prepared all types of equipment for the rescue, the rescue divers were wearing their primitive neoprene suits, and the cooks prepared their finest broths, so they would be able to offer something hot as soon as they had crossed the gangway.[2] The doctor and nurse were also part of the welcoming committee and had prepared everything the ship had to offer (which was not much when it came to medical matters). However, the liferaft sighted was empty. Ten minutes later, they started to see wreckage from the liferafts and, from 12:00 to 16:00 h, they managed to rescue 41 survivors.

---

[2] Opening in the side of the ship to allow the entry of people and/or goods.

The first group found was made up of 12 liferafts. The raging storm had separated them and the crewmembers were forced to cut the ropes tying them together to avoid unnecessary damage to the structure. Rescue operations were further complicated by the violent rolling of the ship, since the seas were still rough. Seeing that it was impossible to use the accommodation ladder, the landing net was hung from the bow. All the shipwrecked men found climbing the net to be highly difficult and had to be personally assisted. As they boarded the ship, *Bouchard*'s crewmembers quartered the rescued according to their specialties, so they could be among and supported by colleagues with whom they had shared schools, courses, or other units, after so many hours of sorrow, cold, hunger and uncertainty. In addition, the crew of *Bouchard* gave to each shipwrecked men one of their own lifejackets, not only so that they may feel safe, but also as a symbol: "We'll share the same fate".

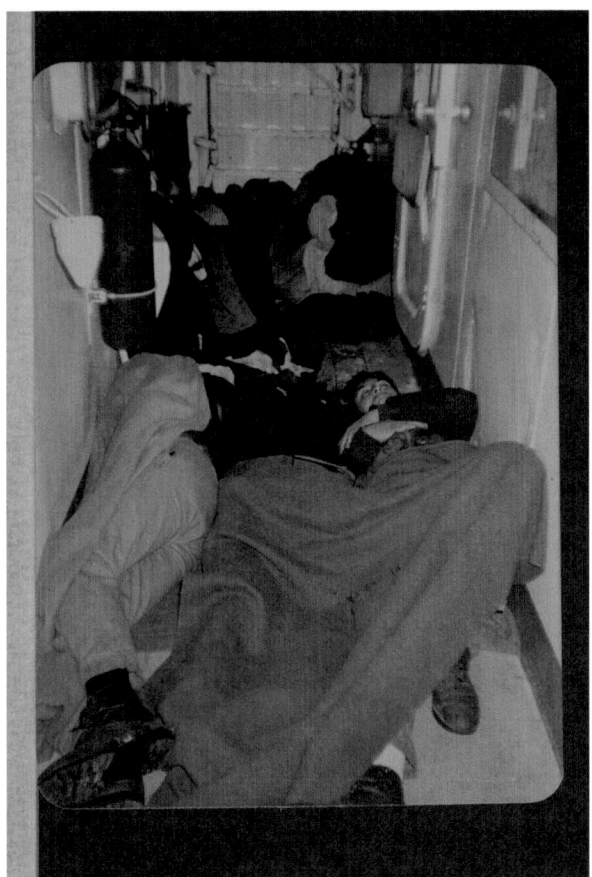

All the shipwrecked men boarded and were received by the deck crew, the doctor and some Senior Staff members. The officers in the liferafts were the last to board and, once they did so, they only went to the wardroom when they were sure that all the men under their charge had been properly tended to and lodged.

After the first rescue, the ship approached a group of three liferafts. They tossed ropes to hold them fast and secure them to the ship, and thus proceed to rescue them, but the hands of the survivors were numb by the cold and could not grasp the ropes. The officer in charge of the manoeuvre tied a rope to a rescue diver and ordered him to head to the liferafts, an order that the petty officer was already anxious to carry out for some time because of the situation. Once in the water, he swam towards the liferafts. Of the three rafts, one was in good conditions, one was half-sunken with a destroyed roof, and the last had a ruined roof and three corpses inside. The latter was the one the diver came to first, but he quickly moved on to the liferaft that was full. New ropes were tossed, but it was all futile, the diver's hands were also frozen and he could not secure them. The group of rafts began to drift away. Facing so many difficulties, it was decided to leave the rescue of the deceased for those with more options available. The diver and survivors were rescued by the fleet ocean tug *Gurruchaga*, which was better suited for the task.

The following liferaft held 32 people, which far exceeded the raft's capacity, but they were in high spirits. A new rescue method was attempted: they were raised two at a time by the stern winch. It was a success. The survivors were in various different conditions: some had recently had appendectomies, others were covered in oil, and some were so frozen that they could not move on their own. Lieutenant Gardiner, in charge of the operation, retells that one of the survivors, a conscript, had abandoned ship with his "most valuable possession", a radio with a recorder. However, when he was being hoisted, the liferaft chief ordered with a shout: "Drop it, kid!" The conscript complied, releasing the last material possession he had left, which fell onto the roof of the liferaft.

The presence of a submarine was clearly evident in the area. At 18:00 h, they went to battle stations and port and starboard watches. The ship was experiencing serious engine problems and could not go below 5 knots, or they would stop inexorably. The low-pressure turbine cooling ducts were completely covered in wreckage from *Belgrano*, which prevented the correct condensation of the feeder water, among other issues. With only 41 survivors on board, and the engines at a highly diminished capacity, the ship began sailing a circuit around the liferafts, but without being able to conduct more rescue operations. Meanwhile, the survivors in the wardroom and other areas were giving their accounts as a sort of catharsis, always maintaining an unimaginable dignity and pride; with only a few exceptions, no man was seen broken by despair. The war was over for them, but peace was still a long way off.

Darkness was very close, and the state of the seas and weather was not appropriate to be in a liferaft. The temperature of the sea was a little over 49 °F (6 °C) and the waves were over 10 feet (3 m) high. The southwesterly winds bestowed greater energy on the waves, since its intensity had gone from 22 to 35 knots, under an absolutely overcast sky and with a temperature of about 41 °F (5 °C), and a much lower wind chill factor. Being unable to continue with the rescue was extremely painful for the entire crew. Survivors shot their pistols from the liferafts to alert them to their presence. They had already been seen, but the risk of attempting a rescue was much higher than the chances of it being successful.

The fleet ocean tug *Gurruchaga* was doing a fantastic job, with its low gunwale and motivated crew rescuing every survivor they could. The ship was full: cabins, rooms, stores, passageways, crewmembers from *Belgrano* could be found everywhere. Similarly, *Bahía Paraíso*, a polar cargo ship built in the country, not only rescued the survivors, but was also able to recover the corpses of those who had died at sea from the cold or their injuries.

The clear and present submarine threat was no longer an issue, and the harassment from sporadic radar pinging was ignored. They could not abandon their colleagues and friends at sea; they would give up their very lives if that was necessary. Everyone knew that solidarity at sea had been present in man since he first dared to ride the waters on rivers, lakes and seas. Perhaps this same feeling was shared by the enemies who stalked them below the surface. However, an order issued by the Admiralty would have been enough for them to sink the vessels that were undertaking the rescue operation of the *Belgrano's* survivors, almost with no risk to themselves. At 22.09 h, and thanks to the lights of the flares, they spotted other liferaft and communicated the good news to the *Piedrabuena*.

From the first hours on May 4, the wind began to reduce its strength and the sea its fury. The temperature also dropped noticeably, and was barely over 35 °F (2 °C). Almost at 08:00 h, *Piedrabuena* ordered *Bouchard* to approach to continue rescue operations. At 08:50 h, another group of liferafts was detected and a zodiac was lowered to rescue the survivors while the ship sailed at almost 5 knots, adding 22 men to the list of survivors. Each new passenger was a source of joy for the crew of *Bouchard*, regardless of whether it was a conscript, NCO or officer, all they wanted was to have the chance to help those who had undoubtedly spent ghastly hours at sea.

After covering liferaft after liferaft, they sunk the empty raft to avoid needless double or triple rescue manoeuvres. Others were marked with paint for the same reason. At around 15:30 h, they set a general bearing westwards to head towards Ushuaia. On the way, they checked every liferaft they came across, always with negative results, and they adopted the method of sinking or painting some to avoid false alarms. As regards their navigation, they adopted a pattern of changing their bearing to avoid facilitating the firing solution for submarine torpedoes. Although this measure would have been the right one in the '40s, it was not for the seeking torpedo technology that homed towards the noise generated by a ship, which *Bouchard* could do little against. Nevertheless, they used every tool at their disposal, even when they knew that it would have little effect against the sophisticated weapons of the enemy.

Fifteen minutes after the watch change at 16:00 h, the sonar gave the alarm due to a strong hydrophone contact at the bow. They immediately went to battle stations for anti-submarine combat, and they investigated without being able to detect anything. They raised the condition 30 min later and returned to port and starboard watches. The enemy maintained their presence in the area as a warning, to harass those who were carrying rescue operations. It was later found that the alarm was raised by an underwater electrical pump for the transfer of water from one tank to another that had been activated by personnel from the electrical department without being authorised to do so by the bridge. This noise is similar to a quick propeller, i.e., similar to that of a torpedo in the water.

The alarm caused much unrest among the survivors, who did not want to relive their previous experience and already knew well what it meant to be sunk. In any case, the *Bouchard's* crew did everything they could to support them and give them shelter. They had rendered their own clothes, blankets and the only lifejackets they had. But even *Bouchard's* complement was unaware that the liferafts on the ship were useless, since a few days later, in a test performed in Ushuaia, it was determined that they either did not inflate at all or they just inflated partially.

During the entire night, the engineers tried to solve a problem that was not theirs: as they sailed, they were not able to remove the wreckage from the cruiser that had entered into the cooling system. They tried small adjustments to the pumps and circuits, but failed to meet the needed results. The ship could not go below 5 knots, otherwise, the plant would stop and they would have to be towed to port, an unthinkable option given the operational environment. A submarine stalked the ships loaded with shipwrecked, even though the alternative of attacking a rescue ship would repulse any naval officer in the world, the British political needs could call for another sinking, even of a ship that was only performing rescue operations: it was a warship and that was surely enough.

Once more, the night was not for resting. While the survivors enjoyed a warm environment in every sense, the crew stayed on watch, ready to lend a hand to any in need. Those people had suffered greatly and they could not be abandoned.

The ship would arrive in Ushuaia on May 5, but the dock was still a long way away. The submarine threat was still very much apparent. The men on watch at the CIC exhaustively assessed the electromagnetic spectrum. They no longer cared about communications, only about submarine radars. The sonar swept passively,[3] seeking the slightest noise not coming from local fauna. While this happened in the cubicles, the remaining men fulfilled the radar emission plans, prepared the bearing changes for their zigzagging, and revised operational plans, searching for a task still undone or reports that were to be sent to higher command.

Focal areas are those places which concentrate maritime transport, for operational or geographical reasons. Those in charge of submarine patrols place the submarines in these areas so that they lie in wait for the forced passage of a ship. *Bouchard* was approaching one of these areas, which lies near the Isla de los Estados and the entrance to the Beagle Channel. Every war or merchant ship that is heading for Puerto Williams (Chile) or Ushuaia (Argentina), or that must sail through Tierra del Fuego's channels to Chile or towards Cape Horn, must traverse this area. In order to cross, *Bouchard* adopted anti-submarine battle stations, to reinforce its port and starboard watches and maximum sealing condition. Once the depth and geographic features made the presence of a submarine very unlikely, they ended the anti-submarine battle stations and prepared the vessel to enter the port of Ushuaia. In addition, once far from the threat of submarines, and after enjoying their breakfast, they lifted the sealing condition and brought out berthing ropes and towing hawsers so that they would be ready for when they were needed. The officers reviewed the repairs needed to carry on the campaign with their teams and division chiefs. The quartermaster for the manoeuvre joined the bridge at first call. His special skill in navigating granted him the privilege of the Commanding Officer placing his trust in him to command the wheel, so that he could lead them with soft touches and a sure hand towards the headings ordered by command. After so much had been shared between them, the Commanding Officer barely had to speak, they understood each other with just a glance.

This ship was already in Ushuaia bay. This time, "stop the engines" was a final order, there was no chance to go forwards or backwards. The manoeuvre could not then be corrected. If the Commanding Officer made a mistake, the ship would be stranded in the middle of the bay without any propulsion, or it could crash into the vessels already berthed. Everyone in the bridge was calm; the only excitement came from the shipwreck survivors who saw the end of their war only a few metres from the ship. The fleet ocean tug *Yamana* approached *Bouchard* and gave a "courtesy" towing hawser, which in navy parlance means "just in case". At 13:10 *h*, the Commanding Officer ordered the engines to be shut down and, except for the generators, the whole propulsion system was completely out of service. The ship slowly neared the dock, where *Piedrabuena* was already berthed. The turbo generators were still online, but

---

[3] That is to say, the sonar only listened.

they lost power and were disconnected, and the ship was left in darkness. The ship stopped alongside *Piedrabuena* at 13:25 h. Ten minutes later, the ship had completed berthing procedures.

The ship docked with less than 30% of its fuel load, far from the 50% it was authorised with, without using sea water as ballast in its tanks to increase stability. This was done with the aim of being able to sail immediately, or as soon as it was ordered, to continue combat operations. Should the tanks be used for ballast, they would have to be boiled to desalinate them, which takes many days, even more without the seasoned technical staff of Puerto Belgrano Naval Base. Both ships were berthed at Ushuaia's old commercial dock. The local Admiral received the units and, a few hours later, the former crewmembers of *Belgrano* had disembarked to be transferred north, where families and friends awaited them. The ship was assigned a telephone line so the crew would be able to communicate with family members, and the Commander of the Austral Naval Area prohibited all personnel from landing to avoid conflict with the civilian population. This measure was deemed ridiculous to the whole crew, regardless of their place in the hierarchy.

The destroyers ARA Piedrabuena and ARA Bouchard berthed in Ushuaia after rescuing the shipwreck survivors from the cruise ARA General Belgrano

In the ARA Bouchard

A few days later, some of the crewmembers from *Bouchard* received family members on a flight coordinated by the Navy to offer support to the crews of the ships still in combat. Local hotels also generously offered lodgings to the families and the Ushuaia Naval Base provided significant logistical support.

Several different dives were necessary to clean the areas affected by the wreckage and to conduct other repairs, to be able to continue operations. In spite of the local limitations, nothing was withheld from the ships so that they may improve their limited capabilities.

Distribution of the Rescue of the *Belgrano's* Survivors

Ship	Survivors	Deceased	Total	Percentage (%)
Bouchard	64	0	64	8
Gurruchaga	363	2	365	46
Bahía Paraíso	70	18	88	11
Piedrabuena	273	0	272	34.5
Belokamensk	0	3	3	0.5
Total	770	23	793	100

Chapter 11
Rebuffing the Attacks Attempted by Commandos (From May 14 to May 19, 1982)

Abstract The domestic and international context and the hostilities. The attempts of the British Special Forces to attack the Argentine continental area are rebuffed. On May 15 and 16, setting sails to patrol in front of Río Grande. The detection of raiding ships. Guns fire on them and their flight as the ship weighs anchors to pursue. The night of May 17 to 18, Day of the Argentine Navy. The detection of a raiding helicopter. Land troops are notified. The search starts. The flight to Chile without setting one foot on sovereign soil. An analysis of the operation from both the British and Argentine perspectives. The assassination attempts on pilots, mechanics and service personnel; the destruction of aircraft and missiles. What each side saw, felt and did. Intelligence on each side.

The Domestic and International Context and the Hostilities (Vv. Aa., IRI, 2012) (Vv. Aa., *Historia de la Fuerza Aérea Argentina* [History of the Argentine Air Force], 1998) (Vv. Aa., informe oficial del Ejército Argentino, *Conflicto Malvinas* [Official Argentine Army report on the Falklands/Malvinas War], 1983) (Rattenbach B., 1983)

On May 6, the UN submitted a peace proposal with several requirements, such as the withdrawal of both Argentine troops and the Royal Navy, the UN administration of the Falklands/Malvinas and the suspension of the economic sanctions imposed upon Argentina.

Since British warfare had subsided significantly, Argentine transport aircraft seized the chance of making several logistic flights to the islands, among which were the retrieval of the wounded as a result of the bombing. In the meantime, both logistic and supply ships assembled at Ascension in preparation for a massive assault.

On May 7, reciprocal complaints were lodged: the United States held Argentina responsible for the failure of its proposal, while Argentina held England accountable for its obstinacy and for its misrepresentation of UN resolutions. England responded by announcing a naval blockade beyond 12 miles from the coastline, where it would attack any Argentine military ship or aircraft, declaration that elicited protests to the OAS and the UN. Moreover, England increased the flow of support to the forces deployed, and it was later discovered that British C-130 and Canberra aircraft had been stationed in the South of Chile.

On May 8, British bombing of Argentine positions near Puerto Argentino (Port Stanley) intensified, and 20 fighter planes landed on Ascension to reinforce British forces. The submarine ARA *San Luis* reported that it had torpedoed an underwater target and then a powerful explosion was perceived. Up until today it is still unknown what the outcome of that attack was.

As regards international affairs, Brazil and Peru issued a joint statement about the TIAR, implicitly criticising the United States for supporting England. Argentina decided to impose restrictions on the entry of British citizens and made public the possible seizure of British companies and the cancellation of pending contracts with British companies.

On May 9, a squadron of British warplanes attacked the Argentine fishing trawler *Narwal*, which was later captured by Royal Marines and sank while being towed the following day. The Argentine Navy stopped using its obsolete Neptune aircraft on search flights, due to their wear and tear and the lack of spare parts.

On May 10, during the TIAR Meeting of Consultation, Argentina again denounced new British acts of aggression. On the islands, British forces received reinforcements and logistics from Ascension and from the Pacific Ocean (sailing to the south of Cape Horn).The HMS *Alacrity* sank the Argentine merchant vessel *Isla de los Estados*, and the naval gunfire of Argentine positions nearby Puerto Argentino (Port Stanley) intensified. The submarine ARA *San Luis* reported having unsuccessfully torpedoed a surface target (possibly a frigate or a destroyer).

That same day the *Gaceta Argentina* (Argentine Gazette) was founded in Puerto Argentino (Port Stanley). It was the first Argentine periodical to appear on the Falklands/Malvinas.

On May 11, Margaret Thatcher announced that she would refuse to take part in any negotiation that might give Argentina the impression that it had regained sovereignty over the islands.

On May 12, the ocean liner RMS *Queen Elizabeth 2* set sail from Southampton with 3000 troops aboard from the 5th Infantry British Brigade, who were supposed to land on the Falkland Sound (San Carlos strait) as per the orders of the British high command. On the same day, the destroyers HMS *Glasgow* and HMS *Brilliant* shot down three Argentine Skyhawks. In turn, the HMS *Glasgow* was put out of commission by a bomb released during that aerial attack and later, both destroyers were attacked by Argentine Air Force fighters and were severely damaged. Meanwhile, the Royal Navy continued bombarding Argentine positions, and an Argentine Puma helicopter on its way to rescue the crew of the *Narwal* was shot down by British planes.

On the next day, May 13, all Argentines who had been taken prisoners on South Georgia arrived in Montevideo on an aeroplane chartered by the International Committee of the Red Cross. Meanwhile, opinion surveys conducted in London reflected strong popular support for the unwavering stance the Government had taken to handle the crisis: one of the objectives of the forced war had been attained. In an attempt to re-establish dialogue with the Argentine Government, the United States sent another General to Buenos Aires. The Secretary-General of the United Nations announced that negotiations were at a crucial stage, and Pope John Paul II asked the Argentine Government to avoid prolonging the war.

On May 14, the Soviet Union protested to the British Government against its arbitrary expansion of the maritime exclusion zone, and the Brazilian Government asked the West German Foreign Minister to intercede with the British Government to tone down the warfare.

On May 15, the SAS struck a lethal blow at the airfield on Pebble Island (isla Borbón), destroying five Argentine aircrafts. This operation was supplemented by a naval bombing from the destroyer HMS *Glamorgan*, which depleted the ammunition and fuel stockpiles at the airfield.

In the international arena, the Member States of the Andean Pact agreed to take action to relieve Argentina's economic emergency resulting from the embargo imposed by Europe and the United States. For its part, Chile offered its icebreaker *Piloto Pardo* to transport the wounded from the islands to the mainland.

On May 16, British aircraft attacked the Argentine merchant vessels *Río Carcarañá* and *Bahía Buen Suceso*, as well as the military garrisons at Fox Bay and Darwin, among other locations. Meanwhile, the Argentine-made 155 mm guns, which had been put into use a few days earlier, caused an unpleasant surprise to the British warships bombarding the shore, which were forced to withdraw in view of their range and accuracy.

In London, Margaret Thatcher met with her war cabinet and the British negotiating team, and stated that unless negotiations made progress, a massive attack would be ordered. Meanwhile, Argentina accused England for sustaining its unyielding stance in the negotiations.

In Buenos Aires, a large group of musicians organised a rock festival to express gratitude for Latin American solidarity and their support for Argentina in the conflict.

On May 17, the King of Spain granted an audience to a Venezuelan delegation, which reported to him that all of Latin America supported Argentina's claim. Furthermore, considering Italy's and Ireland's opposition to the economic sanctions imposed upon Argentina, the EU Foreign Ministers decided to maintain them for only one more week. In Lima, Peru, the Minister of War stated that Peru's support for Argentina should materialise in the shape of the immediate shipping of aircraft, ships and weapons to aid in the war. US government spokesmen in Washington, DC, reported that it was working hard on finding a solution to the conflict.

On May 18, in view of the deep differences between the parties, the UN declared the negotiations a failure. NATO offered its full and unconditional support to England and condemned Argentina for its aggression.

On May 19, London announced that its fleet, having received reinforcements by way of ships, soldiers and aircraft, was now in a position to make a landing on the Falklands/Malvinas and recover the islands. Whilst aerial and naval bombardment on Argentine positions continued, the Argentine Air Force Hercules aircraft successfully carried out the first logistics launch operation in the combat area, dropping eight containers carrying assorted supplies, such as foodstuffs, ammunition and fuel.

The UN offered to send delegates to both parties. While Argentina accepted the offer, Britain refused it. Argentina requested a meeting of the UN Security Council to discuss the Falklands/Malvinas issue, and the United States reaffirmed its unconditional support for Great Britain. In the international arena, Senegal granted overflight rights to British military planes carrying troops to the theatre of operations, while Venezuela and El Salvador declared their support for the Argentine cause.

On May 20, England gave the order to land and, that same night, a flotilla of warships and troop transports sailed into the Falkland Sound (San Carlos strait). After a destroyed British helicopter was discovered near Punta Arenas, the Chilean Government pretended to protest to Great Britain and hastened to provide explanations to the Argentine Government. Then on May 23, the Chilean Navy reported that no British helicopter carrier ship was operating in Chilean waters. Finally, that day, the negotiations between Britain and Argentina were effectively declared concluded by the UN.

On May 21, Operation "Sutton" began when 19 British ships entered the Falkland Sound (San Carlos strait). As soon as the British troops landed, they were received by heavy gunfire from the scarce Argentine forces deployed there. The Argentines succeeded in shooting down two helicopters and damaging a third. In the course of aerial attacks, two British Harrier jump jets and seven Argentine planes were shot down, while one British frigate was severely damaged and three others sustained light damage.

On May 22, an Argentine Navy training aircraft sank the HMS *Ardent* in the Falkland Sound (San Carlos strait). On land, in the Patagonian city of Comodoro Rivadavia, an air raid alert was announced after coastal radar detected helicopters flying nearby. Britain announced that it had consolidated a beachhead. By then 3000 British troops were ashore with sufficient equipment to advance inland.

As regards international affairs, Venezuela condemned England for these actions, accusing it of endangering world peace; the UN General Assembly demanded the Security Council for an urgent ceasefire, and the Pope implored the Governments of Argentina and Great Britain to cease all hostilities.

In ARA the *Bouchard*

With the sinking of the cruiser ARA Belgrano, the Task Group lost their only helicopter, which was lightweight and had no anti-submarine capabilities. All possible measures were employed to avoid an attack or minimize its potential damages, within the serious technological restrictions that they were under. These were the result of combat experience shared by friendly navies during joint exercises, or based on the experiences acquired by Navy personnel assigned to various courses abroad.

May 14

Beginning its 87th journey since raising its flag, the destroyer ARA *Bouchard* sailed from the city of Ushuaia on May 14, at 06:30 h, to patrol the area between Cabo del Medio and the Magallanes lighthouse. At 15:00 h, it was forced to anchor in Puerto Español due to engine malfunctions. It set sail at 09:00 h the following day to continue patrolling, after the exhaustive work undertaken by the engineers below deck. At this point in time, several failures occurred due to the wear and the lack of the right personnel in the workshops needed to conduct the best possible repairs.

May 15 (Vv. Aa. Historical Book Bouchard 1982a:467)

It was a pleasant day for journeying, without problems, which was taken advantage of to adjust the mechanisms that were causing drawbacks. At 09:30 h they left Puerto Español and anchored near Cape San Pablo, from where they sailed at 22:00 h to arrive, the following day, near Cape Domingo.

May 16 (Vv. Aa. War Diary Bouchard 1982c)

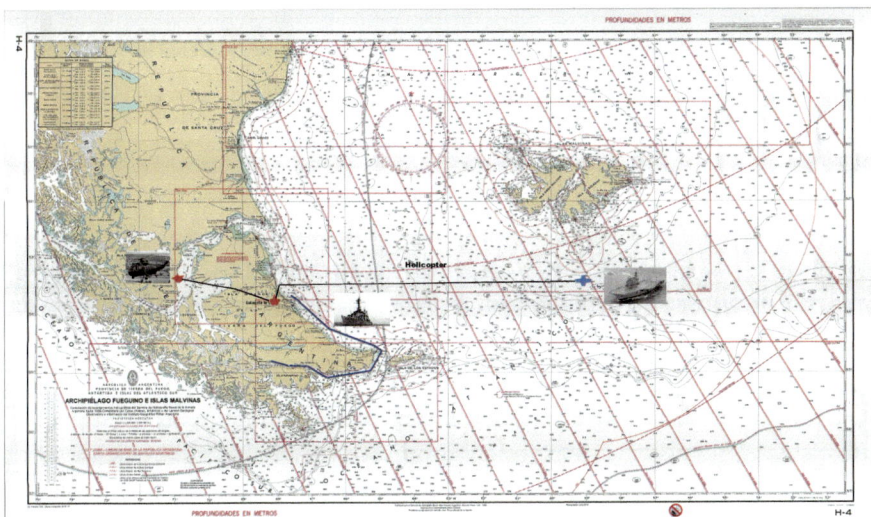

The destroyer ARA *Bouchard* anchored at 10:42 h at Latitude 53° 35' S and Longitude 67° 55' W, between Cabo del Medio and Cape Domingo, exactly two nautical miles from the coast and marking azimuth 235° from Cape Domingo, which was seven miles away (Vv. Aa. Logbook Bouchard 1982b). The Sea was calm; the small ripples barely rocked the ship. The sky was completely covered by clouds and the sun remained hidden the entire day. Nevertheless, visibility was relatively good and the temperature was low (between 35 and 43 °F; 2 and 6 °C). The weather was accommodating for the time of year, considering the ship's latitude and that they were on the open seas. The men on watch were grateful for these conditions, compared to other days which made remaining vigilant impossible amidst constant rains or snowfalls, strong winds, and low temperatures. At 48 °F (8.8 °C), the sea was deadly to anyone entering without protection. That day, the sun rose at 08:37 h and set at 17:49 h. The wind was not strong and calmed even more as the day entered twilight. The destroyer ARA *Piedrabuena* was anchored at azimuth 154°, at a distance of 3.1 miles.

At 16:30 h, the Chief of Submarine Weapons of *Bouchard* and another officer accompanying him at the ship's stern felt a sonar emission consisting of a sonar ping[1] every 5 or 7 s, for intermittent 15 or 30 min periods. At 17:00 h, they went to stations for an anchoring manoeuvre. With the disappearance of the emissions, they returned to normal operations and finished the manoeuvre. The ship remained anchored. This same situation was repeated at 17:10 h, but this time they were able to listen through the hydrophone, confirming a sonar emission with the equipment on board. At that point, they could determine that it was not a sonar emission from the destroyer ARA *Piedrabuena* (Barcena 1982).

The radar repeaters where kept to a short scale, especially on the wheelhouse, so that the officer on watch could verify that the ship had anchored correctly (as they say in the navy, "to verify anchorage"). In the CIC they were maintained to a long scale, to conduct a search at distance. The look-outs were on high alert, searching for periscopes or enemy aircraft. The Task Force Commander had established that the group's radar watch be as follows: ARA *Bouchard* would keep its radar on *stand-by* on even days, and ARA *Piedrabuena* would do so on odd days. Thus, each day one of the two destroyers would undertake aerial and surface watch with their old SPS 40 and SPS 10 radars respectively.

The sonar was listening hydrophonically. The ESM (Electronic Support Measures) equipment,[2] an old WLR 1 "superheterodyne" receiver, which had detected a large number of emissions, had to be kept listening and manually sweeping the I band, seeking emissions from submarine radars. As regards the artillery, the crew was working on the central turret and from fire control they could only fire with the express authorisation from the Chief Defence Officer, since the ship was in a focal area of their own aviation. The missions heading towards the Falklands/Malvinas left from Río Grande.

The ship was well supplied with ammunition for its 5-inch guns and 12.7 mm anti-aircraft machine guns. In addition, it had all its MM38 missiles and two MK44s and three A244S torpedoes, 533 hedgehogs, and six MK9 depth charges. Victuals, as

---

[1] A navy jargon term used to describe the sound produced by a sonar emission on a metallic hull.

[2] Electronic warfare equipment used to listen for and detect emissions.

well as the supply of fuel and water for the boilers and crew, were at a level sufficient to allow them to conduct operations properly for several days.

Between 19:05 and 19:10 h, in total darkness and in the emission period set by the active plan, the radar operator and CIC officer on watch detected a small and intermittent echo at 3000 yards from the ship at true azimuth 070°. They immediately requested authorisation through the communication channels connecting both combat information centres to continue with the emissions and to verify the contact. As the minutes passed, the contact stopped being intermittent. At 19:12, it became three clear echoes, with a very intense point and a "V" that was in the opposite direction to its relative movement, typical of "zodiac" type boats which radar operators had so often observed on their repeaters. After the hectic efforts of the CIC team (everything had to be done manually), they were able to determine a course of 340° and a speed of 18 knots. The three echoes moved in formation, steadily, and showed an intelligent movement (which was impossible for fauna or natural phenomena to copy). The closest they passed the ship was 1200 yards and then moved away to 3000 yards.

At 19:14 h, four minutes after the boats were detected, they went to battle stations, but the sonar added a sense of drama to the situation. At 19:18 h, they reported a hydrophonic noise at azimuth 070°. At that point, the echoes were found in an arc that covered from 350° to 010°, at a distance of 4000 yards. The MK 25 fire control radar managed to acquire the targets at 19:22 h and, simultaneously, permission to open fire with the 5-inch guns from the main battery was requested from the Officer in Tactical Command (OTC), who was the Commanding Officer of the destroyer ARA *Piedrabuena*. The men in the CIC expended great efforts to maintain the contact since, at that time, there only had one firm and two intermittent echoes, but still moving in formation and at calculated course and speed. The adjustments to the gain and filters was an issue of vital importance undertaken by the radar operator, who had acquired a level of subtlety that almost made him seem a part of the equipment.

At the bow, they were raising anchor to have freedom to manoeuvre in order to pursue their targets and avoid being exposed to a subsequent submarine attack. The presence of such a unit was highly probable given the events of the morning and afternoon, as well as to the hydrophone noise detected that also pointed towards the presence of a submarine in the area. At 19:25 h, authorisation was received to open fire. With a firm contact in the fire control radar, the Commanding Officer gave the order to the Chief Artillery Officer so that the ship's main battery would perform the task it deserved for the first time during that war. The guns opened fire with two volleys, and later added a third. The whole complement felt their blood rush hotly through their veins. It was almost like taking revenge for all the repressed anxiety, for the waiting, for the long watches at night, for endless feelings that were locked up behind the walls of professional duty, and which were now aired to the world and shared with no hierarchical constraints. However, those who were amidst the action had to redouble their efforts to closely watch the boats. They did not have to wait long for a response, the echoes fanned out, moving away from the ship, and the radars could only detect them intermittently.

At 19:55 h, the bow notified the bridge that the ship had weighed anchor (Vv. Aa. Logbook Bouchard 1982b). Nevertheless, they remained at the bow completing the arrangements and leaving both anchors ready to be lowered, as the art of seamanship indicates. The ship was left adrift. The CIC and fire control team tried to maintain the contacts, which became inconsistent in a few seconds. They decided to search for them, but the fog prevented visual confirmation, in spite of turning on the available spotlights, some of which were exceedingly strong. Focusing on the mirror-like water, and after an extensive search, they anchored at 20:40 h, virtually in the same place as before.

Night from May 17 to May 18, Day of the Argentine Navy

The night was peaceful, after the previous day's events. The men were riveted to their screens and they seized advantage of the few emission minutes that the plan for silence allowed them. The WLR 1 operator, the ESM equipment, eagerly swept the assigned frequencies, trying to distinguish a concrete or intelligent signal that could lead to the enemy amidst the noises and static. The sky was completely overcast. The atmospheric pressure decreased by the hour, the temperature outside was not above 46 °F (6 °C), and the wind coming from the north-northeast gradually increased. However, the sea was barely stirred, also from the north, and its temperature held at 42 °F (9 °C). The ship was still anchored in the same place as the day before, with a minimum distance of two nautical miles from shore.

A few minutes after the 04:00 to 08:00 CIC watch began, they were to emit with their radar. At approximately 04:08 h, the radar operator reported to the officer on watch at the CIC that he had detected something and requested him to approach to the repeater. The watch officer confirmed the presence of an echo. The operator moved to the bridge to simultaneously operate the Decca radar which could distinguish more clearly what had been detected by the SPS-10 thanks to its I band emitter. Shortly after, the echo was confirmed and both radars were kept emitting. The contact was reported to the destroyer ARA *Piedrabuena*, which was required to confirm whether it managed to see it at true azimuth 340°, at a distance of nine miles (Latitude 53° 26.7' S and Longitude 68° 00.2' W, and only three miles from the coast). Confirmation arrived one minute later. The CIC watch officer ordered the aircraft be hailed on all possible frequencies, receiving no response. In addition, he ordered to communicate with Río Grande to ask whether it was a friendly aircraft and to report the contact to the Base. Faced with the inability to establish contact in the communication plan pre-set circuits, the CIC watch officer suggested to the OTC (D-29) that Río Grande be notified. Meanwhile, the aircraft, that seemed to be a helicopter due to its flight profile, continued its trajectory towards dry land.

At 04:26 h, the D-26 sent another communication to the OTC warning that the potential helicopter was over the coastline and continued moving further into the island. They also restated the need to notify Río Grande and the D-29 informed that they were trying to do so. Despite the arduous task that required maintaining the echo with both radars, at 04:31 h, the D-26 attempted once again to unsuccessfully hail Río Grande.

At 04:22 h, after working intensely, the D-29 notified that they had been able to reach Río Grande and that there were no friendly aircraft flying over the area. They suggested investigating the situation. The news motivated the CIC team to maintain the echo at all costs. At 04:46 h, the D-26 reported that the detected aircraft had descended and been lost near the "La Sara" ranch,[3] in the nautical chart (Latitude 53° 26´ S and Longitude 68° 11.5´ W). Meanwhile, the adjustments to the detection equipment continued, to find an echo in the amber spot that was appearing on the repeater. Soon after, the aircraft regained altitude and the tension to detect it returned. The contact was maintained for only 10 min. Later, at 05:02 h, the D-29 reported that it would have reached the border with Chile. The OTC ordered the monitoring to be heightened.

At 08:04 h, the ship sailed and the Force headed towards Ushuaia where both destroyers berthed alongside each other, on the fuel dock. The manoeuvre ended at 00:19 h on May 19, when a gangway ladder was connected to ARA *Piedrabuena*. With their usual sacrifice and hard work, the engineers began the operation to replenish the ship's fuel for the next voyage.

The British Continental Operations: The Perspective of the Parties Involved

We begin with the memories of two direct participants, which reflect the points of view of the helicopter pilot and a member of the commando group that was involved.

The true enemy of the success of British operations in the Falklands/Malvinas theatre of operations was, without a doubt, the Exocet AM39 air-sea missile, carried by the Argentine Navy's Super Étendard strike aircraft. The final result of the British actions was solidly tied to the fate of that menacing missile-airplane pairing (Southby-Tailyour 2014:viii). After the loss of *Sheffield,* Admiral Sandy Woodward himself, together with his Chief Operating Officer, Commanding Officer Jeremy Sanders, agreed that the real danger lied in the "Super" (Southby-Tailyour 2014:107). Coronel Richard Preston stated the same, stressing that the threat needed to be eliminated, whether by a commando strike or by placing an anti-aircraft picket line between the islands and the continent (Southby-Tailyour 2014:107–108). The Admiral judged that the survival of the fleet's capital ships depended on the operations conducted on Argentine soil by the Special Forces (Hutchings 2014:125). This last situation caused Michael Havers, the General Auditor, to form and submit an opinion on whether these measures fell within international law (Hutchings 2014:124).

The helicopter pilot who transported the commandos, Richard Hutchings, writer of the book *Special Forces Pilot: A flying memoir of the Falklands war*, asked himself

---

[3] "La Sara" ranch is a few metres from National Route 3,. 26 miles from Río Grande and only 15 nautical miles from the Chilean border.

at the beginning: "Will we, won't we?" (Hutchings 2014:3) He was referring to the initial decision to attack the islands. He later talks about the history of the commandos and the need to deploy them and have them once again be a part of the pages of military history, which they had not achieved in some time.

The history of British Special Forces (Hutchings 2014:4–5) units begins on April 1, 1943, with the creation of Squadron 846 (disbanded in 1945, and then reformed in 1962), which was given the nickname "The Junglies", and operated and fought in Borneo against guerrilla groups. It was disbanded once again soon after, and then reassembled in 1968, when it operated with Wessex V helicopters. This model was highly versatile, reliable and robust, and they used it until 1979, when they were equipped with the modern Sea King IV. This was a naval helicopter, excellent for shipboard operations, with a solid landing gear, automatic rotor folding, corrosion-resistant, prepared to operate at extremely low temperatures and freezing conditions, and fitted with state-of-the-art avionics and electronic navigation aids with exceptional performance. However, it had still not been used in real operations, it did not have the Wessex's operational agility (the cabin of which could hold up to 27 operatives, depending on their equipment) and had a "cavernous" compartment. Although the Sea King could transport heavy loads for a long distance, with its inertial navigation system, it could fly up to six hours with 10 equipped men. The author mentions that at the time the war developed, they still did not have NVGs (night vision goggles) compatible with real operations, and also that the pilots preferred the old Wessex.

By the time the war began, the Special Forces were formed in three squadrons, with their own hierarchies and organisation, which could act independently or jointly, in conjunction with the army or in amphibious operations, with aerial projection or in lengthy land incursions. Hutchings clearly states that they already knew the situation in the South Atlantic on April 1, and that the squadron leaders were ready to deploy to "kick some Argentine butt". (Hutchings 2014:5) To this end, Squadron 846, 180 formidably trained men, began training for flexible approach operations, which were a part of "The Junglies" operational doctrine. Morale and confidence were very high, despite the constant changes, orders and counter-orders. Finally, only a small deployment of commandos was allowed, with very limited helicopter support. This did not lower morale, and everybody wanted in on the action.

Hutchings was chosen to fly one of the Sea Kings —selected for British operations on the continent—, and he brought back his former co-pilot, Alan "Wiggy" Bennett, who had been assigned to the modern Lynx squadron. They had formed a very efficient and harmonious group of combat pilots, who were peculiar in having a reciprocal and deeply held belief for survival, something that is not always attained. When they had called for volunteers, Hutchings felt that he had to come forward since he was a marine, had operated with them in the past and knew them well, and was additionally trained in evasion and survival behind enemy lines. Likewise, when his CO on the vessel asked him to choose his co-pilot (who would be assigned should he had volunteered), Hutchings did not hesitate in choosing Alan Bennett. (Hutchings 2014:128).

Two foreign pilots, one Australian and one American, were a part of the combat teams, but they were not allowed to deploy. This was a very complex war as regards international relations and required the greatest care in how it would be carried out. (Hutchings 2014:8) Somehow, this affected the operability of the aircraft, because the American was a helicopter test pilot who was then testing the NVGs for navigation. They had been significantly improved and required tests to be certified. While Hutchings highlights this as being a complex problem, the truth was that the NVGs they had were very suitable for the times, and the Argentines had no comparable or equivalent technologies.

Richard Hutchings mentions one of Winston Churchill's maxims: "The Great defence against the air menace is to attack the enemy's aircraft as near as possible to their point of departure". (Hutchings 2014:123).

To destroy the abovementioned combination (missile-airplane), the author of the book *Exocet Falklands: The untold story of special forces operation*, Ewen Southby-Tailyour, recounts that the United Kingdom had three operations that would be carried out by the Special Forces in mind:

1. Operation **Plum Duff**, which would be carried out by eight men of the 6th Troop, B Squadron, 22nd Special Air Service Regiment. They were to reconnoitre and, if presented with the opportunity, destroy the target. (Southby-Tailyour 2014:viii) The operation was to be in the Río Grande Naval Aviation Base, where the Super Étendards had been deployed. The data collected would complete the information gathered by Chilean intelligence services, which, for some years, had a significant spy network in the area that provided relevant data for the planning of British operations.
2. Operation **Mikado** (a pick-up sticks game), also called "operation certain death" (Hutchings 2014:131) by the participating officers and NCOs, which was to take place after analysing the intelligence gathered by Operation **Plum Duff**. Two Hercules C-130 RAF (Royal Air Force) airplanes would transport 60 SAS operatives from the 47th Special Forces Squadron. (Southby-Tailyour 2014:viii) This operation was also to take place in the Río Grande Naval Aviation Base, and had the same objective: to destroy the naval airplanes and associated weapons.
3. Operation **Kettledrum**, an unknown operation the implementation of which would have changed the international context of the War for the Falklands/Malvinas. It was to be carried out by a SBS (Special Boat Service) group, launched from the submarine *Onyx*. The objective was a naval and aviation deployment in Puerto Deseado, which was on the continent and far from the theatre of operations, making it a fundamental change in the war, since it would have placed it in South America or, at least, outside the unilaterally declared "exclusion zone". (Southby-Tailyour 2014:viii) According to the author of the book cited, this operation was cancelled a day after the submarine had left the Falkland Sound (San Carlos strait) heading towards Puerto Deseado.

One of the issues stressed by the author is that the Brigadier General, responsible for the security at the Río Grande airport, had issued an order of operations on May 6, to meet his responsibilities. Two days later, he was forced to change them and redistribute his forces to adopt another plan, in response to having received troubling information from the military intelligence services (most probably from the Naval Intelligence Service). (Southby-Tailyour 2014:69) The watch and guard on the airport from which the "Supers" operated from were reinforced on May 8. (Southby-Tailyour 2014:viii).

He also mentions that one of the protected areas outside the perimeter was the CAP meat processing plant, where the pilots and airplanes were to be found on the night of May 16. (Southby-Tailyour 2014:viii).

Southby-Tailyour also praises Captain Miguel Pita, a noteworthy superior officer, who had attended intelligence courses in England and several other courses in the United States, and who knew exactly the capabilities of the English commandos and was not willing to give them any opportunities in his operation plans and security framework. (Southby-Tailyour 2014:viii).

He also asserts on several occasions that, notwithstanding the support of Chilean citizens, they knew little about the situation at Río Grande, and that if there was ever a chance when the British Secret Service was to have undertaken an information gathering operation no doubt it would have been here, despite having scarce and inaccurate information to ensure the success of a commando operation. (Southby-Tailyour 2014:viii, 88,113, 117–118) He also mentions there being no intelligence for Operation Plum Duff, and that they only had an aerial map of the Isla Grande de Tierra del Fuego provided by Canada. (Southby-Tailyour 2014:129) This is a significant departure from what was written by Hutchings, who says that they had high-quality satellite photos (probably from the USA) and some maps. (Hutchings 2014:129) This only supports the speculation that the Argentine destroyers' location, at that specific date and time, prevented the realisation of the operations that were allegedly planned.

He also mentions that the crews of the Hercules airplanes were ordered to practice the risky operation, which led to coining the phrase "air-land" to differentiate it from the typical "air-drop" operation, since they were to land on this occasion. The crews and Max Robert himself, leader of the airplane crews that transported SAS o SBS troops, concluded that the operation would in all likelihood end in disaster (Operation Mikado), and that it was a far cry from the operation carried out at Entebbe, since the overall situations were substantially different. (Southby-Tailyour 2014:91).

A point raised by the author, which is no small thing when analysing the behaviours of these units, is that the SASs were desperate to participate and thus to keep the myth of the Special Forces alive and well. (Southby-Tailyour 2014:110–111).

He indicates that the SAS Director, Brigadier Peter de la Billière, took charge of the operation's planning, after ruling out the options of a naval bombardment and an aerial bombing using a Vulcan taking off from Chile. (Southby-Tailyour 2014:111) According to the author, Operation Mikado was already set by May 6. The operation had two phases. The first was to reconnoitre to gather intelligence, to be undertaken by the 6th Troop, B Squadron, 22nd SAS Regiment, together with another team from the 9th Troop, to study Río Grande; this would be named Operation Plum Duff. (Southby-Tailyour 2014:111) The second phase of the operation would be the one code-named Mikado.

The War Cabinet was not very pleased with operating on the continent due to the possible political consequences and the international backlash from increasing the theatre of operations. Therefore, authorisation had only been given to begin training and the authorisation for the operation itself would be issued closer to the execution date.

For Operation Plum Duff, they considered inserting an SBS team deployed from the *Onyx* submarine. The team would penetrate on boats, gather the intelligence needed, and return to the submarine in a typical in-and-out operation. According to the author, this group had already been deployed to the South Atlantic and reached the Falkland Sound (San Carlos strait) on May 31. The other option was to use a Task Force helicopter, which would take off from Chilean waters. However, the helicopter would have to be sabotaged (destroyed by crew), since it would not be able to return to where it had taken off from.

Once the operation's planning was finalised, the objective was broadened to destroying the airplanes and associated missiles, and assassinating as many pilots as possible. (Southby-Tailyour 2014:116) Had this occurred, Operation Mikado would not have been necessary and many material losses and lives would have been saved, as it had been proven during training. (Hutchings 2014:131).

The highly successful SAS attack on the airplanes stationed at Pebble Island (Isla Borbón) revitalised those who pushed for these operations and offered some sureties to the people who had doubts regarding operations on Argentine continental territory. (Hutchings 2014:124).

On May 15, the complements of the Hercules airplanes XV 179 and XV 200, who were to support Operations Plum Duff and Mikado, had been at Ascension Island for three days. RAF Flight Lieutenant Burgoyne received a secret message to prepare his crew to fly to the South Atlantic. He was to deploy cargo and personnel near the auxiliary ship *Fort Austin*, which would make him the first Commanding Officer in refuelling a C-130 in flight. Operation Plum Duff had begun!

After a verification meeting, they began calculations that, among other things, indicated they would take off 2.5 tons over the maximum manufacturer recommended weight. (Southby-Tailyour 2014:127) The pilots were used to flying with too much weight. They knew full well that flying at 10,000 feet they would have a chance, but if something were to go wrong during take-off, a disaster was all that awaited them. The only thing to do was trust the ground team and the robust build of the Hercules.

We can place the beginning of phase 1, Operation **Plum Duff**, around May 15, where a veteran captain was to lead a group of highly experienced and trained commandos to Río Grande. They were to carry out a preliminary reconnaissance of the area of operations (AO) and, if offered the chance, the captain was to begin the operation himself, assassinating the naval pilots and destroying the Super Étendard-Exocet combination. "If offered the chance" is to be understood as follows: if the forces safeguarding the objectives did not offer resistance or the surprise caused sufficient chaos to allow them to achieve their objective, the operation would be extended and would become the main operation. None of this happened and the Naval Infantry forces protecting Río Grande showed a high level of training and professionalism.

Three avenues of approach had been considered: submarine, air via a helicopter, or speedboats. According to the author, none of the three were possible: there was no submarine in the area, the helicopter did not have the range nor could they have a ship approach to a reasonable distance, and the British Navy had had no speedboats since the 60 s. Hutchings shows a new inconsistency here: when planning the operation, he posed that, after the raid, the helicopter would return to the aircraft carrier with a stop to replenish with a submarine, (Hutchings 2014:132) which would provide fuel. This idea was discarded due to the danger to both units, not because there was no submarine in the area as Southby-Tailyour says.

Orders were that the 22nd SAS Regiment was in charge. Cedric Delves and Euan Houston were in command of D and G Squadrons, respectively. Everybody was to be ready for deployment. (Southby-Tailyour 2014:129).

Initially, the thought was to reconnoitre with two four-men patrols, one in Río Gallegos and another in Río Grande. However, once it was confirmed that the Super Étendard airplanes were stationed only at Río Grande, the Río Gallegos site was cancelled and all eight men were to go to Río Grande. (Hutchings 2014:124) This uncertainty was only quenched by intelligence and so the origin of the Naval Aviation attacks was quickly clarified by the information obtained on site by Chilean intelligence, who had woven a wide and well-placed espionage and surveillance network. However, the War Cabinet ordered the SAS to continue planning Operation Mikado. (Southby-Tailyour 2014:130).

Through the operational analysis it became apparent that, even should they be successful, the withdrawal hiking towards the Chilean border would be difficult and in highly adverse weather conditions, with enemy forces stationed alongside any route they could choose.

In this case, the higher command did not ask whether the operation was possible, they merely ordered its execution. Those who planned it saw significant obstacles to be overcome on the path towards the objectives. Notwithstanding the fact that the lack of intelligence is restated, it is very clear that this was not an issue. In the years following the conflict, it was revealed that Great Britain had a wealth of intelligence and information of their own, as well as from Chile and the NATO members. This is why this excuse cannot be accepted, other than to recognize the professional performance of the Argentine forces in the territory and the precision with which they were deployed to deter the free action of enemy troops. The British troops were not afraid of the unknown; on the contrary, the detailed knowledge of the real situation was what scared them. It was no walk in the park. They did not face children, but well-trained and highly-motivated professionals. They were not fighting the forces of a backwater banana republic, but forces with leadership and training to be feared, despite the difference in technological and logistics capabilities. This was no Entebbe, as the higher command had dreamed. As they planned and studied the mission, they grew to see that the situation was far from similar. (Southby-Tailyour 2014:131).

The directives issued by the authorities were strict, but not free of all doubts and uncertainties. They were given with a lot of energy, but filled with unanswered questions. "You will leave here at 05:00 h tomorrow for RAF Brize Norton. From there, you will fly to Ascension Island via Dakar where your VC 10 will be refuelled. [...] Your equipment will be transported separately to Ascension Island, while you travel in civilian clothes. There you will change into uniform for the remainder of the mission. No badges of rank. No regimental insignia. [...] From Ascension Island you will fly in a C-130, specially equipped with long range fuel tanks, to a Royal Fleet Auxiliary vessel off the Falklands. Approaching the Drop Zone, the aircrew will determine whether conditions and enemy air activity are suitable for the drop. If not, you will return to Ascension and try again another day. [...] If you do parachute I'm advised you will need wet suits. The water is quite cold. [...] You will be picked up and transferred to an aircraft carrier, most likely HMS *Hermes*. [...] There a number of options to get you from *Hermes* to the mainland. The first is a Sea King. [...] Moving on to the second and third possible methods. [...] We transfer you to a submarine or a fast patrol boat, from where you will move into a position just off the coast and be taken to the mainland in an inflatable craft. [...] Once there, you are to ascertain the location of the Super Étendard aircraft, the missiles and the defence device for the subsequent combat operation. However, if circumstances permit, you will kill the pilots, destroy the airplanes and missiles and, should you have the time, you will also kill the planes' ground crew". (Southby-Tailyour 2014:132).

The operatives had suggested infiltrating from the west, from the Chilean border. This clearly shows the unrestricted support offered by that country to Argentina's enemy, since the forces would have to be placed in a complex and surreptitious manoeuvre, requiring the express agreement of the highest authorities of the western neighbour. Nevertheless, the authorities decided on a frontal assault.

After a 13-h flight, the eight men of the Plum Duff squad were dropped into the sea, during the early afternoon on May 16. They were picked up by the logistics ship *Fort Austin*, together with two watertight containers with equipment. (Southby-Tailyour 2014:150–153) Phase 2 of Operation Plum Duff was to begin. (Hutchings 2014:126).

After boarding the vessel with their cargo, they were transported to the aircraft carrier *Hermes*, where they had to repair some of their equipment that got wet as one of the containers got partially broken when coming into contact with the water. There, Admiral Sandy Woodward himself stressed the importance of the operation. They met the crew of the Sea King helicopter that would take them to the Isla Grande de Tierra del Fuego.

The helicopter's crew analysed the landing options and the later sinking of the aircraft in deep waters to prevent leaving any trace; then they could wait a few days for the commandos to do their jobs and then contact the Air Attaché in Santiago de Chile to be repatriated. In the account, it can be appreciated that Chilean "neutrality" required some trivial excuse and that the neighbouring country's authorities would not detain them. Three possible locations were selected due to the required geographical characteristics. Once again we can see the inconsistencies in the report, since they insist that they had no maps, but then, how could they choose an adequate location without any maps?

The first one was located 30 miles west of Punta Arenas in Punta Estrada, at the east entrance to the Silva Palma fjord. The second, 10 miles south of Punta Arenas.

Since the depth near the coast was important, the third and least attractive was on the coast of Inútil bay, which also required crossing the Strait of Magellan before coming into contact with Chilean authorities. The last was implausible from any point of view, since no one can cross the strait without doing so on a government vessel or with the knowledge of the Chilean authorities. (Southby-Tailyour 2014:162–163).

The other issue to be decided was where the VC (Sea King) would take off from, and it was agreed that it would be from an area near Mintay Rock, 33 miles south of East Falkland (Isla Soledad) of the Falklands/Malvinas archipelago. From there, Isla Grande and the objective were 325 miles away at bearing 271°. (Southby-Tailyour 2014:165) The time chosen was midnight from May 16 to May 17.

After arriving to the coast, they would fly bearing south-southeast searching for one of the two landmarks marked on the maps that, according to the author, the British Special Forces had for the operation: These were Sección Miranda and the lake with the same name, and "Las Violetas" ranch and a nearby lake. A compromise solution had to be reached between the proximity to the areas for the Special Forces and the chance the pilots would be detected by radar, outside the Río Grande radar coverage. The northeast area of the Miranda lake was chosen for the landing. (Southby-Tailyour 2014:165).

Despite the plans, a thick fog covered the objective. In addition, the communication equipment, which had gotten wet when dropped into the sea, was still damaged and not completely dry. The operation was postponed 24 h. Due to the low security that *Hermes* and *Invincible* had in the landing area, it would be executed on May 17. (Southby-Tailyour 2014:167) The argument that there was fog in the area on the 16th is absolutely true. However, if they did not have local intelligence assets, how were they aware of the local weather conditions?

At 16:00 h on May 17, they were transferred to *Invincible* on a Sea King, where they had removed all possible weight from the ZA 290, (Hutchings 2014:135) even the anti-noise panels, so that it could have the maximum range possible with the fuel that it would have. They were received by the aircraft carrier's Commanding Officer and began pre-flight checks. Once again, the author makes the Commanding Officer of *Invincible* state the lack of intelligence and absence of information provided by the United States and British Secret Service. (Southby-Tailyour 2014:169).

During that afternoon, there were threats of an air raid that did not materialize (Hutchings 2014:136) and, with take-off confirmed for midnight on May 17, *Invincible* approached as close as its own safety allowed to launch a completely "stripped-down" and fully fuelled VC. The aircraft carrier's Commanding Officer promised to reach the maximum speed possible to achieve a 30 knot relative wind on deck.

The author mentions the presence of the destroyers ARA *Piedrabuena* and ARA *Bouchard*. The facts given regarding the latter are wrong, stating that it was in Ushuaia conducting repairs caused by a storm, when it was removing the wreckage from the cruiser ARA *Belgrano* and improving the emergency repairs of their heading due to the third torpedo launched at the cruiser that had caused serious damages.

He also writes about the events concerning the zodiacs, naming it a sure false echo caused by the thermal inversion of the area, with support from the opinion of experts. (Southby-Tailyour 2014:173) However, those of us who were privileged enough to watch the CIC radar and tower fire control screens can affirm that the zodiacs existed, and that their kinematics and attitude were perfectly intelligent. When the first volley landed on their position, they fanned out, also in an intelligent way, which no "expert" can contest and no false echo would reproduce under any circumstances.

Although he mentions that many of the crewmembers on the ship were inexperienced, this does not mean that we were not professional and highly trained, and those of us in the CIC had already seen zodiac echoes, false echoes, and marine fauna echoes countless times.

The defence that the submarines were far from the area of operations is completely false and inconsistent with the sonar pings heard at the hull and detected by the passive sonar. There is no way it could be confused with any sound found in nature.

Perhaps the answer is that it is still unacceptable to admit that an ancient, poorly maintained, Argentine-crewed Second World War destroyer was able to thwart an impressive commando operation that should have become a landmark for the Special Forces: "destroy the Exocet AM39 missiles, destroy the airplanes, assassinate the pilots and, if possible, the ground crew". None of this occurred because an ancient destroyer, with a resolute and professional crew, prevented it by the shear roar of gun fire, just like in the Second World War.

On the other hand, it is probably also unacceptable to acknowledge that, while the British had extraordinary support and intelligence provided by the US, Chile and their allies, Argentine Naval Intelligence was able to warn the Navy high command so that they could place their destroyers in the exact place where two attacks would occur. The fact that this information was exact, precise and timely is surely still cause for exhaustive analysis by British investigators.

Furthermore, Southby-Tailyour writes about the presence of a spy plane, the Nimrod XW 664, which operated on Chilean soil and was supported by a VC10 tanker. Faced with the failure of Operations Plum Duff and Mikado, the Chilean government under General Pinochet requested that the airplane stop operations on May 22, since it undermined Chilean "neutrality". And yet he stresses that they did not have intelligence. (Southby-Tailyour 2014:174).

The third phase of the operation was the most dramatic one, since it would have been the one to bring them glory and turn them into legends within the British Special Forces.

Once the routine pre-flight checklist had been completed, which on this occasion was extensive due to the distance the VC was to fly and the initial excess weight, which was far beyond the manufacturer recommended maximum, the commandos took their places within the stripped down and noisy aircraft. They had 320 nautical miles ahead of them.

The take-off weight calculations, despite having removed everything they could—including apparatus like fire extinguishers and flotation devices—, significantly exceeded the maximum recommended by the manufacturer. It was therefore necessary to call the American test pilot, who advised taking off with the maximum apparent wind coming from the bow and gave them some guidelines to pilot the aircraft during the first hours of flight. (Hutchings 2014:140) The pilot opposes a comment made by Nigel West regarding supplementary tanks, since they were not used. The maximum range calculations were exhaustively verified, and they adjusted for the carrier *Invincible* needing to approach the South American continent. This included fuel usage during the operation and taking the helicopter to Chile to be destroyed.

Likewise, the author writes about the detailed planning, which considered the amount of money to be carried by each member of the flight, in US dollars, Chilean pesos and they even took 40 pounds sterling. The delivery of the money by an administrative officer was a source of great surprise: who carries money with them on a flight in wartime? (Hutchings 2014:141).

A concern that overcame the pilot during the final planning in the pre-flight room shared with the commandos, were the discussions and lack of common criteria amongst the leaders of the commando team, which he deemed boded a bad start to the operation. (Hutchings 2014:142).

At 03:14 UTC (00:14 local time) on May 18, the VC notified that it was ready for take-off and verified the last position that would be introduced in the navigation system, since the now ubiquitous GPS was not available at the time. (Southby-Tailyour 2014:175).

They were forced to fly under 200 feet for the first two hours due to their excess weight (23,350 lb), until using part of their fuel. They headed 265° towards the darkness of the night. (Hutchings 2014:143).

The surface naval force, *Invincible* and its escorts (the destroyers *Brilliant* and *Coventry*), immediately set a course in the opposite direction to move away from the Argentine threat. (Hutchings 2014:144).

Once again, the author restates that the group lacked intelligence, but he acknowledges that the RAF was aware of the presence of two destroyers in the area and that this had been communicated to the Task Force, but for some reason the Special Forces were not informed. Mistakes like this appear in the narrative, but it is difficult to believe that this type of information would not have been delivered in a timely manner to the planners and participants, not when the Admiral himself was involved in the most important operation for the Task Force.

The whole flight was made in utter silence, with absolutely no electronic emissions. The only exception allowed was in the case of them detecting the aircraft carrier ARA *25 de Mayo*, where they were to break radio silence and immediately transmit the ships position to the Task Force. (Hutchings 2014:144).

Once they were near the coast, in sight of the lights of drilling rigs and after flying for three hours, they began moving parallel to the coast bearing south-southeast. Soon after, they realised that their position was off by 10 miles.

The pilot mentions his concerns regarding fuel consumption, motivated by the mistake for the arrival at Tierra del Fuego and, in addition, the weather forecast had been wrong. (Hutchings 2014:146).

Once they had found their position, an unexpected fog appeared and the helicopter was forced to fly over the sea to avoid crashing into anything on land. According to the author, at this point the radar operators of ARA *Bouchard* detected them. The author indicates that the times given are different and believes that the time must have been taken by a young conscript reading his own cheap watch. (Southby-Tailyour

2014:180) This comment is surely incorrect, since all times were entered in the logs, including the ship's war diary, which were public documents and referred to the bulkhead clock, checked daily and compared with the pattern kept by the Navigation Officer, who in turn checked the top time. This procedure is followed by every navy in the world, perhaps copied from the British Navy, and the mere suggestion of such a lack of professionalism shows the scarce knowledge regarding the Argentine sailors, or perchance it is expressly included in the account to undermine and turn everything into pure coincidence. Nevertheless, the facts show that it was no mere coincidence, but professionalism and fighting spirit.

Without knowing that they had been detected, the pilot descended to sea level and they were able to see intense lights, mistaking them for flares launched by Argentine troops, concluding that the area they believed to be unpopulated did in fact have people (according to the author, the presence of Route 3 was not a part of the "scarce" information that they had). The descent in the thick fog was in the vicinity of the "La Sara" ranch, as indicated by the destroyer ARA *Bouchard's* reports. While this was questioned by other authors, it is confirmed by British literature, which removes any speculation about the geographic site of the first descent of the VC.

Once landed and with strange light reflections that led them to speculate that they had been discovered, aggravated by finding themselves 26 miles away from the target, dangerously close to Route 3 and the "La Sara" ranch, after flying more than three hours—two of which were in Argentine controlled airspace—, they had to make the decision to leave the location, in spite of the fog and reflections from the dangerous flares. Their only option was to cross the border and carry out the operation from a "neutral" location.

According to the author, they had a brief but intense discussion regarding the decision to be made, since the pilot considered that even though they were not close, the operation was not compromised. The commando group's leader, on the other hand, held the opposite view.

When they were about to disembark, they believed they saw lights from approaching vehicles and thought they were falling into an ambush, or that they were very close to an enemy position. However, the pilot did not see the lights because he was facing the leader of the commandos, which added a new source of disagreement.

The pilot was sure that they were close to the "La Sara" ranch. The leader of the commandos told the pilots that he did not trust they were in that location and that it was unacceptable to start the operation. (Hutchings 2014:147).

Hutchings denies what was published by Nigel West, (Hutchings 2014:147–148) and states that there were not many flames from gas venting in San Sebastián's wells, as the commando leader reported, but one single flame, and that it was that flame which initially made them take heading too far to the north and deviate from the planned location at 10 nautical miles distance. Moreover, he writes negative remarks about this publication in an article published by the *Sunday Times* and, a year later, in his own book.

It was later confirmed that no flares were fired that night, and that the reflections leading them to confusion were the towers where the gas from San

Sebastián's oilfields was vented into the atmosphere and burnt, which being random, they resemble pyrotechnics. (Southby-Tailyour 2014:181/183) The British author confirms the absence of troops near the area, with a recent communication to Captain Pita, who was in charge of the airports defences.

While they were making the decision, one of the men landed without the VC's crew knowing. Despite the pressure the group's leader was under due to the mission's importance to the Task Force, he decided that the helicopter would take them to the border and they would return from there to fulfil the mission.

When the helicopter regained altitude to head to the Chilean border, they were detected again by the ARA *Bouchard's* radar. According to the account, they reached an altitude of 750 feet conforming to their radio altimeter. They were in a thick fog, in enemy territory, and believed they had been detected by land forces. They gained more altitude and, at 1000 feet, their electronic warfare equipment warned them that they had been detected by a search radar: indeed, they had been found by the *Bouchard's* SPS 10. Seeing a dark shadow ahead, that seemed like a hill, the pilot made some steep turns to avoid it and decided to ascend another 1000 feet to prevent crashing into the "unknown" local terrain and head straight to the border. A few minutes later, they felt themselves be acquired by a radar and deployed bags of thin metallic pieces called "chaff" from the side door. This counter-measure is used to fool any fire control radar that would launch a missile or fire anti-aircraft artillery at them by creating a false target. This was a highly tense moment due to the abruptness of the manoeuvres and the meaning they had in the middle of combat. Ten minutes later, they were flying in Chilean airspace over the water of Inútil bay. A short time after, they were flying over the beaches of the bay, they landed and the commando group disembarked.

According to their initial calculations, they were 35 miles from the border and another 30 miles from their target.

After landing and analysing the situation, they began their march east. After two stops and the severe worsening of the weather, they decided to set up a small bivouac to rest and shelter themselves in their small tents from the rain and easterly wind. There, one of the men reported a budding flu and, shortly after, begun running a fever. The leader then came to a new crossroads. He decided to leave three men tending to the sick operative and led the other three to complete the mission.

While the squad rested, the VC, or helicopter with the registration ZA-290, had been destroyed with fire in Agua Fresca cove, 11 miles (18 km) south of Punta Arenas. (Hutchings 2014:149) Communications, reports and theatrics regarding the appearance of a British helicopter began being exchanged between governments and embassies. (Southby-Tailyour 2014:196/197) After a failed attempt at sinking it in the waters of Agua Fresca cove, the pilot landed it at the edge of the shore and set it on fire at 09:35 h on May 18 (Hutchings 2014:154/156–205).

The three helicopter crewmembers were to remain undetected for at least eight days and then head to Punta Arenas. They decided to walk only at night to stay hidden. The nights were very dark and soon after beginning their march they regretted not keeping their NVGs, which had been smashed into small pieces. The soil was strewn with fallen trees, probably due to a fire, which made progress very difficult.

The helicopter was discovered on May 20, and the Chileans began searching by air and land; they came very close to finding them, but they were able to remain unnoticed. They climbed a hill, from where they could see Punta Arenas a few miles away and, below it, a small military outpost. They hid there for a few days, until meeting the deadline.

On May 25, they decided to approach the city to call the Air Attaché at the British Embassy in Santiago de Chile. They passed in front of the *carabineros*[4] station at peak vehicle and pedestrian traffic time, without being detected. Once in the city, they were picked up by a *carabineros* vehicle, politely greeted, and then formally interrogated; they also learnt about the significant losses that they had suffered during the eight days they had not received any news (Hutchings 2014:171/173). That same evening, they flew to Santiago de Chile on a C-130 that, according to Hutchings, seemed to be a British airplane due to its paintjob, and the group of F-5 pilots that were also being transported. These pilots were relieved weekly and had been stationed to prevent an Argentine attack on the Picton, Lennox and Nueva Islands. They were surprised by the fact that the pilots did not seem to be Hispanic, but almost all of them were German (Hutchings 2014:174/176). After a hectic day, which included a press conference, a Lan Chile airplane took them to Spain and then to England.

Meanwhile, the Commandos…

The authorities were informed of the events occurred and the developing situation in a difficult radio communication, the first since the VC had taken off. The answer was to continue the operation, since it was crucial to the British campaign in the Falklands/Malvinas. (Southby-Tailyour 2014:194) Once the communication had finished, the feeling by those on the ground was that nothing of what had been informed had been comprehended by the people in Great Britain.

Between the night of May 19 and daybreak on May 20, the squad rested in their tents, recovering and conserving their strength for the exhausting hike and action that awaited them.

During the night on May 20, they headed to the border. The man who had fallen ill had partially recovered and was able to follow the rest of the men. The same routine was followed on the 21st and, following their rest during the day, they realised that the operation was beyond them. During a communication with HQ, they also requested being resupplied with victuals before entering Argentina since they had already finished the four days' supply each of them had. The answer was blunt and final: they were to make an Emergency Rendezvous (ERV) with the Assistant Military Attaché stationed at the British Embassy in Chile, who was also a member of the Special Forces. He had been captured in South Georgia and, upon his release to return to his country, had remained in Santiago de Chile as a communication liaison for the Special Forces, due to his command of Spanish. Thus the operation

---

[4] Translator's note: *Carabineros* are the Chilean national police force.

and first attempt to destroy missiles, airplanes, pilots and ground crew associated with the Exocet AM39 ended. The next option, Operation Mikado, would have to be conducted without any previous reconnaissance.

After many hardships, the members met the British officer in El Porvenir and were transported by a Chilean Air Force (FACh) airplane to Santiago de Chile.

Meanwhile, on May 25, commemorating the Revolution for Argentina's Independence, two Exocet AM39 hit the logistics ship *Atlantic Conveyor*. The vessel was destroyed and this greatly impacted the logistics of the British campaign. This magnificent action reinforced what many had been saying about the importance of destroying these missiles and everything surrounding them. The lethal results for the British naval forces proved those opinions right.

According to the British author's account, the group remained in a safe house in Santiago de Chile between May 30 and June 8. Other sources report that most of the group stayed until the end of the conflict, training the Chilean Special Forces. As a sign of their gratitude and affection, they also left them all the weapons they had brought on their failed mission.[5] This was duplicated at a greater scale with fighters, Army equipment and Navy ships, not only in response to this operation, but also due to the broad and unrestricted support provided by the whole of the Chilean government to British operations, both conventional and surreptitious, and the constant and unlimited intelligence and meteorological information.

Operation Mikado

Ewen Southby-Tailyour states (Southby-Tailyour 2014:207) that Operation Mikado was doomed to fail due to the scarce intelligence and imprecise or inexistent orders, only London's urgent need to end the Exocet threat kept the plan alive. The men who would have to actually participate did not agree with the suicidal plan. Even if both the landing and combat were successful, leading to the unlikely destruction of the missiles, the issue of exfiltration to Chilean territory was unaddressed. The plan was filled with guesswork and little certainty. Another weakness was that no RAF officer had been a part of the planning or training. The chief of the commando group was convinced that the operation, in addition to being a response to the serious threat posed by the missiles, was to be carried out to fan the dying flames of the myth of the British Special Forces. The NCO in charge of the troops was of the same mind and, since none of those involved in this suicide mission would go with the airplane, he requested a transfer and not to participate on the mission. When the chief of the group informed his superior, Brigadier De la Billière, of the request, he seized the chance to express his agreement about Mikado. Thus, two of the most decorated and renowned men of the Special Forces were replaced, becoming the first casualties of Operation Mikado, even before its execution.

---

[5] From an informal conversation among the author and senior officers in the Chilean Navy in 2005.

On May 16, with a new chief, they took off with the vehicles and weaponry destined for the operation. They reached Ascension Island on May 17, with all the secrecy and stealth the operation warranted. (Southby-Tailyour 2014:209).

Then the Hercules XV 179 and XV 200, the two airplanes that would take them to Río Grande, arrived. They were loaded with a huge fuel tank that would allow them to make the long flight, which was over 13 h long. During the stay at Ascension Island, they carried out two flights to the South Atlantic, on May 21 and 23. These flights were prioritised over Operation Mikado, perhaps as evidence of the little confidence they had that the aircraft would be recovered after the operation. (Southby-Tailyour 2014:209).

On May 25, the Navy pilots Roberto Curilovic and Julio Barraza executed a colossal operation in their Super Étendards: they destroyed the logistics ship *MV Atlantic Conveyor*, thus demolishing British logistics and causing significant material losses and an even greater damage to the morale of those in charge of operations. While Argentina only had a single missile left, according to the British intelligence sources, it definitely could cause a lot of damage!

The airborne component of the operation seemed like the most complex one. The maps were not the right ones, although the Defence Mapping Agency´s Aerospace Center (US), located in St. Louis, Missouri, in a few hours printed and sent all the maps they had of the AO. (Southby-Tailyour 2014:224).

The maps were completed with electronic intelligence information, provided by their own services and Chile, regarding the radars and other helpful information, like ranges, shaded areas (places the radar could not detect due to being blind by natural obstacles or the configuration of its emitters). There was also information supplied by a submarine that had been watching the Naval Air Base, and reported the blacking out of the runway at night and the movements of the airplanes. (Southby-Tailyour 2014:231).

This last point confirms the frustrated operation conducted by ARA *Bouchard* on the night of May 16, 1982, as well as the detection of several submarine sonar emissions, which the book denies and is later confirmed.

The target could be approached from two different sectors. They could fly beneath 50 feet above sea level directly towards the airport coming from the east. The other option would be to reach land at Cape San Diego (the easternmost point of the Isla Grande de Tierra del Fuego), then to fly over Fagnano lake, cross the border, head northeast over Blanco lake in Chile and then bear east towards the Río Grande Base, flying over the Laguna de los Cisnes, close to the base; the whole flight would have to be at a very low altitude.

According to the author, although they did not have good maps, what they were most afraid of was that the Chilean air defence would think them Argentine forces. However, this is false, because once the operation ended, the airplanes were to fly 120 miles to the Punta Arenas airports in Chilean "neutral" territory. There is no doubt that despite the unrestrained support offered by Chile, both in terms of intelligence and assistance to the troops, the actions of the destroyers and forces stationed on land prevented the execution of Operation Plum Duff.

Secure communications was another point to be analysed. Here they once again received support from the US. Fort Bragg sent the SAS a briefcase with a cutting-edge satellite communications system, which turned the operation into an undetectable unit.

While they were flying in formation, they were to maintain strict radio silence. Thanks to the combined usage of NVGs and small lights on the wings of the airplanes, navigation was safe.

From the perspective of the RAF, the first stage was particularly risky because they were to refuel in the air, during the day, and in the middle of the sea. If something went wrong, they would not be able to return to Ascension Island and would have to seek landing in Brazil. Then, close to the Falklands/Malvinas and to avoid being detected, they were to fly under 50 feet, follow the flight path, land at night in silence and in a hostile airport within two and a half minutes of each other, and the commandos would disembark. Then the difficult but conventional land operation would begin. Meanwhile, the airplanes had to go to the head of the runways, wait for the return of the operatives, surely in the middle of combat, let them board again, and then fly to Punta Arenas.

The atmospheric conditions were extreme and contrary to flying over enemy territory and off the charts of a landing manual.

They also mention that the submarines HMS *Splendid* and HMS *Valiant* reported the destroyers' passing from the AO towards the Le Maire Strait and Ushuaia, that *Valiant* readied its torpedo launchers to fire on ARA *Bouchard*, (Southby-Tailyour 2014:237) and that they did not fire because the rules of engagement only allowed retaliating in self-defence.

This once again contradicts the earlier statements that they lacked intelligence and that there were no submarines in the area. This is more evidence showing the presence of special troops transported by submarines and aircrafts, and the two operations foiled by the alertness and forceful presence of the destroyer ARA *Bouchard* and its combative response to the threats. Perhaps they were unable to sink the ship due to the weather conditions and the proximity to the coast, and not because of a lack of willingness or the rules of engagement. After all, these were not obstacles when it came to sinking the cruiser ARA *Belgrano*, which was not dangerous or a threat to any British unit.

On June 6, Operation Mikado was cancelled. The author of *Exocet Falklands: The untold story of special forces operations* writes several thoughts regarding the legitimacy and consequences of Operation Mikado, as well as about the other alternatives that were not considered by high command and that would have been more effective than Operation Plum Duff, like the use of paratroopers with the new low-altitude equipment for instance, which had been used at that time in Africa with excellent results.

This way they preserved the only two Hercules airplanes suitable for aerial resupplying and maintained the fleet's logistics chain, especially after the sinking of *Atlantic Conveyor*, since with a single Hercules they could launch and then have it return to Ascension with supplies on its return.

The reiterated lack of intelligence, especially after the failure of Operation Plum Duff, the little empathy between high command and the troops that would conduct the operation, the considerable doubts about the chances of landing held by the air crew, as well as the international consequences to operating on Argentine continental territory with the aim of destroying the last Exocet, did little but raise significant points against the operation. Another argument to tip the scale was that it was never prioritised as expected, since it was postponed countless times to free the airplanes for other logistical tasks. These delays were frustrating and distressing for the operatives, since they would get ready and form up on the platform with all their equipment, only to return to barracks to wait for another opportunity. According to the author, many of them would have preferred to be killed in battle than prolong that torturous agony, which continued until the operation was definitely cancelled. (Southby-Tailyour 2014:240).

Operation Mikado as Described by a British "Historian"

Nigel West, a British author, defines himself as a military and security historian. He is the editor for the *World Intelligence Review* magazine in Europe, (West 1977) and deeply knowledgeable about (and maybe even a member of) the active and professional British Intelligence. Others describe him as a narrator of British Intelligence planning intelligence operations through literature. West decided to analyse Operation Mikado. Notwithstanding his intention, when he wrote the book *The Secret War for the Falklands: The SAS, Mi6, and the War Whitehall Nearly Lost*, he provided historical data that explained the presence of a British helicopter on May 17, 1982, near the city of Río Grande.

As a result of our research and review of several diverse sources, we infer that the presence of the patrol constituted by the two destroyers prevented attacks from the air and the sea on two occasions, on May 16 and 17. In addition, the units on land contributed to stopping these operations.

The SAS (Special Air Service) was created in 1940, to perform tasks in northern Africa, with the objective of raiding the Italian forces stationed there. Their badge is a dagger with wings and their motto is "Who Dares Wins". According to Nigel West, Brigadier Peter de la Billière, Director SAS, had requested and was in command of the planning and execution of an operation that would "strike at the heart of the enemy". (West 1977:139) That heart was Río Grande, where the Navy Neptune scouts operated and the feared Super Étendard–Exocet AM39 missile combination could be found. The General gave the operation the codename MIKADO. In truth, the operation was planned by the British Chiefs of Staff, specifically by Admiral Lewin, who entrusted the 22nd SAS Regiment and the SBS (Special Boat Service of the Royal Marines), under the command of Brigadier De la Billière. To this end, he had some members of G Squadron available, who were on board the HMS *Fearless*, in the South Atlantic Task Force (West 1977:139) (the rest of G Squadron was in Belize). He also had B Squadron at his disposal, under the command of Major John

Moss. This Squadron, after finishing training to participate in a NATO exercise in Germany, "embarked on an intensive training program to practise capturing an airport under enemy control" (West 1977:141).

The general basis of the manoeuvre that the commandos were to execute was to deploy on a Sea King for reconnaissance tasks, which meant identifying the target and the location of the airplanes, as well as evaluating the defences and alertness level. It is worth highlighting that the Navy airplanes were scattered and positioned depending on three options or schemes: close, medium or distant. (Muñoz 2005:53) This would have been an additional obstacle for those who were to execute the reconnaissance tasks. On the night of May 17 to May 18, the airplanes were positioned based on a distant spread (this was the only occasion when this pattern was selected) and the pilots were sleeping in a nearby meat processing plant. (Muñoz 2005:117) This lets us conclude that, even if the operation had been successful, it would still have been very difficult for them to complete the mission for which they had deployed on Argentine soil.

Once they had received the information provided by the reconnaissance team, they had to perform a forced landing on the Río Grande runway, with two C-130 Hercules with 55 men on board. Then they were to destroy five Super Étendard planes and the three missiles that Argentina still had according to the data gathered by British Intelligence, and assassinate all the pilots. The author mentions that the intelligence was poor and insufficient, which is hard to believe since they had detailed information provided by Chilean authorities, as is inferred by the statements made by the more eminent participants of the history of those times.[6] However, as indicated by the author at the Forum of the Spanish Armed Forces and in Jorge Muñoz's book, there were two possible ways of executing the task. One is expressed in the book. The second involved a force of 24 SBS/SAS men, who were to disembark from the *Onyx* submarine and head to the coast by boat. The submarine would have to leave them very close to the coast to prevent the area's inclement weather from affecting the operation. The boats would be loaded with MILAN[7] and LAW[8] missiles, grenade launchers, explosive charges, and other types of personal weaponry. They were to use these weapons to destroy the airplanes and kill all the pilots.

The first option (the aerial) was less accepted by the commandos, since they considered it a sure death and doubted its chances of success. In either case, there was no way to escape. They would have to hike through the frozen tundra of Isla Grande de Tierra del Fuego until reaching Chile, so that they could be picked up and taken to England. They speculated that they could be pursued by Argentine troops, which was very likely considering that the Naval Infantry stationed in the area were highly trained and motivated. Hence, should the operation have been executed, it

---

[6] Public statements by the Commander in Chief of the FACh (Chilean Air Force), General Fernando Matthei, who revealed the level of support provided, and Margaret Thatcher's words on the occasion of Pinochet's imprisonment in England, and the words of General Pinochet himself upon his release.

[7] Translator's note: From the French *Missile d'infanterie léger antichar*, which means "Light anti-tank infantry missile".

[8] Translator's note: Acronym for Light Anti-Tank Weapon.

would have been difficult for them to withdraw without facing tough battles during the retreat and operation.

According to the author, the commandos spent a week practicing the C-130 landings. There was an incident in one of the drills that almost cost them their lives. (West 1977:143) In addition, the RAF had to impersonate the defending Argentine forces and reported detection distances and other parameters, which was discouraging and worrying.

The first phase would be carried out from *Invincible*, where they would take off on a Navy Aviation Squadron 846 Sea King, with the registration ZA 290 (West 1977:146) within the British Navy. It would be configured for troop transport, operating at its maximum range, leaving eight SAS troops to reconnoitre the area around the "Las Violetas" ranch, very close to Río Grande, nearby Cape Domingo, an easily recognizable geographical landmark, even for those who had never flown those skies. Once it had taken off from *Invincible*, both that ship and its escort, HMS *Brilliant*, would return at all speed eastwards to enter the exclusion zone and make a show with fireworks and attack Puerto Argentino (Port Stanley), to make their presence felt to the Argentine forces stationed there. (West 1977:147) However, other authors believe that they left from HMS *Hermes*. The flight met the strict and exacting standards planned, until the pilot was informed that they had been detected by hostile radar and the co-pilot observed a flare. However, they decided to continue onwards. But as they were leaving the helicopter, they saw a second closer light and concluded that they were in danger and so aborted the mission and pressed directly towards Punta Arenas. The men were later transferred to the theatre of operations to replace others who had died in an accident (West 1977:153). In spite of what was expressed by Nigel West, Jorge Muñoz writes that, after the event with the Sea King, both C-130 s were flying close to the objective, meaning that the mission was aborted shortly before its start and the commandos were forced to endure long hours of flight and several replenishments to return to Ascension Island. (Muñoz 2005:115).

Another version of events with the helicopter was that of Jorge Muñoz, who states that sources from the Argentine Naval Intelligence Service had unofficially suggested that the helicopter could have taken off RRS *Bransfield*, which was operating from Punta Arenas or the city's airfield. It would have entered Argentine air space from the west and, once crossing the sea by 40 miles, turned and headed towards "Las Violetas" ranch, until disappearing. It then reappeared and after flying over the area around the "Sara Braun" (Muñoz 2005:110) ranch, headed due 290° towards the Chilean border.

Despite some minor variations, the final version of the operation is quite similar. The ZA 290 left the team and their weapons in a far off area and they marched on a trail. The helicopter's crew set the aircraft on fire near Agua Fresca cove, 11 miles (18 km) south of Punta Arenas. The crew requested help from the *carabineros* and were taken first to Punta Arenas and then to Santiago de Chile. After a brief press conference where they mentioned a mechanical failure, they returned to London. The helicopter's wreckage was quickly covered by a road maintenance vehicle, which prevented any possibility of an investigation verifying the authenticity of the British and Chilean versions of the facts. The SAS commandos took refuge in the wilderness and, a few days later, turned in to the Chilean authorities. Some versions mention that they stayed in Santiago de Chile until the end of the conflict, others that they returned to England without communicating with anyone, while others indicate that they took advantage of their stay to train Chilean commandos as a way to show their appreciation.

In addition, we must add that Intelligence had informed the United States President that the British were planning an operation on Argentine soil. This news was cause for concern, since it could lead to other countries becoming involved and not only extending the theatre of operations, but also incorporating other actors in the conflict. Despite the phone call made by Ronald Reagan, Margaret Thatcher insisted on the need for executing the operation. (Muñoz 2005:19).

Epilogue

The decision by the Navy high command to station the destroyers ARA *Piedrabuena* and ARA *Bouchard* patrolling the Río Grande area was highly successful. We cannot confirm that Argentine Naval Intelligence had precise information regarding the operations planned to be executed, but we think it is no coincidence that they happened to be present in both attempts.

While Great Britain jealously guards information, we can conjecture that, even though on the night from May 17 to May 18 the airplanes and pilots were ordered to organise themselves in a distant spread scheme, something far different occurred on the night of May 16. That night, ARA *Bouchard* probably prevented the landing of commandos approaching from a submarine by detecting the echoes of the three boats and opening fire on them. From that moment on, the element of surprise had been lost and, at least on board the destroyers, the alertness level was highly increased when compared to before that night on May 16.

The version with the helicopter landing near the "Las Violetas" ranch seems to be mistaken in the face of official Argentine documentation and the little that transcends from the British side. The logbooks and war diaries of the destroyer ARA *Bouchard* and the reports sent to the high command indicate that the aircraft was nine miles northwest of the ship, two miles from the coast, and the echo was lost a short distance south of "La Sara" ranch and remained outside radar range. It then gained altitude and headed between five and seven miles towards the Chilean border, where it was lost. The radar operator stopped identifying it, since the land return hid the helicopter's signal. It is unlikely that helicopters coming from Chile would head into the sea to return to land, knowing that two destroyers were patrolling those waters, unless the objective was to be detected.

References

Bárcena W. (1982). Report by the Commanding Officer of the destroyer ARA *Bouchard*. Buenos Aires.

Hutchings R. (2014). Special forces pilot: a flying memoir of the Falklands War. Pen & Sword Aviation. London.

Muñoz J. (2005). Ataquen Río Grande (Operación Mikado). Instituto de Publicaciones Navales. Buenos Aires.

Southby-Tailyour E. (2014). Exocet-Falklands, the untold story of special forces operations. Pen & Sword Military. London.

Vv. Aa. (1982a). Historical book of the destroyer ARA *Bouchard*. Buenos Aires.

Vv. Aa. (1982b). Logbook of the destroyer ARA *Bouchard*. Buenos Aires.

Vv. Aa. (1982c). War Diary of the destroyer ARA *Bouchard*. Buenos Aires.

West N. (1997). La Guerra secreta por las Malvinas, los Exocets y el espionaje internacional (2° Ed.) Editorial Sudamericana. Buenos Aires.

Chapter 12
The Patrol Continues (From May 23 to May 27)

Abstract The domestic and international context and the hostilities. Description of the patrol performed from May 23 to 27.

The Domestic and International Context and the Hostilities (IRI, 1994) (Vv. Aa., *Historia de la Fuerza Aérea Argentina* [History of the Argentine Air Force], 1998) (Vv. Aa., informe oficial del Ejército Argentino, *Conflicto Malvinas* [Official Argentine Army report on the Falklands/Malvinas War], 1983) (Rattenbach B., 1983)

On May 23, Argentine Navy fighters made several raids against British vessels over the Falkland Sound (San Carlos strait) and succeeded in damaging a supply ship and two destroyers. England reported that the Argentine attacks had sunk a frigate, and that six Argentine aircrafts had been shot down.

On May 24, the HMS *Antelope* sank as a result of damage sustained from an attack by Argentine Navy aircraft the previous day. That day, the European Economic Community, with the exception of Italy and Ireland, declared an indefinite economic boycott on Argentina.

On May 25, the RAF attacked Puerto Argentino (Port Stanley) and lost three Harrier fighters to anti-aircraft fire. That day a squadron of Argentine Navy fighters with Air Force support sank the SS *Atlantic Conveyor*, a container cargo ship, using Exocet AM-39 missiles. This represented a tremendous logistics loss for the British Task Force.

At Punta Arenas, the *carabineros* assisted the crewmen of the damaged British helicopter and transported them to the capital Santiago, where they were cared for and repatriated by the British Embassy. That day, England acknowledged that its destroyer HMS *Coventry* had been struck by fire from Argentine Air Force aircraft.

On May 26, having consolidated the beachhead and set the men ashore, the attacks on Darwin and Goose Green were initiated. As regards international affairs, France decided to extend its weapons embargo to Peru due to this country's overt support for the Argentine cause.

On May 27 fighting began at Darwin: the British assaulted Argentine positions with aeroplanes, artillery, helicopters, the Royal Marine vanguard and a paratroopers battalion. British aircrafts also attacked Puerto Mitre (Port Howard), Puerto Argentino (Port Stanley) and Darwin, and one of the planes was shot down. Furthermore, despite the warnings received, the British used the SS *Canberra*[1], which had been declared a hospital ship, as a troop transport in support of the military operations.

The American Secretary of State expressed his opposition to invoking the TIAR, since he did not believe that this attack was issued from an extra-continental power. He thus implied that the sovereignty over the islands was deemed to be British and, consequently, that Great Britain belonged to the continent. Moreover, United States military sources report that American logistical support for Great Britain was comprehensive and unrestricted. Additional evidence that points in the same direction is that large Galaxy military transport aircrafts belonging to United States carried military equipment to Ascension Island after a layover in Panama on May 28, 1982.

On May 28, replying to the charges presented by Argentina for having used a hospital ship as a troop carrier, the British claimed that the SS *Uganda*[2] had only entered the Falkland Sound (San Carlos strait) for half an hour in order to rescue wounded soldiers belonging to both sides.

Besides, Pope John Paul II travelled to England, visited Queen Elizabeth II and advocated for peace. On the other hand, the President of the United States volunteered to be part of a peacekeeping force at the Falklands/Malvinas and proposed to settle the issue of sovereignty once peace had been restored.

On May 29, Argentine forces in Darwin surrendered to the British after sustaining intense gunfire and engaging in bitter combat with them. To the north of South Georgia, an unusual encounter took place when a cargo plane of the Argentine air force flew over an oil tanker, the British *Wye*,[3] and then fired a volley of six bombs, five of which exploded in the water, and the only one which struck the ship failed to explode and caused only minor damage. On Pebble Island (isla Borbón), Argentine Air Force planes rescued two pilots who had ejected from two Mirage fighters that had been shot down, and four wounded sailors; they also retrieved the body of a dead pilot.

As regards international affairs, the OAS condemned the British assault on Darwin and requested the United States to cease aiding the British.

On May 30, 90 nm east of the Falklands/Malvinas, in a joint operation, Argentine Navy fighter planes armed with Exocet missiles and Air Force fighter-bombers attacked a British aircraft carrier and inflicted severe damage. Also, two Air Force planes were shot down. Although the British did not acknowledge the attack, the British aerial activity was considerably reduced thereafter.

---

[1] A 45,000 tons of displacement ocean liner with 820 feet length and capacity for more than 2000 passengers in tourist trips. It was nicknamed "The Great White Whale".

[2] A 541 ft length tourist cruise liner.

[3] A 25,000 tons of displacement oil tanker with 524 ft length.

Britain issued a report on the status of the hospital ships, and the Argentine prisoners were transferred to different vessels that would remove them from the theatre of operations once they were fully loaded.

In the ARA *Bouchard*

The ship set sail from Ushuaia at 01:15 h, sailing in stealth mode, where the ship restricts almost all lights to avoid being detected. Although this could increase the difficulty of being detected, the British and Chilean spy network in the area around Ushuaia and the whole Beagle channel would have made it impossible to hide these movements and avoid the notice of British forces in the South Atlantic.

At 04:00 h, the ship had reached the Becasses Islands in the Beagle. Thirty minutes later, as prevention for passing through the focal area, they went to battle stations for anti-submarine combat and sailed parallel to the coast, maintaining a distance of two miles. The depth was more than enough for the ship, but not for a submarine to operate, and launching a torpedo would have been even more difficult, since it would have probably crashed into the seabed.

At 08:00 h, the ship changed course towards Cape San Diego, the easternmost point of Isla Grande de Tierra del Fuego, and headed north-northwest to patrol the area immediately around Río Grande. The crew went on port and starboard watches and their sensors were listening, with a rigorous emission plan, to once again vigilantly patrol, control and eventually rebuff any forces that would attempt to attack the continent. The patrol continued, although the aft engine could not maintain operation and had to be halted for repairs at 13:00 h. After 5 h of intense work, the aft engine was restarted at 18:50 h and the ship continued sailing with only two shafts propelling. The area to be patrolled was 30 miles long, parallel to the coast and the closest point to the coast was five miles out.

May 24 was a day without significant events; they continued patrolling the coast of Isla Grande. Revolutions were masked to make it harder for any enemy submarine to count them, and therefore easily learn the ship's speed. In the afternoon, shortly after 20:00 h, they were forced to stop the forward engine until, at 20:45 h, they were able to start both shafts. After 21:00 h, the ship anchored facing Río Grande.

The ship remained anchored almost the whole day on May 25, on watch to ensure no attacks like those on the previous days would be attempted. The engines were ready, which would allow them to sail in a matter of minutes. However, the aft engine came offline several times and they had to halt and repair it each time. At 13:25 h, the ship set sail to anchor in San Sebastián Bay, at 17:56. During that time, they tested the engines and repaired the log. Once anchored, the forward engine was disconnected to proceed to change the boiler. They then reinforced the watches and rounds to prevent any unwanted surprise and provide both the ship and Base with the maximum vigilance possible. The situation remained the same on May 26: the aft engine was still out of service.

On May 27, after 01:30 h, the ship set sail, enacting the same anti-submarine measures they had been following during the patrol and the port and starboard watches, which had been somewhat relaxed while anchored to cover other duties. By midmorning, the ships sailed in formation, leaving six nautical miles between them, and passed Río Grande heading south. They went to anti-submarine battle stations when they were near the Le Maire Strait, and dropped noisemaking devices to fool any homing torpedoes, but the devices were not activated. At 20:00 h, they entered Ushuaia Bay and berthed at 20:39 h, alongside *Piedrabuena* on the fuel dock.

Chapter 13
The Last Patrol (From May 31 to June 6)

Abstract The domestic and international context and the hostilities. The last patrol, from May 31 to June 6. The Malvinas/Falklands islands' die was cast.

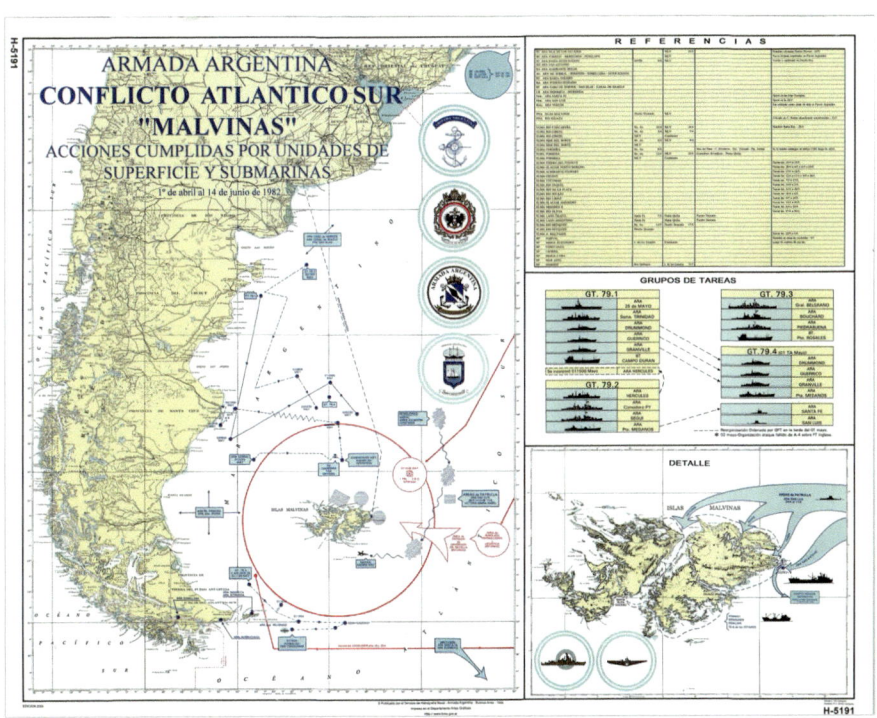

The Domestic and International Context and the Hostilities (IRI, 1994) (Vv. Aa., *Historia de la Fuerza Aérea Argentina* [History *of the Argentine Air Force*], 1998) (Vv. Aa., informe oficial del Ejército Argentino, *Conflicto* Malvinas [Official Argentine Army Report on the Falklands/Malvinas War], 1983) (Rattenbach B., 1983)

By June 1, the British troops had taken positions near Puerto Argentino (Port Stanley), which enabled them to launch a decisive assault on the town. Nearby, the Argentine hospital ship ARA *Bahía Paraíso* was receiving wounded and also Argentines aboard the British hospital ship SS *Uganda*. Sources at the British Ministry of Defence admitted that the aircraft carrier HMS *Invincible* had been attacked, but denied that it has sustained major damage.

A cruel and unusual deed occurred when two British Harrier fighters attacked an unarmed Argentine C-130 Hercules by firing a missile which mortally damaged it, and then finished it off by cannon bursts, causing the aircraft to lose a wing and fall crashing into the sea. The British pilot who carried out these actions was discharged from service at the end of the war.

On June 2, the American Secretary of State informed that Great Britain was unwilling to accept a ceasefire and that it would not even consider the Argentine proposal for ceasing all hostilities. The non-aligned nations, assembled in Havana, Cuba, condemned both Great Britain for its aggression and the US for its support for Great Britain.

On June 3, Margaret Thatcher demanded that the Argentine military leadership retreat from the islands before a final assault would take place. She was thus implicitly transferring to Argentina the responsibility for any forthcoming deaths in combat, both on the Argentine and on the British side. The same message, conveyed in different wording, was also leaked from other sectors of British power.

The same day, two Brazilian fighter jets forced a British Vulcan strategic bomber to land at a Brazilian airfield, in reprisal for entering Brazilian airspace while armed.

On June 4, British forces deployed on Kent, Challenger and Two Sisters hills sustained Argentine aircraft and artillery fire.

As regards international affairs, Brazil refused to allow the Vulcan to depart until the Argentine request that the aircraft and its crew be interned, within the scope of the TIAR, had been granted. Peru complained to France for its embargo on Exocet missiles, and Guatemala offered to send elite troops to fight the British on the Falklands/Malvinas. At the UN, Great Britain and the United States vetoed a proposal for an immediate ceasefire submitted by Spain and Panama.

On June 5, while Argentine aircraft were still attacking Kent and Two Sisters hills, several British surface vessels withdrew from the combat area on account of the damage inflicted on them by Argentine aircraft. That day, thanks to the coordination of the International Committee of the Red Cross, a rendezvous between both the Argentine and British hospital ships was held for them to exchange the wounded.

On June 7, bitter fighting continued between British and Argentine troops. Argentina deployed four Learjet aircraft to scout out and photograph the Falkland Sound (San Carlos strait) area, but one of them was shot down by an anti-aircraft missile launched from a British ship.

On June 8, Argentine fighter aircraft attacked three British ships, RFA *Sir Galahad*, RFA *Sir Tristam* and HMS *Plymouth* in Bluff Cove, causing great human and equipment losses. Fifty-one men died and 200 were injured in the attack, the greatest number of casualties sustained by Britain in a single encounter since the Second World War. Besides, both supply ships were lost.

On June 10, the British assault on Argentine positions near Kent and Langdon hills became fiercer. Likewise, British forces intensified their attacks on the positions held by the Argentine 5th Naval Infantry Battalion, an artillery battery and an Argentine Army Infantry regiment. Fighting continued and both sides showed exceptional courage.

On June 11, British forces made a concerted push toward Argentine positions near Puerto Argentino (Port Stanley). That night, there was an intense naval bombardment of the area. An Argentine Hercules transport plane managed to break through the strict aerial blockade and land on the airfield at Puerto Argentino (Port Stanley) to deliver a 155 mm cannon and ammunition.

British forces began infiltrating Argentine positions, which caused the reserves to be mobilised to prevent these advances. Under the intense British assault, the Commander of the Naval Infantry battalion ordered artillery fire on his own position to drive the enemy back and prevent being surpassed.

While fighting escalated on the islands, Pope John Paul II landed in Buenos Aires. That afternoon, he celebrated mass at the Basilica of Our Lady of Luján, where a multitude of 700,000 people prayed for peace.

On June 12, Argentine troops attempted a counterattack on Langdon hill. However, despite their valiant resistance and the numerous casualties they sustained, they were ordered to withdraw toward Puerto Argentino (Port Stanley), which was being heavily bombarded.

An attempt was made to send infantry reinforcements to relieve Argentine troops on Harriet hill, who had been attacked on both flanks at the same time and were also being bombarded by naval guns. Meanwhile, British infantry attacked Two Sisters hill at dawn after being subjected to heavy artillery fire.

In an amazingly creative feat, Argentine troops succeeded in launching an Exocet MM-38 missile from land, striking the destroyer HMS *Glamorgan*. The gadgetry contraption was nicknamed the "Berreta Setup", since in Buenos Aires slang, "Berreta" means "cheap" or "low-quality".

Once the Argentine troops had retreated, and after conquering William, Wireless Ridge and Tumbledown hills, the British troops also recovered Langdon hill. That evening saw the final Argentine air assault with Canberras and a Mirage III firing on British positions. One of the Canberra planes was shot down during that action.

The same day, the Pope flew back to Rome after spending two intense days in Argentina, constantly surrounded by devout crowds imploring God for peace.

Dawn had scarcely broken on June 14 when, in response to reports from the Commander of the 5th Naval Infantry Battalion on the assaults being sustained by his unit, an Army Infantry Regiment was dispatched to reinforce them and Argentine artillery began firing to repel the intense British attack.

In the dawn twilight, British artillery pounded the Argentine positions that were still withstanding the Infantry assault. Not long afterwards, the British took Tumbledown hill and the area surrounding Moody Brook. That morning, only the 5th Naval Infantry Battalion remained standing between Tumbledown and William hills, having failed in a counterattack due to the disparity on forces and support. By mid-morning, an Argentine cavalry reconnaissance squadron launched a counterattack on Moody Brook in an attempt to halt the British advance, regroup forces and thus regain the initiative. Shortly after noon, the 5th Naval Infantry Battalion was ordered to retreat towards Puerto Argentino (Port Stanley). The battle had clearly been lost, and to prolong it would have merely caused unnecessary casualties. At 1 p.m. the Military Commander of the islands accepted to meet the Commander of British forces at 4 p.m. to agree on the terms for surrender.

On June 17, British troops seized and destroyed the Argentine Corbeta Uruguay scientific station located on Thule Island, and captured the staff exerting unusual violence. The same day, General Fortunato Galtieri was asked to resign, while the wounded aboard the hospital ships ARA *Bahía Paraíso* and ARA *Almirante Irízar* were being evacuated, action which would last until June 27.

Finally, on July 14 the ferry St. Edmund transported the last remaining Argentine prisoners from the Falklands/Malvinas to the Patagonian port of Puerto Madryn.

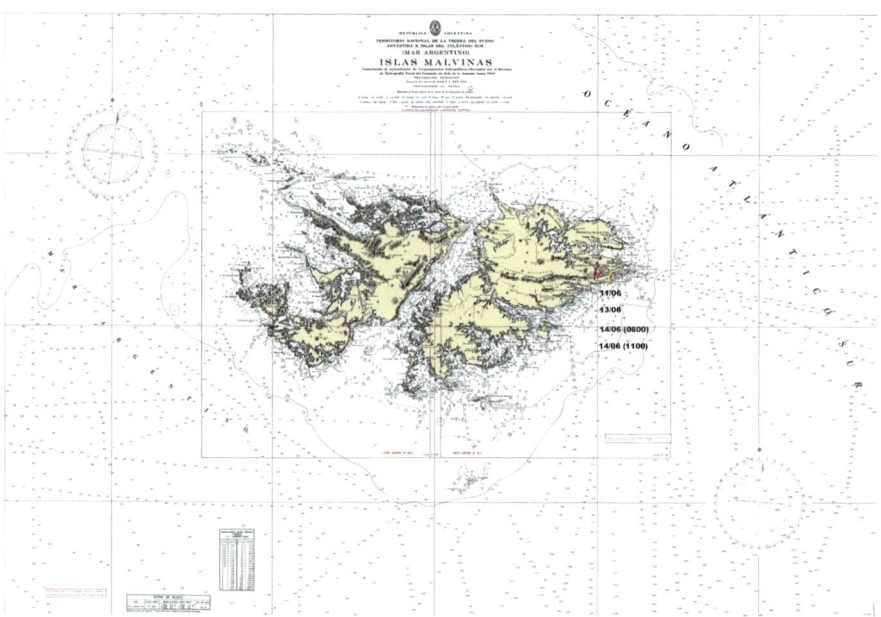

In the ARA *Bouchard*

After 08:00 h, they sailed from Ushuaia's commercial dock, following their routine while patrolling. Once they were near the focal area,[1] they hid their revolutions and, 400 ft away, they implemented the maximum sealing condition and the crew went to anti-submarine battle stations (without activating the Fanfare[2]). They also blacked-out the vessel. Only then was the vessel ready to cross the Le Maire Strait. Once past Cape San Diego, it headed northwest and reduced the alertness level, maintaining port and starboard watches as was usual during the whole conflict. They patrolled between 3 and 5 miles from the coast, in front of the city of Río Grande.

After sailing the whole night, the ship anchored in San Sebastián Bay, passed 09:30 h, with the usual reinforcements to the watches and rounds in these situations. The weather worsened as the day progressed. The wind increased slightly and the temperature decreased, reaching 36.5 °F (2.5 °C). The aft engine behaved as expected, it stopped due to loosing vacuum and had to be repaired.

On June 2, at almost 09:00 h, the ship sailed and began patrolling the area of San Sebastián Bay, since they were expecting a helicopter from Río Grande that had been cancelled the day before. The helicopter arrived at 14:00 h, the Executive Officer boarded and then it left. The ship continued patrolling the coast of the Isla Grande de Tierra del Fuego. Almost at midnight, it anchored to the south of Río Grande. The aft engine suffered another malfunction and they were forced to sail with a single shaft until anchoring.

On June 3, the ship remained anchored at the same location. The only break in the routine was the detection and identification of the Navy cargo ship, *Canal Beagle*, which was transporting cargo to Ushuaia. The ship sailed at 18:00 h and anchored near Río Grande, close to the lighthouse at Cape Domingo. The wind began to increase, coming from the north and northeast. The area did not shelter the ship and the sea's conditions worsened. Before 08:00 h, it was ordered that the engines be readied and they lowered an extra length of chains (around 82 ft, 25 m) so that the anchor would hold in the inclement weather. The measure was successful and the ship did not move from its anchorage, despite the wind and the sea.

As is good practice, every four hours they released between six and ten chain links to prevent the same links from always bearing the brunt of the ship's pressure, which could damage one of them, causing the anchor and a whole section of chain to fall into the sea. With the ship being rocked and the waves crashing, this was no easy task. However, the members of F Division (seamanship and manoeuvres) went to the bridge every four hours to request authorisation to conduct the manoeuvre.

On June 5, the ship remained anchored near Cape Domingo. As the wind and sea conditions returned to reasonable parameters, they decided to stop trying to modify

---

[1] An area of the sea where navigation routes are focused and ships sail past. Submarines seek to damage enemy maritime passage with less effort in these areas, since they are ensured that vessels will pass through.

[2] A device that produces noise destined to deceiving torpedoes. They head towards the device and not the ship's propellers.

the chain links situation and to reduce the engines' readiness. The ship's complement devoted themselves to corrective and planned maintenance of all machinery, aiming at completing all the tasks which had been set aside due to the operations.

The ship set sail during the early hours of June 6. The wind increased its speed to such an extent that the anemometer was damaged when it showed over 40 knots. The sea raged, with over 16 foot (5 m) waves that literally swept the stern. In spite of the weather, they still kept to their routine of going on anti-submarine battle stations, releasing noise devices, hiding their revolutions, etc. The wind and bad weather remained with the ship until it docked, around 17:00 h.

Chapter 14
The Return to Puerto Belgrano After the Defeat

Abstract The ship returns to Puerto Belgrano after the defeat. The cold reception at the Naval Base. The subsequent visit to the dry dock to fix the damages caused by the torpedo external explosion.

After the patrol, the ship sailed on June 29, at 04:45 h, amidst the night's gloom, heading towards its station, the Puerto Belgrano Naval Base. On this occasion, the focal area was crossed without taking any measures, since they were no longer necessary. They took advantage of the favourable weather to conduct an abandon ship drill, then ate and covered their normal watches. As the day ended, they sighted Cape Virgins, the southernmost point of the Province of Santa Cruz. The ship was crossing the Strait of Magellan.

The Frigate Lieutenant Eugenio Luis Facchin on watch at the gangway of the destroyer ARA *Bouchard*, at Ushuaia's harbour

By midday on June 30, the ship was parallel to Puerto Santa Cruz. That same day, at midnight, it was in the San Jorge Gulf. They sailed hugging the coast so that the bridge teams could learn more about the Patagonian coast. Identifying the coastal landmarks, the lighthouses and buoys, which are so crucial for sailors, made the voyage less painful and the time pass faster.

On July 1, at 10:40 h, one of the liferafts that had recently been installed in Ushuaia fell into the sea. It inflated immediately and, luckily, was recovered within a few minutes. The incident brought no pleasure to the Area Maintenance Officer,[1] who had to complete several administrative procedures with different departments, in addition to writing a brief to determine responsibilities and justify the event. However, there was a clear silver-lining for the rest of the crew, who still remembered the tests of the "other" liferafts: these ones worked! During the afternoon, the aft engine once again gave the engineering team the chance to work tirelessly to solve the endless issues. The only uncommon event during the routine voyage was the presence of a Polish ship, *Mazury*, which was heading to Golfo Nuevo.

On July 2, they were in the waters close to Segunda Barranca lighthouse, at the southernmost point of the Buenos Aires Province. They entered the main channel to Bahía Blanca at 07:30 h. Then, at 10:07 h, they moored at berth 34 of the Puerto Belgrano Naval Base. They were completely alone, only the Base' watch officer was there to receive the ship, together with the armoury's watch officers, to take note of the issues shown by the systems and equipment. This was how a ship that took part in the Falklands/Malvinas conflict was received. The families were waiting for their arrival in their homes.

Everyone, no matter the rank, experienced a strange feeling, that no one dared voice. Should they be ashamed for something? Why were they received so impersonally and coldly? The answers would come later. Now, it was the time for meeting their families, for those who were close, or to make an urgent phone call and visit a friend or colleague for those whose families were far away. The burden of defeat would be taken up by those who fought; the commanding officers would come under question to answer for responsibilities that were not their own. Was the condition of the ships dependant only on its crewmembers? Was the technology on board chosen by its operators? The judgments by those who investigated to identify responsibilities seemed to be made by professionals unconcerned with the prevailing reality. The men who were subjected to long questionnaires felt, on more than one opportunity, that there was a complete lack of empathy towards those who had suffered hours of anguish, the pain of loss and the bitter taste of defeat, despite all their efforts.

The ideological use of the defeat was also no small matter. Even today, it turned the veterans of the war in abusers on one hand, and cowards on the other. None of this happened on *Bouchard*, nor in most of the units that fought and that in 2021,

---

[1] An officer responsible for the materials of a department. He is responsible for the whole inventory of an area and must maintain and repair it so that it is at the appropriate level for the Operator—Maintainer.

almost 40 years after the end of the war, continue to meet with the sole reason of commemorating that "we were all there together and fought for something that we believed was right, shoulder to shoulder, without care for ranks, which were only felt when it was time to man our battle stations". It falls to history to clear the lies that damage the memory of those who dedicated their lives. Those who were there know the truth, and it will not be silenced. Long Live Argentina!

Appendix A
List of Commanding Officers

Destroyer ARA *Bouchard*
  Commanding Officers

Rank	Surname and Name	Assigned[1]	Relieved
Commander	Degano Guido Emilio	08/07/1972	07/02/1973
Commander	Otero Edgardo Aroldo	07/02/1973	05/02/1975
Commander	Girling Eduardo Morris	05/02/1975	03/02/1976
Commander	Zaratiegui Horacio	03/02/1976	31/01/1977
Commander	Cúneo Osvaldo Roberto	31/01/1977	12/01/1978
Commander	Diamante Ernesto	12/01/1978	14/03/1979
Commander	Osses Emilio	14/03/1979	07/02/1980
Commander	Catolino Miguel Oscar	07/02/1980	28/12/1980
Commander	Pellegri Cesar A	28/12/1980	10/12/1981
Commander	Bárcena Washington	10/12/1981	6/12/1982
Commander	Barilli Mario Dante	06/12/1982	6/03/1984

---

[1] Translator's note: All dates are represented using the dd/mm/yyyy method.

Appendix B
Voyages of the Destroyer ARA *Bouchard* Under the Argentine Flag

Year 1972

Voyage	Sailing directions and outbound actions	From	Until	Nautical miles
1	Philadelphia—Puerto Belgrano	18/10 to 17/11		7089.9
Year 1974				
2	Puerto Belgrano—El Rincón	07/04 to 08/04		281.5
3	Puerto Belgrano—El Rincón (1º Sea Stage of the Fleet)	15/04 to 18/04		609.7
4	Puerto Belgrano—El Rincón	07/05 to 08/05		267.7
5	Puerto Belgrano—Golfo Nuevo	13/05 to 24/05		1918.3
6	Puerto Belgrano—Golfo Nuevo	21/06 to 02/07		2072.9
7	Puerto Belgrano—El Rincón—Golfo Nuevo	30/07 to 10/08		2223.9
8	Puerto Belgrano—El Rincón Operation "Cimarrón" with the Uruguayan Navy—San José Gulf—Mar del Plata Naval Base	02/09 to 13/09		2441.1
9	Puerto Belgrano—El Rincón Operation "Unitas XV"—Necochea Area—Mar del Plata	28/09 to 03/10		1280.7
10	Puerto Belgrano—Golfo Nuevo–San Jorge Gulf—Le Maire Strait—Ushuaia—Isla de los Estados	07/10 to 18/10		2460.5
11	Puerto Belgrano—Mar del Plata—El Rincón	11/11 to 20/11		1641.1
12	Puerto Belgrano—Mar del Plata	06/12 to 12/12		659.2
Total				16,986.2

(continued)

(continued)

Voyage	Sailing directions and outbound actions	From	Until	Nautical miles
Year 1975				
13	Puerto Belgrano—Mar del Plata Drills after receiving the fast attack craft ARA *Intrépida*	13/02 to 02/03		773.1
14	Puerto Belgrano—El Rincón	05/04 to 09/04		395.6
15	Puerto Belgrano—El Rincón	15/04 to 18/04		585.5
16	Puerto Belgrano—El Rincón	20/05 to 24/05		709.3
17	Puerto Belgrano—Golfo Nuevo	27/05 to 31/05		1035.6
18	Puerto Belgrano—Mar del Plata	03/06 to 07/06		983.7
19	Puerto Belgrano—El Rincón—Mar del Plata	19/07 to 25/07		1716.3
20	Puerto Belgrano—San José Gulf	27/07 to 03/08		1379.3
21	Puerto Belgrano—Puerto Madryn	13/09 to 26/09		3387.2
22	Puerto Belgrano—Rio de Janeiro (Brazil) Operation "Unitas XVI"	18/10 to 05/11		3992.7
23	Puerto Belgrano—Puerto Madryn—Camarones Bay	11/11 to 18/11		2061.5
Total				17,129.4
Year 1976				
24	Puerto Belgrano—Mar del Plata—Puerto Belgrano—Mar del Plata	06/04 to 18/04		1815.4
25	Puerto Belgrano—El Rincón	14/05 to 16/05		244
26	Puerto Belgrano—San José Gulf	21/05 to 23/05		544.6
27	Puerto Belgrano—El Rincón	03/06 to 05/06		423.1
28	Puerto Belgrano—El Rincón	01/08 to 04/08		1039.7
29	Puerto Belgrano—Mar del Plata	20/08 to 22/08		705.6
30	Puerto Belgrano—San José Gulf	03/09 to 05/09		600.7
31	Puerto Belgrano—El Rincón Tests for the Exocet MM38 missile installation	05/10 to 07/10		376.6
32	Puerto Belgrano—Golfo Nuevo	26/10 to 31/10		1046.3
33	Puerto Belgrano—Mar del Plata	02/11 to 07/11		1121.1
34	Puerto Belgrano—Golfo Nuevo—San Matías Gulf	13/11 to 22/11		1753.3
35	Puerto Belgrano—Ushuaia—Isla de los Estados—San Matías Gulf	06/12 to 17/12		
Total				12,114.4
Year 1977				

(continued)

Appendix B: Voyages of the Destroyer ARA *Bouchard* Under the Argentine Flag

(continued)

Voyage	Sailing directions and outbound actions	From	Until	Nautical miles
36	Puerto Belgrano—Mar del Plata	06/02 to 27/02		1994
37	Puerto Belgrano—Mar del Plata—El Rincón	12/04 to 27/04		2553
38	Puerto Belgrano—Puerto Deseado—Puerto Madryn	01/05 to 19/05		1566
39	Puerto Belgrano—El Rincón Tests after receiving the Exocet MM38 missile	14/06 to 15/06		214
40	Puerto Belgrano—San Matías Gulf—San José Gulf—El Rincón—General Mosconi Platform Escort for the Military Committee visiting the platform	01/07 to 21/07		2294
41	Puerto Belgrano—El Rincón	25/10 to 26/10		290.5
42	Puerto Belgrano—Golfo Nuevo—Puerto Madryn—El Rincón	07/09 to 12/09		1050
Total				9911.5
Year 1978				
43	Puerto Belgrano—El Rincón—Boarding of the Navy Chief of Staff, Commander of Naval Operations and Naval Commander—Replenishment with YPF tanker *San Lorenzo*	08/01 to 13/01		787.5
44	Puerto Belgrano—El Rincón Searching for the sailboat *Shangla*	27/02 to 01/03		540.2
45	Puerto Belgrano—Mar del Plata—El Rincón—Le Maire Strait—Río Grande	07/03 to 23/03		3573.9
46	Puerto Belgrano—El Rincón—Golfo Nuevo—San José Gulf	05/04 to 13/04		1646.7
47	Puerto Belgrano—Puerto Santa Cruz—Punta Quilla Dock—Puerto Deseado—Isla de los Estados—Survey of the coves of the Beagle Channel's Adjacent Islands—San José Gulf—El Rincón—San José Gulf	23/04 to 09/05		3130.7
48	Puerto Belgrano—Mar del Plata—El Rincón	06/07 to 13/07		1046.3
49	Puerto Belgrano—El Rincón—Golfo Nuevo—San José Gulf—El Rincón—Naval Review	15/08 to 26/08		2403.6

(continued)

(continued)

Voyage	Sailing directions and outbound actions	From	Until	Nautical miles
50	Puerto Belgrano—Faro Buoy (access to the Bahía Blanca Canal)	05/10		106.8
51	Puerto Belgrano—El Rincón—Mar del Plata—Porto Alegre Operation "Fraterno 78" with the Brazilian Navy—Rio de Janeiro (Brazil)—El Rincón	11/10 to 28/10		3805
52	Puerto Belgrano—El Rincón	22/11 to 24/11		430.6
53	Puerto Belgrano—El Rincón—Isla de Los Estados (replenishment by the YPF tanker *San Lorenzo* and the tanker ARA *Punta Médanos*)—On the 15th and 19th they went to battle stations due to a Chilean scout airplane, that was forced to leave by the Combat Air Patrol—San Jorge Gulf	08/12 to 25/12		4250.8
Total				21,722.1
Year 1979				
54	Puerto Belgrano—El Rincón Test voyage with the new command	07/02		104.2
55	Puerto Belgrano—El Rincón—Mar del Plata 1st Sea Stage with the 1st Division of destroyers and the submarine *Santa Fe*	23/04 to 02/05		1891.1
56	Puerto Belgrano—Puerto Deseado—May 25th in Puerto Deseado—Meeting with *Punta Médanos* at Isla Pingüino—San José Gulf—Puerto Madryn to disembark an ill member of the crew. San José, firing tracers and exercises with the Ocean Fleet—El Rincón, Firing and Tactics	22/05 to 09/06		4064.7
57	Puerto Belgrano—Strait of Magellan, 3rd Sea Stage with the Fleet—July 8 to 12, Ushuaia	03/07 to 16/07		No official data. Estimated: 2640.0
58	Puerto Belgrano—El Rincón	24/09		No official data. Estimated: 105.0
59	Puerto Belgrano—El Rincón	28/09		No official data. Estimated: 105.0
60	Puerto Belgrano—Valdez Peninsula, 5th Sea Stage—Puerto Madryn	07/10 to 13/10		No official data. Estimated: 305.0

(continued)

Appendix B: Voyages of the Destroyer ARA *Bouchard* Under the Argentine Flag

(continued)

Voyage	Sailing directions and outbound actions	From	Until	Nautical miles
60[2]	To Mar del Plata. Anti-submarine exercises. As they left port they hit a shoal with the sonar dome, damaging it and leaving a 40° forward blind spot—Puerto Belgrano	21/10 to 25/10		No official data. Estimated: 860.0
61	Puerto Belgrano—Comodoro Rivadavia. Tactics with the whole Ocean Fleet—November 10, Naval Review by the Commander in Chief of the Navy in front of Comodoro Rivadavia—Combat firing	06/11 to 13/11		No official data. Estimated: 1140.0
62	Puerto Belgrano—El Rincón Exocet missile calibration tests	29/11 to 30/11		No official data.[3] Estimated: 105.0
Estimated Total				11,320
Year 1980				
63	Puerto Belgrano—Near Banco Víboras, assisting the fleet ocean tug *Somellera* that was adrift	04/03		168.9
64	Puerto Belgrano—El Rincón, 1st Sea Stage—On March 25, they entered port for replenishment—Then to Mar del Plata for anti-submarine exercises	18/03 to 01/04		2639.1
64	Puerto Belgrano—Puerto Deseado, 2nd Sea Stage, tactics and various exercises	6/05 to 20/05		3033.8
66	Puerto Belgrano—El Rincón, 3rd Sea Stage. Enters port on July 2 and sets sail on July 3	27/06 to 10/07		3408.2
67	Puerto Belgrano—Puerto Madryn, 4th Sea Stage	19/08 to 28/08		1874.5
68	Puerto Belgrano—El Rincón 5th Sea Stage, Tactics	07/10 to 13/10		1679.0
Total				12,800.0
Year 1981				
69	Puerto Belgrano—El Rincón	31/01 to 01/2		258.3

(continued)

---

[2] The voyage number is repeated in the ship's historical book. Data entered this way by Chief of Navigation, Corvette Lieutenant Horacio M. Rodríguez and ratified by the Commanding Officer, Commander Emilio Oses.

[3] During the second semester, the information regarding the miles sailed was not entered into the historical book. Data not entered by Chief of Navigation Corvette Lieutenant Horacio M. Rodríguez and ratified by the Commanding Officer, Commander Emilio Oses.

(continued)

Voyage	Sailing directions and outbound actions	From	Until	Nautical miles
70	Puerto Belgrano—El Rincón	24/3 to 25/3		187.0
71	Puerto Belgrano—Mar del Plata 1st Sea Stage—Visit to and registration of a fishing boat—Fire in Boiler C3, boiler is halted—Enters Puerto Belgrano for replenishment on April 5. It weighs anchor on 06/04	01/04 to 09/04		1709.3
72	Puerto Belgrano—Ushuaia—Monitoring mile 200 with a Neptune airplane—Commercial dock on April 24—Return to monitoring maritime traffic	20/04 to 01/05		2400.3
73	Puerto Belgrano—Ushuaia 2 nd Sea Stage—Tactics in an insular area—Fuel dock on May 18—San José Gulf—Coastal bombardment	12/05 to 28/05		3554.5
74	Puerto Belgrano—El Rincón Group landing exercises in Baliza Chica, stranded launch and personnel rescued by amphibious vehicles—Enters port for replenishment on June 18. It weighs anchor on June 20. Mar del Plata—El Rincón	16/06 to 25/06		1551.0
75	Puerto Belgrano—Area of Operations—Joint Operation "Ocean Venture"	08/08 to 09/08		482.0
76	Puerto Belgrano—El Rincón—Golfo Nuevo–It berths at Storni docks on August 16, 4th Sea Stage	11/08 to 19/08		1693.0
77	Puerto Belgrano—El Rincón	30/10 to 31/10		178.0
78	Puerto Belgrano—Ushuaia—6th Sea Stage—Launching depth charges and hedgehogs—Effective firing on small island in the Beagle Channel—Fuel dock on November 11—Area of Operations	07/11 to 19/11		2961.3
Total				14,974.7
Year 1982				
79	Puerto Belgrano—El Rincón	03/02		86
80	Puerto Belgrano—Punta Ancla Buoy (Bahía Blanca access canal)	16/02 and 17/02		80
81	Puerto Belgrano—El Rincón	04/03		345

(continued)

Appendix B: Voyages of the Destroyer ARA *Bouchard* Under the Argentine Flag 165

(continued)

Voyage	Sailing directions and outbound actions	From	Until	Nautical miles
82	Puerto Belgrano—El Rincón (1st Sea Stage of the Fleet)	17/03 to 19/03		306
83	Puerto Belgrano—El Rincón Operation "Cimarrón VI" with the Uruguayan Navy and the submarine ARA *Santa Fe*	20/03 to 22/03		507
84	Puerto Belgrano—El Rincón	23/03 to 25/03		340
85	Puerto Belgrano—To form up with the TG with ARA *25 de Mayo*, ARA *Py* and ARA *Piedrabuena* for Operation Malvinas—Replenishment with ARA *Punta Médanos*—Flight Operations—April 1, 10:20 h, the Polish fishing boat *Milenio* is intercepted and ordered to remain north of Latitude 50° S—Due to non-compliance, battle stations are manned and a zodiac with two officers is sent to verify the issues reported by the fishing vessel—April 2 and 3, patrol to the north of the Falklands/Malvinas—April 4, replenishment with ARA *Punta Médanos*	29/03 to 07/04		2847

(continued)

(continued)

Voyage	Sailing directions and outbound actions	From	Until	Nautical miles
86	Puerto Belgrano—April 17, a negative sonar contact is investigated—Replenishment with ARA *Punta Médanos*—April 20, replenishment—April 22, hydrophone noise detected, investigation unsuccessful—April 23, replenishment with ARA *Punta Médanos*—April 24, ARA *Piedrabuena* and ARA *Bouchard* are ordered to meet with cruiser ARA *Belgrano*—April 27, they enter Puerto Deseado due to engine failure; fuel, water and victuals are resupplied—April 28, sailing to Isla de los Estados—April 29, meeting—April 30, replenishment of the Task Force—May 01, replenishment of cruiser *Belgrano*—14:00 approach to the exclusion zone begins—From 14:00 to 17:00, meeting of the commanding officers aboard *Belgrano*—24:00, they went to battle stations and the war flag was raised—May 2, they continue general bearing east—05:10, they are ordered to head northwest—16:05, evidence that the cruiser was torpedoed—*Bouchard* and *Piedrabuena* scattered at maximum speed and conducted evasive manoeuvres—At 17:15, course is inverted to verify the cruiser's situation, without any trace—Ordered to head to the Isla de los Estados at maximum speed—May 3, 01:30, return to the site of the sinking—At 14:10, the first liferafts are sighted—At 16:10, two liferafts with 41 survivors are rescued—At 18:10, the rescue is suspended due to engine malfunctions—May 4, 22 survivors are rescued with a zodiac—At 16:00, they head to Ushuaia—May 5, they dock at 14:00	16/04 to 05/05		4407

(continued)

Appendix B: Voyages of the Destroyer ARA *Bouchard* Under the Argentine Flag 167

(continued)

Voyage	Sailing directions and outbound actions	From	Until	Nautical miles
87	Ushuaia—Patrol between Cabo del Medio and the Magellan lighthouse—At 15:00, they anchor in Puerto Español—May 15, they anchor at Cape San Pablo—May 16, at 10:15 and 17:10, active sonar emissions are heard on the hull—At 19:10, battle stations due to radar echoes—At 19:25, the main battery opens fire—At 19:30, they set sail—May 18, a helicopter flying is detected—At 23:00, docking at Ushuaia	14/05 to 18/05		571
88	Ushuaia—Patrol between Río Grande and San Sebastián Bay	23/05 to 27/05		939
89	Ushuaia—Patrol between Río Grande and San Sebastián Bay	31/05 to 06/06		802
90	Ushuaia—Puerto Belgrano Due to a failure of the life raft holding container lashing, a life raft falls into the sea and is recovered	29/06 to 02/07		1207
91	Puerto Belgrano—El Rincón Engine tests	23/12		187
92	Puerto Belgrano—El Rincón Engine tests	30/12 to 31/12		75
Total				12,964.5
Year 1983				
93	Puerto Belgrano—San Matías Gulf—Monitoring maritime traffic	12/01 to 14/01		961.1
94	Puerto Belgrano—San José Gulf—Monitoring maritime traffic, diving and landing exercises	19/01 to 23/01		1104
95	Puerto Belgrano—El Rincón 1st Sea Stage	12/04 to 20/04		1636.8
96	Puerto Belgrano—El Rincón Exocet missile system test	04/05 to 05/05		156.1
97	Puerto Belgrano—El Rincón Exocet missile system test	05/05		94.2
98	Puerto Belgrano—El Rincón—San José Gulf—2nd Sea Stage—Entered port on the 23rd and sailed on the 25th	21/05 to 31/05		1830

(continued)

(continued)

Voyage	Sailing directions and outbound actions	From	Until	Nautical miles
99	Puerto Belgrano—San José Gulf 3rd Sea Stage, anti-submarine exercises	16/06 to 20/06		1090.8
100	Puerto Belgrano—El Rincón Firing with students from the Navy Officer's School	22/06 to 23/06		139.3
101	Puerto Belgrano—San José Gulf 4th Sea Stage	11/08 to 20/08		2350.4
102	Puerto Belgrano—Mar del Plata 5th Sea Stage, anti-submarine exercises, tactical diving	15/09 to 22/09		1559.4
103	Puerto Belgrano—El Rincón Effective firing	17/10 to 18/10		407.3
104	Puerto Belgrano—Mar del Plata Anti-submarine exercises	20/10 to 25/10		845.8
105	Puerto Belgrano—El Rincón	03/11		125.5
106	Puerto Belgrano—El Rincón Observing ship to the real launching of a missile by ARA *Drumond*	06/11 to 08/11		503
107	Puerto Belgrano—San José Gulf Landing of the Task Force	16/11 to 22/11		1325.2
108	Puerto Belgrano—Ushuaia Tactics with the Fast Attack Craft Grouping	30/11 to 14/12		2331.5
Total				17,299.3
Total flying the Argentine flag				154,312.0

Appendix C
Captain Barcena's "Farewell Address" to his Crew

The farewell address of a commanding officer, his last farewell to a team of men that was there for his tenure, is a transcendent and supremely important event, and an incredible responsibility.

Thus I will try to express my true and authentic feelings, in the hope of contributing positively to the bearing of worthy and noble men, with whom I shared a valuable year of my life.

It was a 1982 filled with difficult and significant circumstances institutionally and nationally, some of which were felt around the world, and which has given us extraordinary experiences that we will have to capitalise on in the benefit of a promising future, in a positive, conducive and fruitful way.

This is why I'm addressing you exclusively, my men, to remind you what you did and reach concrete conclusions.

First of all, I want to tell you that what you did, you did well.

You all fulfilled your duty.

When we act according to our duty, we shouldn't expect anything else other than the personal satisfaction of having done the right thing. However, as your Commanding Officer, I feel the need and even the moral obligation to congratulate you and briefly remember your landmark actions, both during times of peace and war.

While the war was one of the most significant events of the year, 1982 wasn't solely occupied by the conflict. During peace times, you carried out important tasks, such as crewing this ship in circumstances where, together with the submarine ARA *Santa Fe* and Uruguayan units, the "Cimarrón 7" Joint Operation was conducted. In addition, some of our superior officers participated in the planning of the amphibious Operation "Fraterno 4", with the Brazilian Navy.

Beyond the mutual professional satisfaction, you were able to foster traditional bonds of friendship at a regional level.

In times of peace, you also seized every favourable opportunity to prepare and train for the fight, be it by scheduled training or through the interim servicing that you're finishing.

But you also waged war, a war that represented the most important event that has happened in our country in the last few years. You had the pride, satisfaction and honour of facing our enemy in the defence of our sovereignty of the South Atlantic.

You supported the landing on April 2, patrolling the area near the Falklands/Malvinas Islands and controlling the maritime traffic in the area.

When *Bouchard* was headed to join the Task Group with the C4 that was in the Isla de los Estados, it suffered a serious failure in front of Puerto Deseado. Your determination and tenacity allowed the ship to be quickly repaired and able to fulfil its mission.

You were the target of duplicitous and immoral enemy behaviour, who, outside the exclusion zone, torpedoed the cruiser *Belgrano*, and also this vessel without sinking it, though causing four strikes that were later sealed in a dry-dock, by applying a metal patch with a surface greater than 118 ft^2 (11 m^2).

You began the rescue of the *Belgrano's* shipwrecked survivors when one of our own planes, returning to base due to fuel autonomy, reported seeing churning from propellers near the liferaft field that we were heading towards regardless.

You remained for two days rescuing survivors, with malfunctions that wouldn't allow the engines to be stopped to save lives.

You remained in the area with liferafts, in spite of the breakdowns and existing risks, for far longer than was authorised, entering port in Ushuaia with only 30% of your fuel.

You acted with the solidarity and love towards your neighbour that is a hallmark of a noble person, giving your own clothes, coats and lifejackets to the survivors.

You fired your guns in front of Río Grande during the night and amidst a thick fog, attacking radar echoes that headed towards the coast, suggesting that a mere six hours after this fact, and near our position, an enemy helicopter that had been set on fire appeared.

You spent many months working indefatigably to keep the ship operational.

You faced serious risks each and every time you entered and left Ushuaia.

You dedicated your whole self and all possible attention on the use of the sensors and preparing our weapons.

You offered valuable support to the air forces.

And as far as I'm concerned, you gave me one of the most beautiful and meaningful moments of my life, when together, on the signal bridge, scant hours before the *Belgrano's* sinking, we raised the war flag. A ceremony that we felt like a burning light braving pitch darkness.

You accomplished all this, and far more, during this war.

I already told you in July, and I repeat it here today: it is not honourable for a man of the sea to consider himself a hero for fulfilling his duty.

Remember your experiences at war and use them positively, but humbly.

You are not gods of war for having done what you did.

Unfortunately, war gives rise to many things. There are those who feel like heroes just because they did their duty. There are those who manufacture heroes in order to benefit groups or institutions. There are still others that lightly and with a complete

Appendix C: Captain Barcena's "Farewell Address" to his Crew

lack of professionalism, call themselves judges of situations they deeply misunderstand. These are prone to quick comments and disruptive gossip, showing an unmanly personality. They attempt to show themselves as the best suited to difficult situations, some of them compounding the affront by never having been exposed to the sublime risk brought by war.

But war also offers the space for the intelligent, serene and thoughtful attitudes that the post-war situation requires. It is here where, unhurried but also without pause, all the experiences must be seized, capitalising on even the most trivial of events, so that the results can be used to improve the body, procedures, doctrine and men.

Our Navy is committed to this task and rest assured, it will do it the right way.

We should not waste the restless nights, the anguish and the pain, both our own and from our families, who supported our actions.

Let us remember and honour our dead heroes, from the Navy, Army and Air Force, and join every Argentine to build a great future. But to this end, we must begin with the basic cells, in our case, the ship and our home. We shall give the best of ourselves and, from those two places, we'll begin to rebuild what might've been destroyed.

This is the only way in which we will be able to become strong and fulfil our desire to recover the islands of the South Atlantic that belong to us.

It does not matter when, but rest easy knowing that one day, not too far in the future, we will have the sovereignty that today we are denied.

This distinctive honour we bear on our breasts is our commitment.

Mr. Captain Barili, I give you an expert group of men, trained and valiant, in addition to a ship that is in pristine operating conditions despite its age.

Knowing your professional qualities and personal values, I'm fully certain that your command will be excellent.

I cannot end my words without addressing you, noble destroyer and dear friend *Bouchard*. You have given me the enormous satisfaction of having commanded you for a whole year, with several months of war.

I pray to God that He continues blessing you, as well as those who command and crew you until the end of your days, and that He'll always be with you in your voyages to glory and honour, for the good of the Navy and the Country.

Appendix D
List of Crewmembers

Rank in 82	National Identity Document	Surname	Name	Currently alive
Commander	4678212	Barcena	Washington	Yes
Corvette Lieutenant[4]	10305662	Ortiz	Eduardo Pablo	Yes
Frigate Lieutenant	11184675	Amatore Rodrigue	Marcelo Marcos	Yes
Midshipman	14256409	Buscazzo	Miguel Ángel Abel	No
Frigate Lieutenant	10780350	Facchin	Eugenio Luis	Yes
Lieutenant Commander	5400006	Ferrer	Roberto Augusto	Yes
Lieutenant Commander	5512059	Gómez	Guillermo Alberto	Yes
Corvette Lieutenant	10811253	Gardiner	Miguel Ángel	Yes
Midshipman	13570012	Ulloa	Roberto Augusto	Yes
Frigate Lieutenant	11889178	Garay	Roberto Daniel	No
Ship-of-the-line Lieutenant	10517562	Bogliolo	Carlos Antonio	Yes
Lieutenant Commander	4637603	Fontanarrosa	Roberto Pablo	Yes

(continued)

---

[4] Translator's note: The Corvette Lieutenant is a rank roughly equivalent to a Royal Navy Sub-lieutenant or a US Navy Ensign.

© The Editor(s) (if applicable) and The Author(s), under exclusive license to Springer Nature Switzerland AG 2022
E. L. Facchin, *The Untold Story of a Fighting Ship*,
https://doi.org/10.1007/978-3-030-92624-3

(continued)

Rank in 82	National Identity Document	Surname	Name	Currently alive
Midshipman	11889369	Rey Álvarez	Rafael	Yes
Frigate Lieutenant	8069970	Ferrari	Ricardo Amilcar	Yes
Frigate Lieutenant	10077160	Zaragoza	Rubén Horacio	Yes
Ship-of-the-line Lieutenant	8069959	Castrilli	Alejandro	Yes
Midshipman	13316345	Borgogno	Cesar Luis	No
Ship-of-the-line Lieutenant	7618345	Picardi	Edgardo Roberto	Yes
Frigate Lieutenant	8591896	Morena	Marcelo	Yes
Petty Officer Third Class	13763706	Arrech	Raúl Antonio	Yes
Petty Officer Second Class	13080807	Portaluppi	José Alberto	Yes
Petty Officer Second Class	13928879	Fernández	Mario	Yes
Petty Officer Third Class	13762642	Camargo	Juan Isidro	Yes
Petty Officer Third Class	13948207	Stratta	Pedro Horacio	Yes
Petty Officer Second Class	13754728	Velazques	David	Yes
Petty Officer Third Class	13058000	Kelly	Mario	Yes
Petty Officer Third Class	13970170	Verdechia	Horacio Alberto	Yes
Petty Officer	10135596	Alegre	Cesar Oscar	No
Seaman	13000951	Bergeonneau	Sergio Rubén	Yes
Petty Officer Third Class	12972910	Angarano	Jorge David	Yes
Petty Officer Third Class	13934561	Salone	Alejandro Rubén	Yes
Petty Officer Third Class	13213137	Pinnola	Carlos Alberto	Yes
Petty Officer Second Class	13559645	Villaji	Rolando Eugenio	Yes
Petty Officer Second Class	13754736	Acosta	Héctor Daniel	Yes
Petty Officer Third Class	13751521	Cativa	Luis Antonio	Yes

(continued)

Appendix D: List of Crewmembers

(continued)

Rank in 82	National Identity Document	Surname	Name	Currently alive
Petty Officer Third Class	13712429	Ramos	Mario Desiderio	Yes
Petty Officer Third Class	13985473	Pactac	Jorge Alberto	Yes
Petty Officer	8623248	Prado	Ricardo Héctor	Yes
Petty Officer Third Class	13396802	Cuello	Luis Alberto	Yes
Petty Officer Third Class	13549787	Williams	Federico Alfredo	No
Petty Officer Third Class	13520407	Serrano	Ricardo Alfredo	Yes
Petty Officer Second Class	13693342	Robles	José Horacio	Yes
Petty Officer Second Class	13409993	Zarapura	Hugo Cesar	Yes
Petty Officer Third Class	13288320	Cejas	Carlos Camilo	Yes
Petty Officer Third Class	14894513	Vallejos	Walter Lucio	Yes
Petty Officer Third Class	14607671	Giménez	José Alberto	Yes
Petty Officer Third Class	14610389	Cancino	José Rafael	Yes
Petty Officer Second Class	11705454	Aubrun	Néstor Horacio	No
Petty Officer Second Class	12043441	Morelli	Gerardo Luis	No
Petty Officer Third Class	12083633	Pensa	Guillermo Gabriel	Yes
Petty Officer Second Class	12308106	Palacio	Daniel Benito	Yes
Chief Petty Officer	10195674	Aranda	Francisco Hermogenes	Yes
Petty Officer Third Class	14703827	Álvarez	Osvaldo Sergio	No
Petty Officer Second Class	11590369	Junco	Bernardo	Yes
Petty Officer Third Class	14894519	Venica	Sergio Daniel	Yes
Petty Officer Third Class	14894541	Salinas	Alberto Cesar	Yes

(continued)

(continued)

Rank in 82	National Identity Document	Surname	Name	Currently alive
Petty Officer	5404539	González	Raúl Abel	Yes
Petty Officer Third Class	14894686	Libertelli	Héctor Daniel	Yes
Petty Officer Third Class	16894573	Compiano	Roberto Andrés	Yes
Seaman	12409710	Maiza	Ernesto Enrique	Yes
Petty Officer Third Class	12308389	Villegas	Ernesto Omar	Yes
Petty Officer	10811141	Palacios	Alfredo Noel	Yes
Petty Officer	10135954	Ramírez	Carlos Andrés	Yes
Petty Officer	10135982	Ferreyra	Ramón Nicolás	Yes
Petty Officer Second Class	12959608	Guerrero	Diego	Yes
Petty Officer Third Class	14172548	Flores	José Alberto	Yes
Petty Officer Third Class	14174741	Pérez	Mario Antonio	Yes
Petty Officer Third Class	14188572	Santillán	José Marino	Yes
Petty Officer Third Class	14578636	Rodríguez	Enrique Miguel	Yes
Petty Officer	10811094	Fernández Britez	Omar	Yes
Petty Officer Third Class	14399413	Rucci	Juan Carlos	Yes
Petty Officer Third Class	14189044	Truffa	Daniel Ramiro Roque	Yes
Petty Officer Third Class	14189058	Garro	Néstor Alcides	Yes
Petty Officer Third Class	14189523	Campos	Víctor Hugo	Yes
Petty Officer	10937152	Innamorati	Luis Basilio	Yes
Petty Officer	11033845	Dubanced	Elio Carlos	Yes
Petty Officer Second Class	11578926	Velazquez	Hugo Roberto	Yes
Petty Officer Third Class	13875094	Alarcón	Mario Benjamin	Yes
Petty Officer	10225522	Bade	Juan Carlos	Yes
Senior Chief Petty Officer	5496270	Girardi	Carlos Norberto	Yes
Petty Officer	8527281	Bobis	Jorge Alberto	Yes

(continued)

Appendix D: List of Crewmembers

(continued)

Rank in 82	National Identity Document	Surname	Name	Currently alive
Chief Petty Officer	8362040	Iddon	Jorge Roberto	No
Petty Officer	8397290	Fernández	Enrique Domingo	Yes
Petty Officer	8435574	Ubeda	Marciano	Yes
Petty Officer	8435737	Sarria	Juan Domingo	No
Petty Officer	5314868	López	Américo Mario	No
Petty Officer	4701293	Ojeda	Eugenio Damián	No
Petty Officer	5398202	Ibáñez	Oscar Hugo	Yes
Chief Petty Officer	4581877	Molinari	Luis Ángel	No
Petty Officer	5505265	Olivera	Francisco Manuel	Yes
Petty Officer	10420560	Sosa	Juan Carlos	Yes
Chief Petty Officer	10424706	Báez	Héctor David	Yes
Chief Petty Officer	10456507	Montenegro	Hugo Ernesto	Yes
Petty Officer	10489304	González	Jorge Alberto Ramón	Yes
Petty Officer	10489388	Garatti	Francisco Adrián	Yes
Chief Petty Officer	5333737	Serrano	Miguel	Yes
Senior Chief Petty Officer	7283220	Mamani	Víctor	Yes
Petty Officer	6083790	Meneghini	Juan Carlos	Yes
Chief Petty Officer	6145589	Bullon	Rubén Marciano	Yes
Senior Chief Petty Officer	6239319	Acosta	Ignacio	Yes
Command Senior Chief Petty Officer	4366132	Navarro	Elio Rubén	No
Senior Chief Petty Officer	4388798	Bosquiazzo	Edgardo Martín	No
Petty Officer	6903261	Moreno	Roberto	Yes
Petty Officer	4992334	Castrogiovanni	Lucio Eduardo	No
Senior Chief Petty Officer	7257214	Figueroa	Miguel	Yes
Petty Officer	11045139	Molina	Eusebio Rolando	No
Senior Chief Petty Officer	7329955	Velasco	Luis Rodolfo	No
Chief Petty Officer	8209787	Almada	Braulio	Yes

(continued)

(continued)

Rank in 82	National Identity Document	Surname	Name	Currently alive
Petty Officer	8005050	Silva	Rubén	Yes
Chief Petty Officer	8145094	Cosmi	Carlos Humberto	Yes
Chief Petty Officer	8244419	Burgos	Luis Alfredo	Yes
Chief Petty Officer	8256706	Silva	Juan Carlos	Yes
Chief Petty Officer	6906480	Luic	Nicolás Ángel	No
Petty Officer	8298554	Funes	Marcelo Vicente	Yes
Petty Officer Second Class	11958141	Bevilacqua	Roberto	Yes
Petty Officer Second Class	11958658	Mesina	Ramón Miguel	Yes
Petty Officer Second Class	11966499	Ríos	Jorge Omar Alberto	Yes
Chief Petty Officer	8270919	Lanciotti	Daniel Armando	Yes
Chief Petty Officer	8270961	Chávez	Ramón Dolores	Yes
Petty Officer	8282633	Di Cesare	Alberto Arturo	Yes
Petty Officer	10626043	Vara	Fortunato Enrique	Yes
Petty Officer Second Class	12170478	Rosas	Rubén Aníbal	Yes
Petty Officer	7682566	Bazan	Ángel Estergidio	No
Petty Officer Third Class	12368712	Martínez	Cesar Enrique	Yes
Petty Officer	8468249	Tolaba	Jorge Martín	Yes
Petty Officer Third Class	12423803	Lamas	Agapito	Yes
Petty Officer	8527293	Tula	Miguel Carlos	Yes
Petty Officer Third Class	12265216	Romero	Francisco	Yes
Petty Officer Third Class	12815272	Escobar	Transito Rodolfo	Yes
Petty Officer Second Class	12168801	Escalante	Omar Enrique	Yes
Petty Officer Second Class	11343834	Paredes	Juan Domingo	Yes
Petty Officer Second Class	12944633	Bottiroli	Carlos Alberto	Yes

(continued)

Appendix D: List of Crewmembers 179

(continued)

Rank in 82	National Identity Document	Surname	Name	Currently alive
Petty Officer Second Class	11045211	Díaz	Pascual Mariano	Yes
Petty Officer Second Class	11089674	Bianchi	Edgardo Amilcar	Yes
Petty Officer Second Class	11109506	Zurita	José Ramón Antonio	No
Petty Officer Second Class	11184853	Fernández	Alberto Candido	Yes
Petty Officer Third Class	11255940	Jesús	Ramón Alejandro	Yes
Petty Officer Second Class	11957882	Sager	Carlos Alberto	Yes
Petty Officer Second Class	11331247	Laciar	Alejandro del Valle	No
Chief Petty Officer	7695289	Cabrillana	Salvador Urbano	No
Petty Officer	5507358	Quiroga	Félix Rufo	Yes
Chief Petty Officer	5507395	Soto	Rogelio Víctor	Yes
Chief Petty Officer	5513500	Romo	Rene Raúl	Yes
Petty Officer	5517179	Parodi	Rubén Alberto	No
Chief Petty Officer	5517398	Patron	Héctor Samuel	Yes
Chief Petty Officer	5519824	Soria	Pedro Irineo	Yes
Petty Officer Second Class	10676813	Cardozo	Manuel Eduardo	Yes
Petty Officer	11286226	Biggnon	José Manuel	Yes
Seaman	16502781	Álvarez	Adalberto Damian	Yes
Petty Officer Third Class	14612334	Velarde	Hugo Orlando	Yes
Petty Officer Third Class	14556642	Macedo	Pastor Antonio	Yes
Seaman	14544205	Hauron	Abelardo Néstor	Yes
Petty Officer Third Class	14533688	Caretta Álvarez	Gustavo Adrián	Yes
Petty Officer Second Class	14528934	Escobar	Juan Carlos	Yes
Petty Officer Third Class	14524747	Segura	Ramón Manuel	Yes
Petty Officer Third Class	14516716	Martínez	Juan Carlos	Yes

(continued)

(continued)

Rank in 82	National Identity Document	Surname	Name	Currently alive
Petty Officer Third Class	14502681	Gronek	Enrique Ángel	Yes
Petty Officer Second Class	14291591	De La Cruz	Sergio Rolando	Yes
Seaman	14278844	Bustos	Mario Dante	Yes
Petty Officer Second Class	14256636	Arcangelo	Claudio Néstor	Yes
Petty Officer Third Class	14894629	Aliano	Pedro Oscar	Yes
Petty Officer Third Class	16926035	Martínez	José María	Yes
Petty Officer Third Class	14454943	Serenelli	Eduardo Néstor	Yes
Petty Officer Third Class	14662677	Segovia	Carlos Armando	Yes
Seaman	17068023	Garayalde	Juan Alberto	No
Petty Officer Third Class	17045849	Nichea	Gustavo Darío	Yes
Seaman	17019178	Lovey	José Luis	Yes
Seaman	16993835	Lencina	Andrés Abrahán	No
Petty Officer Third Class	16945731	Riquelme	Néstor Ricardo	Yes
Seaman	16926184	Lugo	Ángel Ramón	Yes
Petty Officer Third Class	16926163	Moran	Aresio Santos	Yes
Petty Officer Third Class	16926154	Rodas	Omar Alberto	Yes
Petty Officer Third Class	16926147	Peralta	Ricardo José	Yes
Petty Officer Third Class	16926102	Trangoni	Silvio Dante	No
Petty Officer Third Class	16926082	Bais	Carlos Alberto	No
Petty Officer Third Class	16926075	Torres	Manuel Farnecio	Yes
Petty Officer Third Class	14189785	López	Walter Fernando	Yes
Petty Officer Third Class	16398322	Sarome	Juan Ricardo	Yes
Seaman	17019166	Herrera	Gerardo Cesar	Yes

(continued)

Appendix D: List of Crewmembers

(continued)

Rank in 82	National Identity Document	Surname	Name	Currently alive
Seaman	17019162	Gómez	Rubén Rodolfo	Yes
Seaman	17019149	Figueredo	José Martín	Yes
Seaman	16631935	González	Gustavo Javier	Yes
Petty Officer Third Class	16630709	Escobar	Cesar Adolfo	Yes
Petty Officer Third Class	16622937	Pena	Juan Ramón	Yes
Petty Officer Third Class	16622919	Ojeda	Walter Ricardo	No
Petty Officer Third Class	16601753	Gainza	Jacinto Roberto	Yes
Petty Officer Third Class	16557711	Aranda	David Jorge	No
Petty Officer Third Class	16502672	Rosas	Pedro Miguel	Yes
Petty Officer Third Class	16502648	Rodríguez	Enrique	Yes
Petty Officer Third Class	16502644	Maidana	Oscar Antonio	Yes
Petty Officer Third Class	14626585	Peruchena	Juan Francisco Javier	Yes
Seaman	16412559	Aducci	Néstor	Yes
Petty Officer Third Class	14643493	Ferreyra	Carlos Edgardo	Yes
Petty Officer Third Class	16296813	Esquivel	Raúl Oscar	Yes
Petty Officer Third Class	16296766	Fleytas	Carlos Alberto	No
Petty Officer Third Class	16296717	Altamirano	Marcos Nemecio	Yes
Petty Officer Third Class	16279570	Medina	Julio Antonio	Yes
Petty Officer Third Class	16125694	Alcaraz	Daniel Osvaldo	Yes
Petty Officer Third Class	16125015	Ibarra	Otilio Aníbal	Yes
Petty Officer Third Class	14949778	Martínez	Elio Rubén	Yes
Petty Officer Third Class	14940449	Dezi	Néstor Enrique	Yes

(continued)

(continued)

Rank in 82	National Identity Document	Surname	Name	Currently alive
Petty Officer Third Class	14906531	Medrano	Oscar Francisco	Yes
Petty Officer Third Class	14900101	Vásquez	Sergio Emilio	Yes
Petty Officer Third Class	14876553	Paz	Carlos Enrique	Yes
Seaman	14859083	Gutiérrez	Ramón Alberto	Yes
Petty Officer Third Class	14473571	Lasser	Alfredo Oscar	Yes
Petty Officer Third Class	16502636	Gómez	Juan Carlos	Yes
Petty Officer Third Class	12711283	Fernández	Víctor Hugo	Yes
Petty Officer Third Class	16088312	Prieto	Juan Manuel	Yes
Petty Officer Third Class	14057243	Sueldo	Raúl Félix	Yes
Petty Officer Second Class	14012123	Restelli	Héctor Edgardo	Yes
Petty Officer Third Class	13991971	Quiroga	Braulio Rubén	Yes
Petty Officer Second Class	16089635	Sosa	Saúl Marcelo	Yes
Petty Officer Third Class	12641844	Arenas	Francisco Lorenzo	Yes
Petty Officer Second Class	13851621	Alanie	Néstor Cesar	Yes
Petty Officer Second Class	13796443	Bernier	Luis Omar	Yes
Petty Officer Second Class	14058575	González	José Gabriel	Yes
Petty Officer Third Class	13792152	Monti	Juan Carlos	Yes
Petty Officer Second Class	13852142	Ascurra	Carlos	Yes
Petty Officer Third Class	12723517	Ferro	Julio Sergio	Yes
Seaman	16320506	Abreliano	Miguel	Yes
Petty Officer Third Class	16926029	Segovia	Anselmo Osvaldo	Yes

(continued)

Appendix D: List of Crewmembers

(continued)

Rank in 82	National Identity Document	Surname	Name	Currently alive
Petty Officer Third Class	14219908	Argüello	Domingo Alberto	Yes
Petty Officer Second Class	16305707	Vázquez	Sergio Francisco	Yes
Petty Officer Third Class	13105413	Costilla	Alfonso Eleodoro	Yes
Petty Officer Third Class	12790422	Choqui	Julio Roberto	No
Petty Officer Third Class	12775098	Trinchin	José María	Yes
Petty Officer Third Class	12698123	Wendler	Ernesto Sebastián	Yes
Petty Officer Third Class	14109345	Maidana	Filomeno Nicolás	Yes
Petty Officer Third Class	14426740	Del Canto	Daniel Ignacio	Yes
Petty Officer Third Class	14434899	Aguirre	Carlos Rubén	Yes
Petty Officer Second Class	12682256	Torriel	Oscar Félix	No
Petty Officer Third Class	16926007	Cardozo	Aldo Daniel	Yes
Petty Officer Third Class	14060595	Valdez	Jorge Alberto	Yes
Petty Officer Third Class	14165251	Ruitort	Carlos Roberto	Yes
Petty Officer Second Class	14144764	Funes	Francisco	Yes
Petty Officer Third Class	14428898	Moyano	Jorge Daniel	Yes
Petty Officer Third Class	14900035	Arias	Carlos Alberto	Yes
Petty Officer Third Class	14172235	Schwal	Carlos Eduardo	Yes
Seaman	14999008	Ayarzabal	Enrique José	No
Petty Officer Third Class	14068590	Orellano	Juan Alberto	Yes
Petty Officer Third Class	12483043	Villegas	Carlos Oscar	No
Petty Officer Third Class	14105391	Vega	Jorge Carlos	Yes

(continued)

(continued)

Rank in 82	National Identity Document	Surname	Name	Currently alive
Petty Officer Third Class	14900058	López	Eduardo Aníbal	Yes
Seaman	16926023	Fernández	Alfonso Isidro	Yes
Petty Officer Third Class	14094365	Taborda	Miguel Ángel Edgardo	Yes
Petty Officer Third Class	12493479	Barrios	Daniel Eladio	Yes
Conscript	16128759	Suárez	Ricardo Ramón	Yes
Conscript	16735078	Zambrano Videla	Luis Marcelo	Yes
Conscript	14402515	Verón	Miguel Ángel	Yes
Conscript	16211452	Bedini	Henry Felipe	Yes
Conscript	16116538	Buccolini	Roberto Constantino	Yes
Conscript	16159346	Moreno	Julio César	Yes
Conscript	16220301	Ariaz	Miguel Ángel	Yes
Conscript	16064507	García	Héctor Omar	Yes
Conscript	16239708	Contini	Sebastián Eugenio	Yes
Conscript	16252791	Cherin	Claudio José	Yes
Conscript	16255912	Soria	Luis Romualdo	Yes
Conscript	14572688	Cornero	Ángel Nelson	Yes
Conscript	16196900	Chocobar	Armando Manuel	Yes
Conscript	16369712	Barbero	Daniel Alejandro	Yes
Conscript	14681791	Ramos	Claudio Adrián	Yes
Conscript	14688067	Villalba	Carlos Oscar	Yes
Conscript	16050183	Bufanio	Juan Carlos	Yes
Conscript	14832392	Dentaro	Marcelo Vicente	Yes
Conscript	16023183	Yachinto	Oscar Alfredo	Yes
Conscript	16085612	García	Alejandro Esteban	Yes
Conscript	16201093	Leoz	Eduardo Dante	Yes
Conscript	16494765	Rodenas	Juan Carlos	Yes
Conscript	14847382	Machado Basaldua	Roberto Antonio	Yes
Conscript	14612476	Giorgi	Luis Ricardo	Yes

(continued)

Appendix D: List of Crewmembers 185

(continued)

Rank in 82	National Identity Document	Surname	Name	Currently alive
Conscript	14561970	López	Reynaldo Armando	Yes
Conscript	14554187	Serrano	Carlos Mamerto	Yes
Conscript	16446397	Maza	José Armando	Yes
Conscript	14637940	Hansen	Rubén Enrique	Yes
Conscript	14481314	Lizondo	Miguel Alberto	Yes
Conscript	16332863	Aranda	Pedro Antonio	Yes
Conscript	14964002	Osores	Gregorio Justiniano	Yes
Conscript	14089680	Posadas	Víctor Hugo	Yes
Conscript	16138230	González	Alberto Ricardo	Yes
Conscript	16036244	García Renes	Daniel Omar	Yes
Conscript	14134627	Gómez	Hugo César	No
Conscript	13609467	Jara	Luciano	Yes
Conscript	14525740	Riedweg	Rubén Clemente	Yes
Conscript	14854876	López	Roberto César	Yes
Conscript	14970922	Rocha	Pedro Pablo	Yes
Conscript	14943612	Barreda Faccaro	Luis Octavio	Yes
Conscript	14924708	Casco	José Mario	Yes
Conscript	14917171	Apaza	Alberto Antonio	Yes
Conscript	14914489	Escobar	Jorge Alberto	Yes
Conscript	16348688	Macri	Osvaldo Luis	Yes
Conscript	16315962	Avalo	Jorge Daniel	Yes
Conscript	14974583	Reniero	Gabriel César	Yes
Conscript	14844382	Córdoba	Enrique Rubén	Yes
Conscript	14829130	Alderete	Carlos Ernesto	Yes
Conscript	14816235	González	Marcelo Fabián	Yes
Conscript	14795186	Di Gargorio	Orestes Hernando	Yes
Conscript	14661467	Carabajal	Carlos Daniel	Yes
Conscript	14653878	Iñiguez	Daniel Antonio	Yes
Conscript	14649860	Royano	Mario Rómulo	Yes
Canteen	11595057	Boriglio	Realdo Roberto	Yes
Canteen	10388538	Lavios	Rubén Eduardo	Yes

Epilogue: An Undeserved End

Abstract: An undeserved end. The empty ship is used for missile target practise, launched from both surface ships and aircraft. The ship was later scrapped to take advantage of its metal.

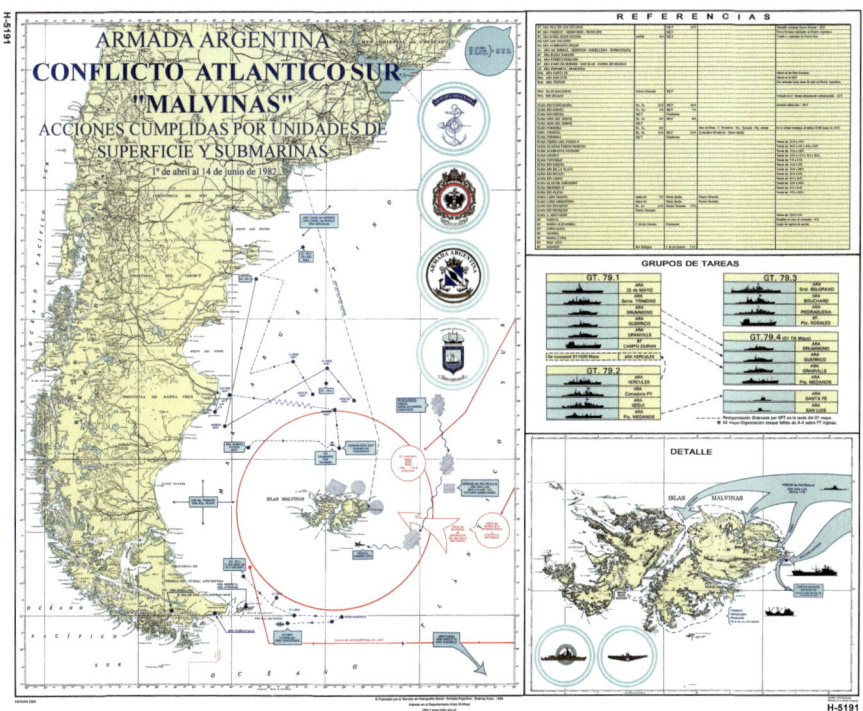

In the early hours of November 9, 1988, the old destroyer ARA *Bouchard*, unarmed, cold and with no equipment, fuel, ammunition or life, was towed to Mar del Plata's waterfront. Its hull had knifed through those waters again and again on the different national and international operations and trainings, as well as for the ubiquitous anti-submarine trainings, with the participation of the patient submariners posing as the enemy that, year by year, began with the bare basics to train the combat teams aboard the Ocean Fleet's ships.

The ship at open seas seconds before being hit by two Exocet missiles

Both the silence and the creaks from the mast cables knocking against surfaces, badly closed doors and loose metal plates, gave a ghostly feel to the ancient destroyer, a symbol of a feat as righteous as it was unforgettable. So, without that life that gives character to a mere mortal machine, without the crew that blesses it with continuity and meaning, which would be forever lost on that day, the fleet ocean tug dropped the tow ropes and left it alone, isolated, waiting for its fate that would arrive in just a few hours.

The only witnesses were the observers and the people in charge of the launchings. A few days before, the Naval Hydrographic Service had issued the pertinent warnings so that no one would sail those waters, since they would conduct a live fire exercise. Nothing had been reported concerning the historic tragedy that was about to take place.

At 14:23 h, the corvette ARA *Espora* launched an Exocet MM38 sea-sea missile, from 18 miles away. It hit the General Administrative Office and the laundry room, without a doubt, the places with the most traffic on the ship. No longer could one hear the echoes of the constant bustling, caused by the proceedings that had to be completed and the delivery of the uniforms, that the patient laundry staff cleaned every day to maintain the strict neatness standards that was demanded of all crewmembers. The chatter of those who stopped by for a constitutional drink of mate, always available there could not be heard either. Through the hole made on the main deck, the boilers' ducts could be seen, which had caused so much work for the engineers during the war.

The ship is hit by two Exocet missiles

A Super Étendard fighter later finished the deed with an Exocet AM39 air-sea missile, fired from 23 miles away. It destroyed all the officers' quarters, also on the main deck. The bulkheads were completely deformed; they almost looked like they had never been inflated.

The coming of night let them transport the wreckage to the Puerto Belgrano Naval Base, so that the impacts could be analysed. When the engineers, technicians and operators next visited, they could confirm the destruction unleashed by the two impacts. Had the ship been crewed and bearing its load of ammunition, powder, fuel, lubricants and furnishings, the impacts would have led to its immediate and dramatic destruction, with the certain loss of a large number of crew. In spite of being empty, the extent of the damage was impressive and it was clear that a single impact would have been enough to destroy the ship.

And so, as a sea-sea and air-sea missile target, the decaying destroyer gave its last breath as a gallant fighter of the waves and became scrap, to be auctioned by some obscure bank official and bought by people who only saw steel plates, copper wiring and bronze pieces, and could not see all that was added by the men who crewed it, the Commanding Officer who guided it, and the passion that msoved it.

The ship on an island in the delta of the Paraná River awaiting its scrapping

Without a shadow of a doubt, this ending deprived the nation of being able to keep a seaworthy ship, a ship that played a worthy role in the Falklands/Malvinas War. It also deprived historiography from a privileged party in the historical narrative, which could have offered future generations the opportunity to appreciate it in person and learn how people lived on board such ships, as mere accounts cannot cause the same visceral reaction that can be experienced from a visit.

Bibliography

Books, Magazines and Articles

Bartley W. S. (1954). Iwo Jima, amphibious epic. Historical Branch G-3 Division Headquarters U.S. Marine Corps. Washington.
Burzio H. F. (1967). Captain and Accountant. Capitán de navío Hipólito Bouchard al servicio de la Marina de Guerra del Perú. Departamento de Estudios Históricos Navales, Secretaría General Naval. Comisión Nacional de Homenaje al Capitán de Navío Hipólito Bouchard. Buenos Aires.
Cagle M. W. Manson FA (1957). The sea war in Korea. United Sates Naval Institute. Annapolis, Maryland, USA.
Caillet-Bios T. (1937). Álbum de Historia Naval Argentina. Buenos Aires.
Cardoso, K, Del Kody V. (1983). Malvinas, la trama secreta. Sudamérica. Planeta. Buenos Aires.
Carrero Blanco L. (1957). Historia de la Segunda Guerra Mundial, Tomo X: La guerra aeronaval en el Mediterráneo y en el Pacifico. Ediciones Idea. Madrid.
De Marco M. Á. (2009). Corsarios por la Independencia. Cultural insert of the *La Nación* newspaper, January 24.
Field J. Jr. (1962). History of United States naval operations. Korea. Government Printing Office, Washington.
Hutchings R. (2014). Special forces pilot: a flying memoir of the Falklands War. Pen & Sword Aviation. Great Britain.
Karig W., Cagle M., Manson F. (1952). Battle report, the war in Korea. Rinehart and Company Inc. New York.
Lajous F. (Vice Admiral). (1967). Capitán de navío Hipólito Bouchard, Comisión Nacional de Homenaje al Capitán de Navío Hipólito Bouchard, Departamento de Estudios Históricos Navales. Buenos Aires.
Lajous F., Pereira Liate C., Marti Garro P. et al. (1967). Hipólito Bouchard, marino al servicio de la independencia americana y argentina. Departamento de Estudios Históricos Navales, Secretaría General Naval. Buenos Aires.
Martí P. (1967). Hipólito Bouchard: marino al servicio de la independencia argentina y americana. Comando de Operaciones Navales, Departamento de Estudios Históricos Navales, Biografías Navales Argentinas, Series C, No. 10, Buenos Aires.
Martínez de Campos and Serrano C. (1956). Historia de la Segunda Guerra Mundial. Las campañas del Pacifico y de extremo Oriente, Volume VIII: 1941–1945. Ediciones Idea. Madrid.
Maruyama X. (2003). Noticias del Puerto de Monterey. Q Bull Monterrey History Art Assoc LII(4).

Morrison S. (1960). History of United States naval operation in World War II. Little, Brown and company. Boston.
Muñoz J. (2005). Ataquen a Río Grande (Operación Mikado). Instituto de Publicaciones Navales.
Nichols C., Shaw H. (1955). Okinawa: victory in the Pacific. Historical Branch G-3 Division Headquarters US Corps. Washington.
Piccirilli R. Gianello L. (1963). Biografías Navales. Departamento de Estudios Históricos Navales, Secretaría de Estado de Marina. Buenos Aires.
Rattenbach B. (1983). Comisión de Análisis y Evaluación de las Responsabilidades del Conflicto del Atlántico Sur. Informe Final. Consejo Supremo de las Fuerzas Armadas. República Argentina.
Ratto H. Commander. (1961). Capitán de navío Hipólito Bouchard. Departamento de Estudios Históricos Navales, Secretaría General Naval. Buenos Aires.
Ratto H. Commander. (1941). Hombres de mar en la *Hipólito Bouchard*. Departamento de Estudios Históricos Navales, Secretaría General Naval. Buenos Aires.
Ruiz Moreno I. (1961). "La Armada Argentina y la Soberanía Nacional", Conference given on May 19, in the Law and Social Sciences College of the University of Buenos Aires.
Southby-Tailyour E. (2014). Exocet Falklands, The untold story of special forces operations. Pen & Sword Military. Great Britain.
Uhrowczik P. (2001). The burning of Monterrey—the 1818 attack on California by the privateer Bouchard. CYRIL Books. Los Gatos, California.
Vv. Aa. (1949). Desarrollo estratégico de la guerra naval en el Pacifico 1941–1945. Escuela de Guerra Naval de Argentina. Buenos Aires.
Vv. Aa. (1965). Gran crónica de la Segunda Guerra Mundial: de Stalingrado a Hiroshima, vol III. Selecciones del Reader´s Digest. New York.
Vv. Aa. (1965). La Segunda Guerra Mundial. Editorial Codex. Buenos Aires.
Vv. Aa. (1983). Conflicto Malvinas, informe oficial. Ejército Argentino. Buenos Aires.
West N. (1977). La Guerra Secreta por las Malvinas, Los Exocets y el espionaje internacional. Editorial Sudamericana.

Websites

BBC News. Mundo. https://www.bbc.com/mundo/economia/2010/04/100405_1503_malvinas_falknads_chatarra_cr
Histarmar. https://www.histarmar.com.ar/BuquesMercantes/Marina%20Mercante%20Argentina/Transportes/BahiaBuenSuceso.htm
Informe final Malvinas Ejército Argentino. https://www.argentina.gob.ar/sites/default/files/informe_malvinas.pdf
Instituto de Relaciones Internacionales—Universidad Nacional de la Plata. https://www.iri.edu.ar/publicaciones_iri/anuario/A94/A1MVCRO.html
Irizar.Org. http://www.irizar.org/malvinas-acciones-10.html
Martí C. Guerra de Corea y USA. Monografías.com. http://www.monografias.com/trabajos13/monodos/monodos.shtml
Nav Source Naval History Photographic History of the US Navy. https://www.navsource.org/archives/05idx.htm
Naval History and Heritage Command. https://www.history.navy.mil/content/history/nhhc/
Naval History and Heritage Command. https://www.history.navy.mil/content/history/nhhc/search.html?q=map&start=270&pdf=true
The National Archives and Records Administration. https://www.archives.gov/contact

Bibliography

Other Sources

Crónica de Malvinas. personal diary of Corvette Lieutenant Gardiner.
Data acquired from the South Atlantic Operations Report, File No. 12, destroyer ARA *Bouchard*, Pages 134 ff.
Data from the logbook of the destroyer ARA *Bouchard*.
Data gathered from statements made by the Commanding Officer of the *Bouchard*, Washington Bárcena, to the War Actions Review Board.
Data provided by the report made by the Commanding Officer of the destroyer ARA *Bouchard*, our own and our enemy's tactical procedures, virtues and defects, page 86 ff.
DEBU Office, CMT No. 13/82 "Secret" Operations Report. Annex VIII—1.
Historical book of the destroyer ARA *Bouchard*, Page 467.
Libro historial del buque (Historical Book of the Ship), Publication MI No. 1, Confidential, Copy 142, General Archive of the Navy, Ministry of Defence.
Logbook of the destroyer ARA *Bouchard*, Voyage 3 of the Río Grande Area of Operations, May 16.
Public statements by the Commander in Chief of the FACh (Chilean Air Force), General Fernando Matthei, who revealed the level of support provided, and Margaret Thatcher's words on the occasion of Pinochet's imprisonment in England, and the words of General Pinochet himself upon his release.
War diary of the destroyer ARA *Bouchard*, Pages 77 ff. of the "South Atlantic Operations Report", File No. 12.

Printed by Printforce, the Netherlands